Gower Champion

GOWER CHAMPION

DANCE AND AMERICAN MUSICAL THEATRE

DAVID PAYNE-CARTER

Edited by
BROOKS McNAMARA and STEVE NELSON

Foreword by MARGE CHAMPION

Contributions in Drama and Theatre Studies, Number 87

LIVES OF THE THEATRE
JOSH BEER, CHRISTOPHER INNES, and SIMON WILLIAMS, Series Advisers

Greenwood Press
Westport, Connecticut • London

Library of Congress Cataloging-in-Publication Data

Payne-Carter, David, 1948–1991.
    Gower Champion : dance and American musical theatre / David Payne-
Carter ; edited by Brooks McNamara and Steve Nelson ; foreword by
Marge Champion.
      p.   cm.—(Contributions in drama and theatre studies, ISSN
0163–3821 ; no. 87. Lives of the theatre)
   Includes bibliographical references (p.   ) and index.
   ISBN 0–313–30451–3 (alk. paper)
    1. Champion, Gower, 1921–1980. 2. Dancers—United States—
Biography. 3. Choreographers—United States—Biography.
4. Theatrical producers and directors—United States—Biography.
I. McNamara, Brooks. II. Nelson, Stephen, 1952– . III. Title.
IV. Series: Contributions in drama and theatre studies ; no. 87.
V. Series: Contributions in drama and theatre studies. Lives of the
theatre.
GV1785.C463P39   1999
792.8'2'092
[B]—dc21   98–21954

British Library Cataloguing in Publication Data is available.

Copyright © 1999 by New York University

All rights reserved. No portion of this book may be
reproduced, by any process or technique, without the
express written consent of the publisher.

Library of Congress Catalog Card Number: 98–21954
ISBN: 0–313–30451–3
ISSN: 0163–3821

First published in 1999

Greenwood Press, 88 Post Road West, Westport, CT 06881
An imprint of Greenwood Publishing Group, Inc.

Printed in the United States of America

The paper used in this book complies with the
Permanent Paper Standard issued by the National
Information Standards Organization (Z39.48–1984).

10 9 8 7 6 5 4 3 2 1

Every reasonable effort has been made to trace the owners of copyright materials in this book,
but in some instances this has proven impossible. The editors and publisher will be glad to
receive information leading to more complete acknowledgments in subsequent printings of the
book and in the meantime extend their apologies for any omissions.

Contents

Contents

A photo essay follows page 81.

Series Foreword

Lives of the Theatre is designed to provide scholarly introductions to important periods and movements in the history of world theatre from the earliest instances of recorded performance through to the twentieth century, viewing the theatre consistently through the lives of representative theatrical practitioners. Although many of the volumes will be centred upon playwrights, other important theatre people, such as actors and directors, will also be prominent in the series. The subjects have been chosen not simply for their individual importance, but because their lives in the theatre can well serve to provide a major perspective on the theatrical trends of their eras. They are therefore either representative of their time, figures whom their contemporaries recognised as vital presences in the theatre, or they are people whose work was to have a fundamental influence on the development of theatre, not only in their lifetimes but after their deaths as well. While the discussion of verbal and written scripts will inevitably be a central concern in any volume that is about an artist who wrote for the theatre, these scripts will always be considered in their function as a basis for performance.

The rubric ''Lives of the Theatre'' is therefore intended to suggest both biographies of people who created theatre as an institution and as a medium of performance and of the life of the theatre itself. This dual focus will be illustrated through the titles of the individual volumes, such as *Christopher Marlowe and the Renaissance of Tragedy, George Bernard Shaw and the Socialist Theatre*, and *Richard Wagner and Festival Theatre*, to name just a few. At the same time, although the focus of each volume will be different, depending on the particular subject, appropriate emphasis will be given to the cultural and political context within which the theatre of any given time is set. Theatre itself can be seen to have a palpable effect upon the social world around it, as it both reflects the life of its time and helps to form that life by feeding it images, epitomes, and alternative versions of itself. Hence, we hope that this series will also contribute to an understanding of the broader social life of the period of which the theatre that is the subject of each volume was a part.

Lives of the Theatre grew out of an idea that Josh Beer put to Christopher Innes and Peter Arnott. Sadly, Peter Arnott did not live to see the inauguration of the series. Simon Williams kindly agreed to replace him as one of the series editors and has played a full part in its preparation. In commemoration, the editors wish to acknowledge Peter's own rich contribution to the life of the theatre.

Josh Beer
Christopher Innes
Simon Williams

Foreword

Seventeen years ago this month, Gower Champion died at the age of sixty-one on the day of the opening of *42nd Street*. An entire generation has grown up since then never having seen a production of his Broadway hits or misses—as directed, cast, choreographed, scheduled meticulously, and tinkered with endlessly by him. He may not have invented the "concept musical," but he certainly furthered its development and the art of American musical comedy. His untimely death robbed the theatre not only of his legacy but also, perhaps, of his memory. The recent acclaimed revival of *Carousel* reminds one of Gower's creative concept and direction of *Carnival!* in 1961. The new generation of theatregoers was exposed through LeRoy Reames and Jerry Herman's careful recreation of *Hello, Dolly!* to the wonders of Carol Channing's original performance and the brilliant nonstop flow of its book, music, lyrics and choreography thirty-two years later.

Life has always been good to me in spite of the tragedies of the 1980s detailed in this book. It gave me remarkable gifts: a precious husband, partner and eventual good friend for forty-seven years; two wonderful sons; and an exciting career. In the mid-1980s Karla Champion, Gower's widow, introduced me to David Payne-Carter, a Ph.D. candidate whose dissertation NYU's The Gower Champion Foundation was helping to underwrite. We became great friends, spending countless hours exploring the scrapbooks and letters I had accumulated since the first entry in my diary at the age of fourteen, "Dancing at Del Mar Club with Gower—happy time." No wonder the inscription inside my ring, "More than just happy times," meant so much to me thirteen years later when we married.

My need to fill in some of the historical gaps remembering Gower's contribution to this unique American art form has been greatly realized by the publication of David's dissertation. It has been carefully edited and reviewed by Brooks McNamara and Steve Nelson. I salute all who have worked on this project with gratitude and a profound bow of appreciation.

Marge Champion
August 26, 1997
Stockbridge, Massachusetts

Editors' Preface

David Payne-Carter died of AIDS on November 19, 1991, leaving behind the manuscript of *Gower Champion: Dance and American Musical Theatre*. David, a great student of Broadway, had received his Ph.D. from the Department of Performance Studies in the Tisch School of the Arts at New York University, and was later a much respected and admired member of the school's Department of Undergraduate Drama. In his last days it became clear to David that he would not see this book through to publication, and he asked us to edit it for him. We do so with sadness but with great enthusiasm for what he captured about the career of Gower Champion.

It was not only Champion's energy and thoroughness that made him stand out—although both of these qualities are made abundantly clear throughout David Payne-Carter's book. But beyond that, David's insights into the relationship of Gower Champion to the dance, film, television and theatre worlds of his time are unique. And his account of Champion's career is made all the more powerful and compelling by the way that David meticulously brings out these relationships—how techniques developed for one medium spilled over into every other area of his creative life. For this reason we have retained much of the material on the early career of Gower Champion because it so clearly leads into his later, better-known theatre career, one that culminated in the opening of *42nd Street* on the day of his untimely death.

In particular, as David makes clear, more than any other figure in the Broadway theatre of his day, Champion drew on his dance background to guide him as a theatre director. In fact, for most of his career, he seems to have conceived of few distinctions between directing and choreography. That is part of what made Champion unique as a musical theatre director.

We are delighted with the book for another reason. Certain figures in dance and the theatre have become legendary. Gower Champion deserves to be remembered among the most vital dancers, directors and choreographers in the history of entertainment. His contribution to American dance and theatre was extraordinary. Champion *ought* to be a legend. And David Payne-Carter's book points out the reasons on every page.

It has been a privilege to work on this book. We especially want to thank David's family, who have been so helpful. Among his friends who kindly assisted with its preparation are his colleague, Jan Cohen-Cruz, and Marge Champion, who made so much history with Gower Champion. This book benefits the David Payne-Carter Award Fund of the Tisch School of the Arts, New York University. For help on this project we want to thank Dean Mary Schmidt-Campbell and her assistant, Roberta Kahn. We also want to thank Sylvia Wang for her aid and encouragement.

Brooks McNamara
Steve Nelson
Tisch School of the Arts
New York University

Preface

Gower Champion's career spanned the years during which American musical theatre was transformed from crude popular entertainment into a sophisticated art form. Indeed, he was part of the transformation. To date, however, no full-length study of Champion's contribution to the American musical theatre has appeared. This book attempts to fill that gap. It falls into two main sections: Champion as performer (Chapters 1 through 5), and Champion as director-choreographer (Chapters 6 through 11). The first section treats Champion as he prepared himself for a career as a director. The second is organized around the Broadway musicals that he directed and choreographed; each chapter consists of a history of one or more of those productions, from original concept to opening night—and sometimes beyond, as Champion, ever the perfectionist, sought to improve on what everyone else thought was already perfect.

The research for this book involved three kinds of sources—libraries, scripts and interviews. The basic historical research was accomplished at the Billy Rose Theatre Collection of the New York Public Library at Lincoln Center. The Special Collections of the University of Southern California, the University of California, and the Institute of the American Musical, all in Los Angeles, were also particularly helpful, and I wish to thank both Ned Comstock and Miles Krueger for their invaluable assistance.

Script analysis was essential because Champion was never content simply to stage a text as it was presented to him. Instead, he became an integral participant in the dramaturgy of each production. Thus, the various reductions of the script for each of his shows are filled with his footprints. The Special Collections Department of the Research Library of the University of California at Los Angeles holds a number of Champion's personal copies of scripts, as well as legal pads on which he mapped out strategies for different numbers. Each contains a wealth of revisions, and often frustrated scrawlings as well. For patience and invaluable aid in dealing with this difficult material I would like to thank Hilda Bohem of UCLA. The Theatre Collection of the University of Wisconsin was also helpful in locating scripts. In connection with script analysis, I would particularly like to thank Michael Stewart. His patience and kindness in opening his files to me made the degree of analysis contained here possible. It was at his kitchen table that the lion's share of script analysis was accomplished.

The third major method of gathering information was through interviews. In the course of the research I spoke with persons who had worked with Champion at the very beginning of his career as well as those who were with him when he died. To all those who opened up their memories to my curiosity, and often their homes and hearts as well, I owe a debt, not only of gratitude but of friendship. If a person's real legacy is the friends he leaves behind, Champion truly has blessed me with wealth beyond measure.

I would like to thank Brooks McNamara for his endless patience and expert guidance. I would also like to mention colleagues and friends without whose expertise and support this volume would be not only poorer but slimmer. I would like to thank Ellen Holt and the David Merrick office for their kindness. For their help in research I am especially grateful to John Butz, Barbara Cohen-Stratynor, Don Littell, Julie Malnig, and Tony Manzi. For constant support and friendship, I would like to thank Pat McEnnis and Winn Blostic. And, most especially, I would like to express my gratitude to Bob Littell, without whose patience and perseverance this book simply would not exist at all.

Finally, I would like to thank Champion's partners. In his life and in his career, these were his companions and collaborators. I consider it a rare privilege to have met these remarkable women and to count them among my friends. So, to Jeanne Tyler Estridge, Marge Champion Sagal, and Karla Russell Champion, this book is affectionately dedicated.

David Payne-Carter

Introduction

"I'm in the musical comedy business," Gower Champion matter-of-factly told an interviewer in 1980 during rehearsals for his last Broadway show, *42nd Street*. "It's really all I know." The statement seems a bit disingenuous—the "all" he knew could well fill several careers, not to mention lives. But in the years since Champion's death not even musical comedy remains a straightforward enterprise. Like much in our culture, musicals have been strained through so many critical and stylistic sieves that little of their naive joy and energy remains. In the quarter-century that Stephen Sondheim has held sway on Broadway, even the most innocuous shows are expected to be conceptually elaborate and to reflect contemporary notions of topicality and political correctness.

In 1980, when Gower Champion passed suddenly from the scene, the term entertainment was beginning to sound trivial to many people. But for Champion and others of his and earlier generations, it was label enough, imbued with his singular charm and enthusiasm. He tended, in his words, to "the musical comedy business" with great verve and style, managing to entertain quite a few people along the way.

Gower Champion came of age during the zenith of American musical theatre production, and made his mark on both sides of the curtain: as an individual dancer with his partners Jeanne Tyler and Marjorie Belcher, and as a choreographer and director with a penchant for spectacular numbers that blended dance, staging and scenographic elaborateness. More than any Broadway practitioner of his generation, he knew how to build from the simplicity of a single dancer to a full-tilt, stage-filling showstopper. It was his vision of staging as a seamless blend of dance, movement and design that paved the way for later auteurs of Broadway such as Bob Fosse and Michael Bennett. The debt was acknowledged early on by Fosse, who in his nightclub days with Mary Niles used to introduce their act with the quip: "You've heard of the Champions? We're the runners up." Champion certainly understood his own value to a show: He was the first director/choreographer to receive over-the-title billing ("A Gower Champion Musical"). As John Simon observed, he did "more than anyone to break down the barrier between the prose of mere blocking and the poetry of dance."[1]

Champion's work melded two distinct modes of expression: the dance team realm of the Castles and the Astaires, with its emphasis on intimacy, romantic lyricism and elegance, and the more boisterous jazz-driven rhythms of Broadway and movie musical chorus dancing, as exemplified by the choreography of Busby Berkeley. Like Berkeley (an early idol of young Gower), Champion understood the appeal of youthful vigor and charm tempered by the poise and sophistication of experience. He also knew how to present stars, especially women, to best advantage. His work with Carol Channing in *Hello, Dolly!* remains a masterpiece in the art of creating a star's big moments.

Champion knew instinctively that what made musical theatre effective was its unabashed and self-referential theatricality: it was about "numbers"—not as links between sequences of exposition, but as the central architectural features of a show. Everything built to those spots where music, dance, lighting, costumes and staging created a sustained narrative and emotional flow through sound and motion rather than words. *Hello, Dolly!* is a sequence of ever more elaborate and complex staging patterns which unfold and flow seamlessly before the audience.

Herein lies one of the great misconceptions about Gower Champion's style and its relation to the work of other Broadway dance innovators. In an article written shortly after Champion's death, Frank Rich praises him as the principal torchbearer of the Busby Berkeley school of spectacle, but hesitates to place him in the first tier of director choreographers.

> For all the commercial and critical success Mr. Champion achieved during his lifetime, perhaps he was never fully appreciated on his own terms. That may be because he was an anachronism. He was no innovator like Jerome Robbins or Michael Bennett. He never created his own distinctive choreographic style, like Bob Fosse. He didn't try to tackle daring subjects like Hal Prince.[2]

In assessing Champion's impact on musical theatre, it is important not to use the choreographic terms "style" and "vocabulary" too narrowly. In Broadway dance they are often applied in the microcosmic sense: the hip action of a Fosse piece, the torso and arm moves of a de Mille sequence or the head tilts and kicks of a Michael Bennett number. So tempting is this particular brand of stylistic reductivism that Jerome Robbins' career has (for many) been reduced to a single pose from *West Side Story* which became a logo during the promotion of the show *Jerome Robbins' Broadway*. Typing Broadway choreographers by "signature" moves only goes so far.

In Champion's case, his idiom was one of complete images, not the idiosyncrasies of a specific style. His intention was not to invent a new or unique "vocabulary" for dancers, but rather to erase the lingering notion that dance and movement were somehow second-fiddle to words in telling a story. A Gower Champion show evolved largely by movement and provided its most revealing moments and emotional peaks through the deft use of all his resources in unison: props, lights and costumes were as important to his palette as the subtler nuances of steps and gestures. As musical theatre historian Denny Martin Flinn aptly put it, "[H]is patterns overshadow his steps."[3] Such an emphasis is one of the reasons why Gower Champion's more elaborate numbers achieve their uncanny effect—they come upon you full-blown with no wheels and gears revealing the specific mechanisms underneath.

While praise is heaped upon the ability of choreographers such as de Mille, Robbins and Kidd to "integrate" dance into a musical, Champion's numbers were themselves integrated, as David Payne-Carter frequently observes. His influence on the staging of Broadway musicals may well be more profound than his impact on the styles of individual choreographers and dancers. Unlike Jack Cole, who also came to prominence in Hollywood, Gower Champion was never content solely with the staging of dance sequences—he saw all movement, the entire mise-en-scene, as his province. If one felt compelled to find a link between Champion and other musical theatre luminaries (besides Busby Berkeley), it would be directing legend George Abbott, whose meticulous concern for a unified look and staging concept Champion believed in almost religiously. Like Abbott, he was a consummate Wagnerian and would not have been startled by the resurgence in spectacle musicals wrought by the English and Disney in the mid-1980s. Champion had been staging such no-nonsense crowd pleasers for years.

Champion's style and approach owed much to the circumstances in which his career blossomed. He was fortunate to develop and test his choreographic and staging instincts in an easy and fruitful mix of media—moving comfortably as both performer and director from stage to screen to television at a time when few artists were able to do so. David Payne-Carter properly situates Champion's rise to prominence at the conjunction of two distinct phases of American popular entertainment: the demise of vaudeville and variety shows and the rise of television, which gave the variety form a new lease on life.

The importance of Gower Champion's television and nightclub origins cannot be overemphasized. Like all variety performers, he had to learn the fine art of refining and compacting ideas into the tightest, simplest and briefest possible package. From his first youthful forays into amateur dance team contests, he worked to achieve a crisp, smooth presentation that would entice and reassure an audience. Precision, polish and a highly finished look were central. He also knew how to project an appealing personality—they had to like you, or little else mattered.

There seemed little doubt of that from the very beginning. With his first partner Jeanne Tyler and later with Marjorie Belcher, Gower Champion displayed a vitality and freshness that concealed a fiercely dedicated and relentlessly hardworking dancer who seldom called a routine finished even after it had been performed successfully for years. He knew that novelty and flawless technique were a foundation, but a dance team number had to have a particular spark and chemistry.

It also had to be about something, at least as far as Champion was concerned. The projection of personality was connected to character and character to narrative. In order to like you they had to know you, and that meant telling a story. "It's like writing a book, poetry or a piece of music," Gower explained in a 1949 interview soon after he and Marge became television sensations. "You just have something to say." Marge and Gower Champion managed that deceptively simple proviso so well that they became not merely a successful dance team, but for more than a decade "America's Dance Team."

From their emergence in the late 1940s until Gower's decisive turn to directing with *Bye Bye Birdie* in 1960, the Champions were seldom out of the limelight. They seemed to embody what many Americans wanted to see in the 1950s: clean-cut youthful energy and innocence set forth with unpretentious style and wit. Like so many icons of the period, they were the idealized faces in the mirror—what we wished we were or could be. Much as the decade's landmark domestic television comedies codified the desires and values of middle class white America, the Champions gave its romantic yearnings a face and a name. As the Castles and Astaire and Rogers had done years earlier, Marge and Gower Champion managed to be both accessible and exotic—"average" Americans doing glamorous, exciting things the rest of us could only dream about.

In his nightclub, television and film years with Marge, Champion refined the flair for movement as narrative that would earmark his two greatest Broadway triumphs, *Bye Bye Birdie* and *Hello, Dolly!* In each show, Champion's involvement with and shaping of the book ensured that the production numbers were the central architecture of the story and not merely added punctuation. "The Telephone Hour" sequence from *Birdie* was more than a clever bit of staging. Using the everyday act of talking on the telephone, it captured the entire spirit of teen life and rock-and-roll fandom in a wondrously simple and funny montage.

Likewise, in *Hello, Dolly!*, Champion took a monstrously shopworn cliché—the star's entrance down an upstage staircase—and transformed it into one of musical comedy's most memorable scenes. After a dizzying comic build to Dolly Levi's arrival at the Harmonia Gardens, in which waiters dash and stumble about the stage carrying piles of dishes and huge shish kebabs, the moment arrives. Veteran Broadway chronicler Abe Laufe recalls its impact:

> With the announcement that Dolly Levi has arrived . . . the spotlight focused on the entrance at the top of a center stairway, with the waiters lined up on both sides. Suddenly Channing appeared . . . in a red gown and jewels, and came down the stairs to sing "Hello, Dolly!" As the boys took up the second chorus, Channing went through a shuffle routine on the stage, on the runway, and back on stage to make the song one of the biggest show-stoppers in the history of musical theatre.[4]

Gower Champion was a crowd pleaser in the best sense of the word, always keeping the audience in the forefront with his particular blend of narrative and novelty. He had a performer's sense of what worked, but his true gift was the great director's unerring vision of the whole—what a show needed to look like and what it took to get there. As Harold Clurman observed, Champion had "humor and an unfailing sense of what will surprise, move and strike home on stage."[5] He began with a clear vision of the complete stage picture and a precisely controlled approach that demanded complete focus and discipline on the part of his performers. Champion was not easy, but he knew what he wanted.

Part of what he wanted (and needed) was the theatre itself. Although he always saw himself as a Californian, and came to national prominence through television and film, it was New York that gave him the urgency West Coast life seemed to lack. "I needed the tension and pressure of New York and the immediacy of the theatre," he said in an interview prior to beginning work on *42nd Street*, "The fact that you're opening next Thursday and have to be ready. That's where I feel at home."[6]

Champion's three greatest stage triumphs (*Bye Bye Birdie, Hello, Dolly!* and *42nd Street*) were unabashed celebrations of the power of staging and his own particular gift for creating those potent images that ensconce a performance forever in the memory of an audience. The three shows also had strong links to show business itself and frequent opportunities for the kind of straightforward, irony-free moments of pleasure so rare in contemporary musical theatre. As was the case in his performing career, Champion's success as a director rested squarely on his ability to convey to an audience the unalloyed delight he felt in creating those moments. He was the kid in the candy shop inviting everyone else to join in.

The moments may have seemed free and easy from out front, but they took vast amounts of energy and discipline to achieve. The stories of Champion's unflinching insistance on perfection are legendary, and he left more than a few bruised egos in his wake. On the other hand, his actors were often fiercely loyal and secure in the assured, certain way he went about creating his shows. The man David Merrick referred to as the "Presbyterian Hitler" would have been perfectly at home with Gordon Craig's notion of performers as supple marionettes, pliant to the director's every wish. His own style as a dancer was always there (a controlled torso with a lyrical but precise use of arms and legs) no matter who danced in his shows. Lee Roy Reams, one of the lead dancers in *42nd Street*, put it this way: "When I'm on that stage it's still me, but I have to wear his body." It was not a bad fit for most, but its owner's particular style often eluded description. The finished product, however, seldom left people at a loss for superlatives.

Gower Champion's career was a clear reflection of the path he took across several eras of musical theatre style and practice. His performing life brought to a close the great forty-year tradition of nationally popular dance teams; his choreography flourished during the last great period of movie musical production in the 1950s. It is of more than passing interest that his final stage success, *42nd Street*, was a blend of stage and film spectacle that brought full-circle the aesthetics that shaped his career for four decades. It also carried more than a fair number of homages to Champion hits of the past. As a paean to both Busby Berkeley and Gower Champion, the show was both remembrance and summation.

It also provided, in its garishly melodramatic tale of an authoritarian director and a neophyte chorus girl, an eerie composite of the many faces of Gower Champion, who came to prominence as the personification of youth and innocence and closed his career as the embodiment of *42nd Street*'s most compelling character, the director Julian Marsh—a demanding, lonely perfectionist whose life was his art. At the conclusion of the 1933 film, Marsh lurks outside the theatre to overhear the audience's comments. Unlike the fictional Marsh, Gower Champion never lived to experience the vindication of his last opening night. At one in the afternoon of August 25, 1980, the day *42nd Street* was to open in New York, Gower Champion died at Sloan Kettering Memorial Hospital.

For better or worse, posterity's treatment of Gower Champion and his career are forever linked to the almost surreal circumstances of his untimely death. Suffering from an extremely rare and fatal blood disorder, Champion's death was no doubt hastened by the stressful process of seeing *42nd Street* through under the aegis of his longtime antagonist David Merrick. Immediately after the doctors pronounced Champion dead, producer Merrick forbade any release of the news and promptly left the hospital. Barely five hours later, the show opened to thunderous applause and the unexpected appearance of the producer after the last curtain call. Following Merrick's choked announcement of Champion's death from the stage of the Winter Garden, the crowd of first-nighters, celebrities and press stumbled out into the night utterly bewildered. The opening night party at the Waldorf Astoria went on, but in an atmosphere bizarre even for Merrick's brand of Broadway. "The people here don't really know how to deal with it," Neil Simon told a reporter. "If you ever wrote a scene like this they'd say it was too melodramatic, too sentimental. Life is more absurd than we think."[7]

The startling circumstances of his end prompted an immediate rush to judgment on Champion and his place in musical theatre history. The temptation to view his last show as the end of a particular brand of Broadway was strong at the time—but ultimately premature. Less than a week after Champion's death, Frank Rich wrote in the *New York Times*: "Mr. Champion outlived the brand of old fashioned musical comedy he loved. He didn't leave behind any heirs with his particular calling and gifts.''[8] As the 1980s also saw the deaths of Michael Bennett and Bob Fosse, it may be that Champion's death heralded the passing of an era, but did not necessarily end ''old fashioned musical comedy.''

Nineteen years later, as this book goes to press, the inheritors of his approach are everywhere, albeit not always with Gower Champion's style or taste. The unbroken rise of spectacle in the 80s and 90s (fueled by the extravaganzas of Andrew Lloyd Webber and Disney) proved that while no one filled his shoes, producers continue to fill theatres with the elements he utilized so long and so well. ''Gower was 100% show business,'' Marge Champion recalled soon after his death. It is as good a summation as any for a man who gave as much as he had and then some to ''the musical comedy business.'' That gift, so ably chronicled here by David Payne-Carter, is as fine as a testimonial as anyone in that business could want.

Steve Nelson

NOTES

1. Samuel Leiter, *The Great Stage Directors* (New York: Facts on File, 1994), p. 56.

2. Frank Rich, ''Gower Champion Was a True Broadway Believer,'' *New York Times*, August 31, 1980, sec. D, p. 1.

3. Denny Martin Flinn, *Musical! A Grand Tour* (New York: Schirmer Books, 1997), p. 299.

4. Abe Laufe quoted in Leiter, *The Great Stage Directors*, p. 57.

5. Leiter, *The Great Stage Directors*, p. 59.

6. ''Gower Champion Returns to Broadway,'' *New York Times*, May 30, 1980, sec. C, p. 2.

7. Neil Simon quoted in *David Merrick: The Abominable Showman* by Howard Kissel (New York: Applause Books, 1993), p. 22.

8. Rich, ''Gower Champion . . . ,'' p. 4.

Chapter 1

The Beginnings of a Style
(1919–1936)

When Champion started in the theatre in 1936, vaudeville was in its death throes. He and his first partner, Jeanne Tyler, played the last remaining vaudeville houses, mostly with dance bands, and enjoyed a brief but successful career when vaudeville tried to team with the motion picture. They were also featured in one of the last of the spectacular Broadway revues, *Streets of Paris*, in 1939. The team broke up when World War II began.

After the war, Champion teamed up with the daughter of his childhood dancing teacher and, not too many months later, they were married and made a career for themselves as Marge and Gower Champion. They were the definitive American dance team of the 1950s. Their motion picture career, which was short-lived, came at the very end of the era of lavish MGM musicals.

Champion went on to a successful career as a Broadway director-choreographer, his last show, *42nd Street* opening the day he died, August 25, 1980. He became famous as a result of his Broadway musicals, but his aim had always been to direct motion pictures. Fame in that field eluded him, however, and the few films that he directed were not successful at the box office.

Gower Carlisle Champion was born on June 22, 1919, the son of John W. and Beatrice (Carlisle) Champion, in Geneva, Illinois, a prosperous suburb of Chicago.[1] He was named after his maternal grandmother, Bell Gower.[2] John Champion was an advertising executive with Munsingwear, the underwear manufacturer.[3] In September of 1919 John Champion announced that he had fallen in love with his secretary. John and

Beatrice were divorced and Beatrice was awarded custody of Gower and his older brother John Jr.; their father promptly remarried.[4]

It was soon evident that Mrs. Champion did not want to live near her former husband and his new wife, and she began casting about for other possibilities. She finally decided on Los Angeles, a choice which was to affect Gower deeply for the rest of his life. He came to love California and, although his career centered in New York, he never settled there, always returning to his home in Los Angeles when not actually in production.

The recently divorced Beatrice Champion, with John Jr. and Gower in tow, arrived in southern California early in January of 1922. Although she felt unjustly abandoned, Mrs. Champion maintained communication with her ex-husband, probably because the letters he wrote to her each month included an allowance to supplement the income she was able to earn as a dressmaker.[5] As a result, their position was comfortable, solidly middle class. The letters from Chicago also gave her the opportunity to rehearse again her version of the divorce. She made certain that Gower and John had the image of their father as a worthless bounder.[6]

In the late twenties, Los Angeles was on the brink of its golden period.[7] Burnished with the publicity of the oil and the movie boom, it was a town of movie stars and mock-Spanish architecture. In the fall of 1931, when Gower was 12, Mrs. Champion decided that it was time for her sons to begin cultivating some of the social graces necessary in the Los Angeles circles of which she intended them to become a part. Gower began taking dancing and piano lessons. It was at the Norma Gould School of the Dance on Larchmont Avenue in Los Angeles, within walking distance of the Paramount Studios, that he met Jeanne Tyler.[8]

The dance classes conducted by Norma Gould actually were more etiquette lessons than serious dance training. The boys learned to bow, one hand in front and one in back. The girls were carefully coached to keep their ankles chastely crossed whenever they sat. When couples did dance, the boys held handkerchiefs between their right palms and their partners' dresses, lest the girls' frocks be soiled.[9] Gould, herself a capable ballroom dancer, had performed with Ted Shawn.

Jeanne lived in the San Fernando Valley. Each week, along with several of her cousins, she would board one of the "red cars" and take the twenty-minute ride into Los Angeles to Norma Gould's studio for dancing lessons. After two years with Gould, Gower and Jeanne were obviously ready for some real training. Rather than progressing into the more advanced classes at the Gould Studio, they were enrolled at Elisa Ryan's Studio of Dance in Beverly Hills.[10]

The studio taught more advanced techniques than the polite exercises that they had been used to. Under the expert tutelage of Thomas Sheehy, Gower and Jeanne learned rudimentary ballroom steps and the basic variations: the waltz, the foxtrot, the quick step. The Ryan studio also had a drama department, headed by Ben Bard, and both Gower and Jeanne demonstrated a flair for dramatics. On the evening of May 29, 1933, "The Ben Bard Dramatic Groups in conjunction with the Thos. Sheehy Dancers" gave a recital in the Elisa Ryan Auditorium.[11] One of the offerings was Oscar Wilde's *Birthday of the Infanta*, with Gower Champion as the Count of Terra-Nueva. A tango was interpolated and danced to great acclaim by Gower and Jeanne.

In 1933 Gower attended Hubert Howe Bancroft Junior High School. He was small and spindly, a full head shorter than Jeanne, who never grew much beyond five feet. The lack of a firm father image, compounded by his mother's intense contradictions (she professed that evil could not exist, and yet she was almost maniacally suspicious, and punished Gower for any slight infraction of her strict moral code), made Gower fiercely private and almost obsequiously polite.[12] Some of his classmates found him cold and aloof, a spoiled brat.[13] Everyone called him "The Young Prince."[14]

In history class at Bancroft he sat behind a petite, vivacious blonde named Marjorie Belcher, who was later to become his wife.[15] She had not noticed much about him until, at the end of the year, Gower and Jeanne performed their customary ballroom turns at a talent show. Marjorie had not known that Gower was even remotely interested in dancing. It might, however, have been a topic of conversation between the youngsters, as Marjorie's father was Ernest Belcher, a famed Hollywood silent-film choreographer, known as "the Ballet Master to Movieland."[16] Belcher had a large dancing school and, of course, Marjorie had not only attended, but by junior high was already teaching some classes. At this same talent show she performed her specialty, a Portuguese Hat Dance. Her father had, of course, come to see her. He was impressed with Champion's ability and delighted by his boyish charm and natural stage presence. Belcher made enquiries about the boy's interests and his training.

Belcher's strength lay in his ability to analyze the choreographic exigencies of the camera, and his talent was apparent in his first films. He was soon sought after by such luminaries as D. W. Griffith (for the elegant prologue to *Broken Blossoms* [1919] with Carol Dempster). Belcher planned his work carefully, explaining that "the mere matter of *knowing what you want* simplifies direction."[17] This forthright attitude also surfaced in his casting only dancers whom he had trained himself. With a supply of dancers, trained in his own method, he could produce camera-ready routines "before noon."[18] By 1930, his school had become famous throughout the movie industry and was the largest dancing studio in Los Angeles.[19]

So impressed was he with the youngster's abilities and his potential that Belcher offered Gower a full scholarship to his school. The Ernest Belcher School of Dance was Champion's first experience with systematic dance training. He took ballet lessons twice or three times a week, but he did not really progress very far.[20] He simply was not interested. He continued his ballroom work with Jeanne at Elisa Ryan's, and since Belcher had not offered Jeanne lessons, he did not even mention his own work to her. But the lessons from Ernest Belcher were a beginning— and exposure to the discipline of dance, even if Gower ignored much of it.

In March of 1935, when Gower was 15, he played a part in his first musical. Although the Ben Bard Dramatic Group presented what they called "musical comedies," the shows were really little more than glorified recitals, with numbers designed to show off what the students had learned and plots built around the abilities of current students. On the evening of Saturday, March 30, 1935, Elisa Ryan presented a tabloid version of *Good News*, the quintessential 1920s collage musical. Ryan could not resist interpolating dance numbers into the show—parents wanted to see what their children had learned during the year, and every student had to have his or her time in the spotlight. Gower, along with Eric von Stroheim, Jr., had parts in the chorus. In the second act Jeanne and Gower did their specialty, a rendition of "Darktown Strutters' Ball."[21]

A year later, when Gower and Jeanne heard that the *Los Angeles Examiner* was sponsoring a waltz contest, they entered it as they had entered dozens of others. In fact, because they were only high school seniors, they had absolutely no interest in the prize—a week's engagement at the Coconut Grove. But on February 25, 1936, Jeanne and Gower found themselves finalists in the "Veloz and Yolanda Waltz to Fame." To their utter amazement, they won. Talent scouts were in the audience, and Music Corporation of America (MCA), one of the largest talent agencies, which booked acts into nightclubs and theatres across the country, signed them up immediately.

Since their entry into the contest was a lark, they were totally unprepared for a week's engagement in a nightclub. They had literally just waltzed around, letting the audience get caught up in their youthful charm and enthusiasm. The Coconut Grove agreed to let them have some time to rehearse a minimal act and they asked Tom Sheehy, their teacher at Elisa Ryan's Dance Studio, to help them with a routine. Gower supplied most of the ideas while Sheehy coached. Apparently the routine they composed was a tremendous success, because their week's engagement at the Coconut Grove turned into a six-week run. MCA had already booked them to appear with Carl Ravazza, "San Francisco's Singing Maestro," in the Mural Room of the Hotel St. Francis, where they danced for nine weeks beginning on July 17th.[22] Although they were a solid hit, neither Gower nor Jeanne nor Mrs. Champion, who had accompanied the couple to San Francisco, thought that much more would happen.

But MCA had other plans. The agency had secured a booking in the Gold Coast Room at the Drake Hotel in Chicago. As a result, during that summer, they worked with Ernest Belcher to compose new routines. The Coconut Grove asked them to return for six weeks ending in September. In October of 1936 Gower and Jeanne, with Mrs. Champion chaperoning, set out for Chicago, billed as "America's youngest dance team."[23]

At that point their act consisted entirely of their own dance routines, all choreographed by Gower and coached either by Sheehy or Belcher. (The one exception was "The Veolanda," which they had been taught by Veloz and Yolanda as part of their first prize for winning the "Waltz to Fame.") The Drake had their entrance completely preplanned. They were in skaters' outfits, Gower in a white suit and Jeanne in a short white satin outfit, edged in marabou. They entered down a slide onto the stage, where they performed one of Gower's dances, which at this point were full of the usual ballroom turns—a few modest lifts and tentative drops. But neither Gower nor Jeanne had enough dance technique to support anything more complex. In any case, it was not their astounding technique that endeared them to the audiences. It was their interactions with each other. Their joy and enthusiasm fairly bubbled over when they hit the dance floor, and audiences could not help but get caught up in it. By the end of their act their audiences felt as if they knew them, and were overjoyed to see their friends having so much fun.

Mrs. Champion enrolled Gower and Jeanne in ballet and tap classes, making sure that their days were full. They would usually attend class in the morning, have lunch, and spend the afternoons working on new routines. Even at this point, Gower was sensitive to the team's strongest asset—their freshness; that is, the appearance that they simply enjoyed dancing. Whenever a movement became stale, it was rehearsed and re-worked until a way was found to make it seem spontaneous again.

Champion's later rehearsal habits were forecast even in this early stage. Since his dance training was minimal, he had no working methods to follow. He had to find them himself, and from the earliest days he had the patience to repeat movements over and over again. It was not unusual for him to spend hours working out the choreography to a few bars of music.[24]

Despite the difficulties of the Depression, show business in the 1930s was a highly organized industry. A great variety of live entertainments could be found in every city. Traveling shows were booked into any town that had a theatre large enough to make a profit. Often shows were built around a "name" act—a singer or a big band. Other acts, of vary-ing quality and reputation, would be added to the bill to make up an entertainment of the necessary length. In some cities these shows would last an entire evening. In others, the show might be performed in a movie house, either before, after, or between feature films. The acts might be dance teams, like Gower and Jeanne, ventriloquists, or acrobats. Any-thing that would keep the curtain up was tried. As a result, agencies like MCA had no difficulty booking acts on tours that took entertainment out of major metropolitan centers to smaller cities and towns.

After seventeen weeks at the Drake, MCA sent the team out "on the road" with the Eddie Duchin Orchestra, the first of the team's many tours with big bands. Working with the great Eddie Duchin did have its drawbacks, however. Duchin played by ear, and although his orchestra followed the dance team's special arrangement of the Rachmaninoff "Prelude in C-Sharp Minor," its leader was simply repeating what he thought he had heard. Gower's choreography left no move unplanned, no notes unaccounted for, but Duchin would skip bars willy-nilly. Gower, however, had an uncanny ear, perhaps because of his early piano training, which enabled him to find the precise place Duchin had skipped and continue from that point. Jeanne, on the other hand, would get com-pletely lost. Since spinning was her strong point, she would twirl and twirl until she was caught. Then Gower would guide her until she, too, found her musical bearings.

The two toured with Duchin three times and were working with him as late as 1937. In fact, Gower and Jeanne worked steadily with Duchin, Guy Lombardo, Wayne King, and others, playing Philadelphia, Washington, DC, Boston, Pittsburgh, Chicago and Indianapolis. Tours most often traveled by rail. The amount of equipment necessary to mount a show made traveling by truck or air impractical; the big bands, for example, had to transport instruments, band stands, and the like. Gower and Jeanne traveled with at least five steamer trunks, and Jeanne's gowns filled three of them.

These road shows followed patterns that had been developed over years of trial and error. A typical engagement of this period was the one Gower and Jeanne played at the Metropolitan Theatre in Boston the week of February 11, 1937. They were touring with Eddie Duchin. On the bill with Duchin, his band and his singer, Jane Dover, were Gower and Jeanne, a "mixed trio" (a dance team comprised of two men and a girl), and a pair of tumbling comedians known as The Calgary Brothers.[25]

The next-to-closing spot was traditionally the featured one and, for obvious reasons, was called "the eleven o'clock spot." Coming at this point in the evening it had had, in effect, the rest of the show to warm up the audience. Its job was either to be so exciting that it gave spectators the release that they needed or to wake them up for the finale.

It was highly unusual for a dance team to be given the eleven o'clock spot. Not only that, but Gower and Jeanne were a new act (they had been performing less than a year), and they were a pair of youngsters, not yet eighteen. Furthermore, dance teams were romantic, not exciting. But by this time Gower had produced choreography that was significantly different from the ordinary dance team stuff involving close turns, deep dips, and acrobatic lifts. Undoubtedly influenced by Belcher, the team's style was more akin to ballet than to regulation ballroom dancing.

Their youth, combined with unusual and surprising moves, had led to a generous review in *Variety*: "Gower and Jeanne, mixed team, have the next-to-shut spot. That's a big order for their type of act. Why they are so situated on the bill becomes apparent before they have danced out half their first routine. To say they are distinctive would be understatement; to mention their refreshing youthfulness, their swell routines, surprise lifts would only give a sketchy impression of one of the most unique dance duos to come to Boston in many seasons."[26]

After a succession of tours, first with Duchin, then with Guy Lombardo, and finally with Wayne King, Jeanne and Gower's agency booked them into the Mount Royal Hotel in Montreal. The hotel had opened a new roof garden, the Normandie Roof, and wanted an act to introduce it. On July 17, 1937, the Normandie Roof opened to rave reviews for the room, as well as for Gower and Jeanne. They were on a double bill with Paul Gordon, an acrobat who performed on bicycles. After thirty-two weeks, MCA wanted them to move on, but the hotel seemed reluctant to let go of the act which had opened its highly successful nightclub and begged them to stay on. The club let them go only after they promised to return, and threw them a gala farewell party.[27] Gower kept that promise to return within the year, and he came back again in 1947 with a new partner, Marjorie Belcher, then called Marjorie Bell, the future Marge Champion.[28]

After Gower and Jeanne had spent the bulk of the summer of 1936 rehearsing and had played for a number of weeks in Chicago, it began to occur to him that his dancing was developing into a career. In complete contradiction to his behavior in dance classes with Ernest Belcher, he became punctual, faithful, and diligent at classes in Chicago. The more he worked, the more the work enthralled him and the more he began to realize his gift for dancing. In rehearsals with Sheehy or Belcher, Gower had idly suggested choreographic ideas; in Chicago, he developed a passion for rehearsing. He was developing into a choreographer.

Walter Kerr remembers seeing Gower and Jeanne in vaudeville, probably at the Earle Theatre in Washington, when he was teaching at Catholic University.[29] He recalled that Champion had an incredible elevation, making him seem to soar above the stage effortlessly. And Jeanne was so light that Gower could lift her, dip her, twirl her, as if she were weightless. Kerr also recalls their erect torsos, and the "drawn-up" feeling their posture gave to the performances. Later, Champion's choreography would be particularly distinctive because of this "drawn-up" feeling—in contrast, say, to the jerky angularity of Bob Fosse or the loose-limbed, head-thrown-back style of Michael Bennett. Kerr remembers further that the team exuded a confidence like that of seasoned performers. It could have been simply the youthful ebullience for which they were known. But, in any case, Gower and Jeanne simply performed, never "selling" what they were doing.

NOTES

1. Gower Champion, Birth Certificate for "Gower Carlisle Champion," Cook County Recorder's Office, Geneva, IL. Perhaps because at first the team

was billed as "America's Youngest Dance Team," Champion began paring years off his reported age. While young, Champion was called "Boy" because of his appearance and his pranks. As he grew older he retained his boyish good looks and continued his sense of the ridiculous, with sometimes puerile, practical jokes. During his thirties and forties his reported age fluctuated wildly (see, for instance, *Current Biography*, "Gower Champion, Marge Champion," September 1953, p. 39). At one point their friends joked that Marge was growing older while Gower was growing younger. The birth date of June 22, 1919, is on Champion's birth certificate and is as accurate as any date can be. (Interviews with Marge Champion Sagal, New York, January 6, 1984; Great Barrington, MA, May 25, July 5, and October 10, 1985.)

2. Sagal, Interviews.

3. Interview with Jeanne Tyler Estridge, San Bernadino, CA, June 5, 1985.

4. Estridge, Interview.

5. Estridge, Interview, and Interview with Jess Gregg, New York, January 15, 1985.

6. Estridge, Interview.

7. John Caughey and Laree Caughey, *Los Angeles: Biography of a City* (Berkeley: University of California Press, 1976).

8. Estridge, Interview.

9. Estridge, Interview.

10. "Gower Champion," *Dance Magazine*, March 1964, pp. 33, 82.

11. Elisa Ryan, Program for a recital, Elisa Ryan Studio of Dance, May 29, 1933.

12. Sagal, Interviews.

13. Interview with Tracy Torrey, Washington, DC, May 6, 1985.

14. Gregg, Interview.

15. Sagal, Interviews.

16. Ruth Eleanor Howard, "An Interview with 'The Ballet Master to Movieland,' " *The American Dancer* [*Dance Magazine*], June 1927, pp. 10–11.

17. Ibid.

18. Ibid.

19. Renee Dunia Hawley, *Los Angeles and the Dance, 1850–1930* (Ph.D. dissertation, University of California at Los Angeles, 1971), p. 50.

20. During class he would fall out of the most elementary pirouettes. To cover his error he would break up the class by crawling toward the piano and climbing up on top of it. In fact, Champion would never acquire a substantial or reliable enough dance technique to choreograph technically difficult work.

21. Elisa Ryan, Program for *Good News*, Cathay Circle Theatre, March 30, 1935.

22. Advertisement for Gower and Jeanne, *Variety*, June 19, 1940, p. 43.

23. "Gower Champion," *Dance Magazine*, March 1964, pp. 33, 82.

24. Estridge and Sagal, Interviews.

25. Sidney J. Paine, "Metropolitan, Boston," *Billboard*, February 11, 1937.

26. Chappie Fox, "Met, Boston," *Variety*, February 11, 1937.

27. "Gay Color Marks Normandie Roof," *Montreal Gazette*, June 18, 1937.

28. "Gower and Jeanne Still the Rage on Normandie Roof," *Montreal Daily Herald*, July 27, 1937.

29. Interview with Walter Kerr, New York, April 23, 1984.

Chapter 2

The First Broadway Shows
(1937–1942)

Gower and Jeanne's act was glamorous enough to be booked into the Empire Room at the Waldorf-Astoria for New Year's Eve, 1937.[1] The team was as popular in New York as it had been on road tours, and, by the next week, it opened in the Sert Room in the same hotel, a much more prestigious venue.[2] In fact, the team was the only one in the 1930s to play all three top nightclubs in New York: the Sert Room at the Waldorf, the Persian Room at the Plaza Hotel and the Rainbow Room atop Radio City in Rockefeller Center.[3]

While Gower and Jeanne were playing the Waldorf, Broadway was chalking up one of the worst seasons on record. Although business had been falling off since the crash in 1929, there were fewer shows produced during the season of 1937–1938 than in any of the previous thirty years.[4] An era of Broadway history was coming to a close. With ready money scarce, people were slow to spend hard-earned salaries on entertainment. In addition, motion pictures had cut deeply into the income of the legitimate theatre. Theatre on the road was surviving only by joining with the movies to provide "combination shows"—movies plus live entertainment. Gower and Jeanne had previously put in time traveling and performing with such shows.

One of the staples of the Broadway economy had been the lavish revue, and its influence on the rest of American musical theatre was pervasive, even in 1937. A revue is the quintessence of consumer theatre: acts strung together with no other thought than to entertain. And every musical show, even if it had what passed for a plot in the mid-1930s, also had to have the elements of a revue: gags and girls.

In 1939, Olsen and Johnson, stars of *Hellzapoppin*, were working in

The Streets of Paris, one of the last great Broadway revues.[5] Gower and Jeanne made their Broadway debut in the show. Robert Alton, the choreographer of *The Streets of Paris*, had seen their nightclub act and had requested that it be interpolated into the show. Thus, it was simply inserted into an appropriate spot on the bill. Their contract did call for them to appear in some of the ensemble numbers, however, and so for the first time since Ernest Belcher helped them with routines during the summer of 1936, the team had another choreographer.

Alton was one of the most active choreographers on Broadway at the time, providing the dances for many of the Rodgers and Hart musicals. His style was balletic, and he was famed for keeping the stage filled up with movement, rather than having a chorus strike poses with a solo or duet placed in front of them.[6]

On May 2, 1939, rehearsals for the show started in New York.[7] Alton met with Gower and Jeanne to begin some of their routines, and soon discovered that Gower was himself an even more able choreographer than his nightclub work had shown. Although Gower was bright and eager to learn what he could from this famous Broadway dance man, Alton deferred to him and in the numbers where Gower and Jeanne danced by themselves, Alton encouraged him to take over, and simply facilitated what he had planned.[8]

The Streets of Paris had a tryout run in Boston. It was a hit.[9] Some of the Boston papers speculated that the show was going to be held over a week or more, but the attraction of New York, swollen with visitors to the World's Fair, moved it to Broadway, where it opened at the Broadhurst Theatre on June 19, 1939, three days before Gower's twentieth birthday.

The show was the Broadway debut not only of Gower Champion and Jeanne Tyler, but of Bud Abbott and Lou Costello (a rising comedy team that had played burlesque and vaudeville and who were to make their lasting mark in movies). But the real sensation of the evening was Carmen Miranda, whose mugging eyes and fluttering hands stole the show. She was an immediate, absolute smash. If the show was not the last word in highbrow entertainment, at least it was a lavish entertainment.

The Streets of Paris closed in New York in February of 1940 and began a tour. Philadelphia was the first stop, then Washington. The show continued on to Pittsburgh, Toronto, Detroit, Cleveland, and Chicago, where it closed on May 8, 1940. Billy Rose then bought the rights and staged a revival with Gypsy Rose Lee, which he opened at the New York World's Fair in the summer of 1940—with but few members of the original cast. Gower and Jeanne had left the tour a bit before *The Streets of Paris* closed in Chicago. By May 3 their agency had them booked at the Strand Theatre in New York and by May 17, into the Earle in Washington.

By the middle of June, they were in the stage show at Radio City Music Hall. The William Holden–Martha Scott *Our Town* was the feature film, and the stage show had as its theme "Goin' to Town."[10] Gower and Jeanne were featured in a number that used the central revolve on the immense Music Hall stage. In a segment called "Small Town," an elderly couple (Janice Chambers and Loren Hollenbeck) sang a duet from a park bench, lamenting their lost youth. The stage revolved to discover Gower and Jeanne playing the couple as sweethearts.[11] Champion was to remember this scene years later, when he proposed precisely the same device for a production of a musicalized *Sayonara*, which he was planning to direct after *42nd Street*.[12]

The performance at the Music Hall earned Gower one of the very, very rare bad reviews during his ballroom days. It is clear from the context of the review, however, that the *Variety* critic did not like *any* of the show. "The bench turns around to bring out a youthful couple, the dance team of Gower and Jeanne," he wrote. "Male is very theatrical, over-using his hands and spoiling any illusion that may have been created by the appearance of the old folks. The girl, a charming type, carries the illusion much better."[13]

Dolores Pallet, a Music Hall production assistant at the time, had advised against hiring Gower and Jeanne because they were simply not her idea of what the number needed. After the opening, however, and despite a bad review, she confessed to the couple, "I had to eat crow because you brought down the house!"[14] Pallet was to become a force in the young team's career. She and Jeanne quickly became fast friends, and the two began sharing an apartment.

MCA, Gower and Jeanne's agency, had the same faith in the dance team as did Pallet. On June 19, 1940, the same day that the unflattering review of their Music Hall appearance was published in *Variety*, MCA took out a full-page advertisement for them in the paper. Gower is pictured with Jeanne sitting in front of him in a graceful pose. Radiating from Gower's head like a halo are rays that spell out "YOUTH." Around the couple is a listing of their engagements, starting with their first appearance at Coconut Grove. The list ends with their current engagement at Radio City Music Hall and a plug for their next booking, at the Rainbow Room, where they were to open July 24, 1940.[15]

In October of 1941 "girl and boy dancers" were being auditioned for a new musical called *The Lady Comes Across*. The musical was not entirely new; it had been written around the scenery and a few songs from *She Had to Say Yes*, a Dennis King Production which had tried to reach Broadway the previous season but never made it.[16] In an attempt to salvage some of the original $160,000 investment, the scenery and the songs had been sold to George Hale.[17] Recasting the revised show was a major problem. Joe E. Lewis (with whom Gower and Jeanne had appeared at Loew's State Theater on Times Square barely three months earlier) was finally settled on as the star.[18] Gower and Jeanne, making their second appearance on Broadway, had never auditioned for *The Lady Comes Across*. MCA had simply booked them into the show, as if it were yet another nightclub date.

When the show opened in New Haven, the reviews were anything but raves. Between New Haven and Boston, Morrie Ryskind was brought in to rewrite the book—"principally the second act."[19] The story line was still built around the scenery, however, and it is small wonder that when the show reached Boston, Elinor Hughes of the *Herald* pleaded "that it does seem as though the plot should be allowed to make a little more sense."[20]

The Lady Comes Across opened in New York on Friday, January 9, 1942, and closed Saturday evening, three performances later. The reviewers were unanimous in their agreement that the show did not come across. Willela Waldorf of the *Post* mentioned a detail about Gower and Jeanne's performance: "Their dance featuring a dash of dialogue was nice enough except that dancers who talk when they dance, unfortunately, invariably pant a little, unless they happen to be doing it on screen, where it is possible to do the dancing one month and then wait until a year from next August to record the talking. On the stage, where the Aristotelian unities are more carefully preserved, this sort of thing won't work."[21]

In fact, however, the team was mentioned more or less favorably in every other review. They were variously described as "freshly charming," "engaging young dancers," and "a cute pair of dancing youngsters." One critic thought that Joe E. Lewis's comedy spot was the highlight of the show, but that "second only is the young ballroom team of Gower and Jeanne."[22]

Each time the two were cast in a Broadway show during the next few years, the nominal choreographer deferred to Gower as far as the team's solo or featured routines were concerned. Gower and Jeanne were established as performers, and insofar as Gower's choreography was part of the act, he was now established as a choreographer in his own right.

Gower and Jeanne moved as a team. This is notable because each performed a function in the team. First, Jeanne was the point of connection with the audience; it was through her that Gower, the supporting member, communicated. They were playing love scenes. Choreographically, their dancing related one body to another; dramatically, their dancing related one person, or character, to the other; and theatrically, at least, their dancing had attained an effectiveness that was uncommon.

Their postures were identical, both with extremely erect torsos—erect to the point of seeming "drawn up," as Walter Kerr put it.[23] The positions of their arms and legs, their elevation, and their weight distribution all accomplished what they set out to do, whether it was the process of getting from one spot to another or simply one partner holding the other up. This sort of physical economy is, of course, central to technically correct dancing, and did not, in itself, set Gower and Jeanne apart from any of their competent colleagues. These were two dancers, however, who had been booked into one of the most prestigious nightclubs in the country when they were sixteen years old, before either had developed any serious dance technique.

Their technique—beyond basic ballroom moves—had been acquired either on the job or on the run, attending classes when and where they could. This training in economy would be fundamental to Champion's later development as both a choreographer and a theatrical director. Gower and Jeanne were more than just efficient dancers, and Champion was discovering ways that technical necessities could be turned into choreographic elements, allowing him to relate to his partner not only choreographically but dramatically as well.

Champion developed a number of devices. One involved having all of the team's extension radiate from a single point—that is, having the angles of all four arms and all four legs relate to one another by seeming to originate at a single point. This is an almost unavoidable compositional device when a pair is close, but it is more difficult to attain when they are far apart or when their torsos are on different planes. An example was the deep dip that became a Champion trademark. It appears often in Gower and Jeanne's work and was used again and again in Marge and Gower Champion choreography, as an ending pose or "button" to a number—a sort of dramatic finale to push an audience across the threshold from excitement to applause.[24] The pose is an extended dip, much like a classic tango dip, but the woman descends to within

inches of the stage floor, parallel to it, supporting herself on one extremely bent leg while the other leg is also parallel to the floor. The
male partner, instead of bending over with his arm around the woman's
back as in the tango plunge, straightens up, perpendicular to the floor
and supports the female from their joined hands with a fully-extended
arm. His free arm can echo some element of the overall design. The
radius of this composition is the joined hands, the male's body emanating
from that point, with the female's body relating to the male's via the
same point.

A second device that Champion used was a bent supporting leg. In
the extended dip, this device could be used to lower the radius of the
composition to knee level, where the bent supporting leg provided yet
another angle to repeat the major structural point. In other positions, this
bent leg was used to put the body's plane at an angle to the stage floor
so that a compositional tension would be created that either could be
resolved with right angles or provide a line in a more complex composition. With a tendency to bend his supporting leg, Gower's body was
often at an angle to the stage floor (rather than being perpendicular to
it). His slightly low-slung body position was one way that Champion
achieved a third device that was more dramatic than choreographic—
presentation of the woman.

While he was by no means merely support for Jeanne's moves, Gower
managed to employ the male support function as structural, choreographic, and theatrical elements. He was the context; she became the
statement. This emphasis on his own body as background and the
woman's as object-in-the-foreground became one of Champion's hallmarks. From his first major choreographic assignment, *Lend An Ear*, in
1948, which catapulted Carol Channing into stardom, through *42nd
Street*, in 1980, which showcased the talents of Wanda Richert, he consistently chose productions that essentially were vehicles for the presentation of women.

Within these three devices other elements of the Champion choreographic style may be seen. Both Gower and Jeanne showed extended
backs, with controlled, carefully placed shoulders. (Champion maintained this very disciplined, erect style throughout his career.) Although
their dancing was often described as balletic, Gower and Jeanne show a
minimal turn-out, with the feet either parallel or at a slight angle to each
other. This was due, of course, to their essentially ballroom style. Although they both had studied ballet—at least cursorily—their basic technique was that of ballroom dancers, not ballet dancers working in a

ballroom idiom. As some observant critics pointed out, however, the principal charm of Gower and Jeanne—and their success—was not a result of their dancing per se. There were many other dance teams in the business at the time, and many of them were better dancers; that is, others had a more solid technique. Gower and Jeanne's appeal was their youth and the fact that they were in love.

Between the Broadway shows there were always either nightclub dates or band tours. Gower and Jeanne never auditioned. After that first victory at the Coconut Grove, their agents, MCA, were able simply to book them into the next engagement, whether it be a club, a tour, or a Broadway show. At one point a member of another dance team complained to the agency that Gower and Jeanne were always working while she and her partner seemed to be making endless rounds of auditions and only playing dates every now and then. She asked the agency why the young team was given bookings so often—indeed, continuously. The agent replied, "They ask for them."[25]

Gower and Jeanne were different from most, if not all, the dance teams of the early 1940s. Ballroom dancing had become a craze in the 1910s. The incredible popularity of dancing was in no small part due to the publicity given it by exhibition ballroom teams such as Veloz and Yolanda and their predecessors in the 1910s and 1920s. By the time Gower and Jeanne were dancing, the public had begun to tire of the teams. There was at least one on every band tour, in every nightclub, every movie house, every Broadway revue.

The "standard" dance team was a carbon-copy of every other. The female was slight, with hair pulled back into a chignon. She wore a strapless panné velvet gown that was either black, studded with rhinestones, or white, with endless ruffles. The male had his hair slicked back and his moustache trimmed pencil thin. He wore a dinner jacket or, better yet, white tie and tails. This pattern had grown out of the style of the early dance teams, many of whom specialized in the tango, and seems to have given many teams, even into the 1930s and 1940s, the need to seem foreign.[26] On the other hand, there were the Astaire-Rogers clones, trying to reproduce the sophistication of the famous movie team. Gower and Jeanne, in total contradiction to either of the models, were simply young and enthusiastic. It was precisely this studied lack of self-consciousness that was the key to their success; it was what made them seem so "American."

The team's final Broadway show took place during the following season. *Count Me In* opened at the Ethel Barrymore Theatre on October 8,

1942. As in the case of *The Lady Comes Across*, the show had a con-
voluted preproduction history. It had started life as a college musical at
the Catholic University of America in Washington, DC. Written by Walter Kerr and Leo Brady, it was their third collaboration.

The show was a satire-fantasy. It concerned a family with a long
military history, reaching back at least to the Revolutionary War. The
Father, played on Broadway by the aging comedian Charles Butterworth,
felt uninvolved with World War II and was determined to do something
about it. During several fantasy sequences he participated in the war
effort. In an interview at the time, Kerr said that he and Brady had
created "a wistful little man, over 60, who had missed the last war. We
had him awaken in 1942, to face the terrific fact that he seemed to be
missing this war."[27]

Lester Cowan, who also just happened to be the husband of Ann
Ronell, the composer-lyricist, brought the show to New York. Somehow
the trip from Washington to New York, however, lessened its charm.
The reviews on the whole were mediocre. Cowan had done all the casting, and the authors arrived in New York to find that the roles originated
by students were now filled by "name" performers. Kerr felt that the
transition hardened the show, and that it had "lost its tone." He and
Brady had conceived the show as an exercise in fantasy and fun. "In
the transfer to New York, it had acquired a sense that what was going
on was plausible—it had lost its cartoon qualities, a degree of reason-
ableness that was essential seemed *to be missing*."[28]

The reviews, however, all mentioned Gower and Jeanne, and they
suggested that the critics had once again fallen under their youthful spell.
They were variously described as "pleasant and graceful as always" and
there were "several graceful duos" and "stellar specialties."[29] Once
again, Gower and Jeanne inserted dialogue into their routines, much to
the displeasure of Willela Waldorf who thought that they "would be
much pleasanter if they didn't try to talk while twirling," and to the
delight of *Variety*, which mentioned that the "dialogue with terps fur-
thers the plot."[30]

The show's choreographer was Robert Alton, who had worked with
Gower and Jeanne on *The Streets of Paris*. Alton had not been idle: in
the meantime he had choreographed *Du Barry Was a Lady, Panama
Hattie*, and *Pal Joey*. The choreographic influence of Alton on Champion
at this early stage is, of course, difficult to document. They were later
to work together on the Arthur Freed production of *Show Boat*, and
Alton's influence is evident there. But the tendency of the young Cham-

pion to insist upon "freshness" must have been reinforced by Alton who seemed "always to have some fresh routines in store—or at any rate, a way of seeming freshness about his handling of dance problems."[31]

The photographs of *Count Me In* indicate a development not evident before in Champion's *port de bras*—his arm position and use—which was later to become typical of his style. Champion often used the arms parallel, or roughly parallel, to the placement of legs, making the entire body a unified statement. An analogy to this would be the effect of an entire chorus moving in unison as opposed to a stage of dancers moving in similar, but not identical, patterns.

Further evidence of the careful control of the arms is the fact that they were often at right angles to one another, or to the torso. A right angle, as opposed to an oblique or an obtuse angle, is a much simpler choreographic device; it does not cry out for resolution as other types of angles do. This setting up of a direct, simple, and clear arm-torso vocabulary could be used to advantage in building a routine or number to a climax: with the arms never above the shoulders throughout a number, a final pose of arms extended above the head would be that much more exciting. Years later, Champion was to use this very simple device in his staging of the famous *Hello, Dolly!*. At this point, however, 22 years before *Dolly*, the beginnings of the device are evident in poses with arms and legs parallel, extending outward rather than upward.

Earlier reviews had mentioned the team's smoothness, but not until *Count Me In* was the team described as "acrobatic."[32] While Gower and Jeanne had used devices such as lunges and modest lifts before, Champion had not choreographed such moves into their routines because the team's technique was rudimentary; they simply could not handle the technical demands made by lifts. Even at the height of his career with Marge, Champion was never able to master the technique completely or muster the strength of classic adagio work with extended lifts. Moreover, a very young dance team could not be expected to incorporate virtuoso effects into routines *and* to be consistently described as smooth.

During his time with *Count Me In*, Gower was beginning to become increasingly aware of the war. Although he had received a deferment because he was supporting his mother, he felt it his duty to enlist. The couple talked it over. Gower knew that going into the service would put Jeanne out of work, but she would not listen to that excuse and told Gower to do what his heart told him. Gower enlisted in the Coast Guard—over the objections of his mother.[33]

Count Me In ran a scant six weeks. Unaware that Gower had enlisted,

MCA had booked the team on an international tour, and they were expected not only in Rio de Janeiro but on the Riviera, as well. On their final night together, Walter Winchell suggested that the tears he saw in Jeanne's eyes were for Gower, and ran a column on the parallels between the characters they played in the show and their real-life situation.[34] After the show that night, Gower walked Jeanne back to her apartment. They detoured through Central Park and climbed up in a tree, talking and crying in each other's arms. Gower left for the service the next day.[35]

MCA wanted Jeanne to find another partner, and even suggested possibilities. But she was too deeply in love with Gower even to consider anyone else. Morrie Ryskind, who had discovered Deanna Durbin, also offered Jeanne a crack at Hollywood. She refused, having decided that her career—in entertainment at least—could take place only with Gower. By the time he got out of the service, three years later, she had married and retired from show business. Jeanne never danced professionally again.[36] For Gower Champion, however, Marge, Hollywood, and Broadway still lay ahead.

NOTES

1. Waldorf-Astoria Hotel (New York), *Waldorf-Astoria Daily Bulletin*, December 31, 1937, vol. 7, no. 92, p. 1.

2. Malcolm Johnson, "In the Cafes and Supper Clubs: Casa Mañana opens Tuesday—New Reviews at the Rainbow Room—Other Night Life Notes," *New York Sun*, January 15, 1938.

3. Interviews with Jeanne Tyler Estridge, San Bernadino, CA, March 20, 1985, and June 5, 1985.

4. Gerald Bordman, *The American Musical Theatre* (New York: Oxford University Press, 1978), p. 510.

5. Marjorie Farnsworth, *The Ziegfeld Follies: A History in Text and Pictures* (New York: Bonanza Books, 1956).

6. Robert Baral, *Revue: The Great Broadway Period* (New York: Fleet Press, 1962), p. 206. An approach similar to Alton's was to become one of the hallmarks of Champion choreography.

7. Willela Waldorf, untitled, *New York Post*, May 3, 1939.

8. Estridge, Interviews.

9. Waldorf, *Post*.

10. Radio City Music Hall, *Program*, June 13, 1940.

11. Estridge, Interviews.

12. Interview with Robin Wagner, New York, October 25, 1984.

13. Char, "Music Hall, New York," *Variety*, June 19, 1940.

14. Estridge, Interviews.

15. Advertisement for Gower and Jeanne, *Variety*, June 19, 1940, p. 43.

16. Burns Mantle, "The Lady Comes Across," *New York Daily News*, January 10, 1942.

17. Scho, "The Lady Comes Across," *Variety*, January 14, 1942.

18. "Boston Lauds Hale Show," *New York Herald Tribune*, December 19, 1941.

19. *New York Times*, December 15, 1941.

20. Elinor Hughes, " 'Lady Comes Across,' " *Boston Herald*, December 15, 1941.

21. Willela Waldorf, " 'The Lady Comes Across' New Musical at the 44th Street," *New York Post*, January 10, 1942. Although Gower was doing the choreography for the team's appearances in the show, the dialogue-while-dancing idea was not his but an inspiration of the show's choreographer, George Balanchine.

22. Scho, "The Lady Comes Across."

23. Interview with Walter Kerr, New York, April 23, 1984.

24. See Lehman Engel, *The American Musical Theatre*, rev. ed. (New York: Collier Books, 1975), p. 106.

25. Estridge, Interviews.

26. See Julie Malnig, *Exhibition Ballroom Dancing and Popular Entertainment* (Ph.D. dissertation, New York University, 1987).

27. Kerr quoted in Hazel Channing, "Broadway Goes to College for Hit Musical Show," *Boston Sunday Post*, September 13, 1942, supplement, p. 5.

28. Kerr, Interview.

29. Burns Mantle, " 'Count Me In' Was a College Show Before Broadway Got It," *New York Daily News*, October 9, 1942; Rowland Field, "Broadway Dull Story Handicaps New Musical," *Newark Evening News*; Elie, " 'Count Me In,' " *Variety*, September 16, 1942.

30. Willela Waldorf, " 'Count Me In' Musical Comedy About the Home Front," *New York Post*, October 9, 1942, and Abel, "Count Me In," *Variety*, October 14, 1942.

31. John Beaufort, " 'Count Me In' Expert Dancing Decorates the Show at Ethel Barrymore," *Christian Science Monitor*, October 9, 1942.

32. Robert Coleman, " 'Count Me In' Opens at Barrymore," *New York Daily Mirror*, October 9, 1942.

33. Estridge, Interviews.

34. Walter Winchell, "On Broadway: The Private Papers of a Cub Reporter," *New York Daily Mirror*, November 3, 1942, p. 10.

35. Estridge, Interviews.

36. Estridge, Interviews.

Chapter 3

Marge
(1942–1948)

Late in 1945, Marjorie Belcher, now living in New York and performing under the name Marjorie Bell, got a letter from her father. "Boy is back in town," he wrote. What he meant was that Gower Champion had returned to Los Angeles from Coast Guard duty and was taking classes at the Belcher school. Marjorie knew that her father had always wanted her and "Boy," as he always called Champion, to team up. It had never worked. When they were younger, Gower was already paired with Jeanne Tyler, and no amount of conniving on her father's part could spark a partnership or a romance.[1]

Marge had a partner, too. Louis Hightower was tall, dark, and handsome. Although Champion had neither the looks nor the strength of Hightower (the young Gower was scrawny and short), he possessed an indefinable something that Marjorie's partner lacked. In fact, Marjorie Bell and Louis Hightower had not done badly. Although they never achieved the acclaim of Gower and Jeanne, they appeared in clubs, and even made a short film together—a very early effort by the then 21-year-old George Sidney, called *Sunday Night at the Trocadero*.[2] Their likenesses also had appeared in the Walt Disney classic *Snow White and the Seven Dwarfs*. Disney had sent his scouts to all the Los Angeles dancing schools looking for models for his characters. At Ernest Belcher's School of Dance, they had chosen five candidates for Snow White, Marjorie Belcher among them. They also found a candidate for Prince Charming in Louis Hightower. Both of the young people were hired and became models for the cartoon characters.[3]

During the war, Champion had spent three years in the Coast Guard. The first year he was assigned as a platoon leader on Catalina Island off

the coast of California.[4] It did not take the service long to discover that
Seaman First Class Champion had talent, and the second year of his stint
was spent touring with the Coast Guard musical revue *Tars and Spars*.
Tiring of spending the war on stage, Champion requested sea duty and
was assigned to public relations aboard a troop transport in both the
Atlantic and Pacific.[5]

Champion's part in the revue, however, was to have consequences far
beyond the armed forces. In fact, his first directing assignment was a
result of contacts he made during the show's tour. *Tars and Spars* had
been conceived as a recruiting tool by Vernon Duke and Howard Dietz,
both of whom were also in the Coast Guard.[6] It was a regulation military
revue, much like Irving Berlin's better known *This Is the Army*, and it
played a brief stint in New York at the Plymouth Theatre in 1943. It
starred the most famous member of the Coast Guard at the time, Victor
Mature. The civilian director of the revue was Max Liebman, who would
later go on to fame as the director of the early television success, *Your
Show of Shows*. Through this contact, Marge and Gower Champion were
later to become the first dance team whose reputation was made through
television—on *The Admiral Broadway Revue*.

When he was released from active duty, Champion returned to Los
Angeles. The last thing he wanted to do was begin a new career as a
ballroom dancer with another partner. He took some lessons with Ernest
Belcher (who quickly wrote to his daughter), and made the rounds of
the studios. He also made a screen test for Fox, but was not offered a
contract. Meanwhile, Bell wrote a letter inviting Champion to come to
New York to look around. She could not offer much in the way of
contacts, but she *was* performing, having been cast as the blonde witch
in *Dark of the Moon*.[7]

Champion made his way to New York around Thanksgiving of 1945
and stayed at the St. Moritz for twenty-one dollars a week. Much to their
surprise, Marjorie Bell and Gower Champion got on very well, and even
had Thanksgiving dinner together in a friend's apartment. Soon Champion was offered a contract from MGM.[8] His agent had obtained the
screen test, made at the Fox Studios, and had peddled it to the leading-
man-poor MGM. Gene Kelly was still in the service, Fred Astaire was
still under contract to RKO, and the studio thought that they might be
able to parlay Champion into a leading man. Despite the budding romance with Marjorie Bell, the offer from Metro-Goldwyn-Mayer was
too good to pass up, and Champion returned to California early in 1946.

The relationship seemed to offer enough potential that Bell returned to Los Angeles during the summer to stay with her father. Suddenly, however, the relationship was severed. Perhaps Champion felt, as he had with Jeanne, that he was going to be tied down too quickly; perhaps he was simply afraid of the prospect of marriage. At any rate, after months of frequent letters and weeks of seeing each other every day, Bell found herself reporting to a job in Louisville to do the lead in Jerome Kern's *Sally*, with no word from Champion.

Although Champion was under contract with MGM, he made only "one rotten picture," as he put it.[9] Although MGM thought that they might be able to turn him into another Gene Kelly, they seemed unwilling to take the plunge and give him an important part. The one movie he made for them under contract was *Till the Clouds Roll By*, a fictionalized account of Jerome Kern's life "in which I danced across the screen in strawberry pink hair with Cyd Charisse."[10] Champion was eager to get back into the mainstream of show business, but most of all he disliked being treated as a chorus boy, called in for a fifteen-second clip. "I hated it, but it was the only thing I knew how to do. I could make good money dancing and it was better than working in chop suey joints or grousing around for a job."[11]

Meanwhile, Richard Rodgers happened to see Marjorie Bell in *Sally* at the Papermill Playhouse in New Jersey. He told her that she was just the type to play the lead in one of his shows, but that she badly needed vocal work. He recommended a coach in New York, and she began regular sessions with Clytie Hine Mundy.

Champion was already thinking about directing, and he was frustrated by the fact that his contract with MGM had produced only fifteen seconds of film. He had written to Bell that the last thing he wanted to do was to take up ballroom dancing again.[12] Resuming a ballroom career had the specter of retreat about it. One of his strongest traits was his need to approach work on his own terms. At the beginning of his career, for example, he had refused to accept simple ballroom formulas and had begun to tell stories through the dances. Champion would only agree to direct if he had complete freedom to alter, add, or delete material as he saw fit. He was never one to choose the safe alternative. So, resuming a ballroom career could very well have seemed to him that dreaded safe alternative. On the other hand Champion perhaps felt that almost inextricable pull that New York has always had for every performer. Whatever the reason, he began corresponding with Bell again, and, early in 1947, he was making plans to move east.[13] Bell and a friend, Jess Gregg, welcomed Champion to New York. He found space in an abandoned church south of Houston Street, an area then *terra incognita* to theatre folk.

At this point Bell was free to rehearse with Champion, often for hours at a time. He had not lost his power of total immersion. When he was rehearsing, nothing else existed for him. By the end of a three- or four-hour rehearsal session, Bell would be wild with hunger but often too tired to eat. Sometimes, Champion would ask her to kill time while he continued to work. Sometimes he needed to be totally alone—apart even from the person who was going to perform the dance he was creating at that very moment.

Champion's plan was to try out his new act with Bell at Montreal's Normandie Roof, where he was well-known and well-loved. Montreal was also far enough away from New York City to ensure that no one was likely to come to see them while they worked the kinks out. He called up the office and arranged a date. The management was overjoyed that at least half of their premiere attraction was returning. He also contacted Merriell Abbott, who had been Gower and Jeanne's mentor. She booked them sight unseen into the Palmer House in Chicago for the summer and into the Persian Room of the Plaza in New York for the following fall.[14]

The new act would consist of material reworked from his days with Jeanne, and some new numbers as well. Because there would be two shows nightly, the new team needed at least six numbers. Some customers saw both, so the pair could not use the same material in both shows. Champion taught Bell the choreography to two numbers resurrected from his earlier career, "Vaudeville 1910" and "The Missionary and the Maiden." One of the new ones was called "Three Blind Mice," and was performed as a dance round, that is, with both dancers performing the same steps, but starting on different bars of music. Champion was to use the idea of a dance round a number of times, and "Three Blind Mice" was to have many descendants. His choreography at this point was well-crafted and intricate, rather than difficult, but the work already added up to more than just a series of steps. Even the simplest of numbers had a clear-cut form.

Finances were very tight for the budding team. They had to pay the bills in New York, provide some sort of costumes for Bell, and get to Montreal. Champion received payment for his stint in *Till the Clouds Roll By*, which went for his rent, with enough left over to buy a couple of second-hand dresses that could be turned into presentable costumes. He still had suits from his Gower and Jeanne days—and they still fit.

Bell was still performing at night in the Duke Ellington musical *Beggar's Holiday* at the Broadway Theatre, sewing during the mornings, and rehearsing all afternoon. Champion was, as usual, tireless in attending to every detail. If he was going to open in a new act, the act would have integrity from the first choreographic notion down to the sequins on his partner's costumes.

The new team, of course, needed a name. The friends discussed the question endlessly, considering every possibility, no matter how ridiculous it sounded. Champion thought that since he was known as half of the team "Gower and Jeanne," that "Gower" needed to appear in the name. They considered "Gower and Marjorie," but it somehow did not seem sleek enough. "Gower and Bell" worked, but it was Champion's first name and Bell's last. It was not consistent. They decided to give Champion a new first name and keep "Gower" as a second name. "Christopher" was decided upon as crisp and rhythmically right with "Gower." The act was christened "Christopher Gower and Marjorie Bell"—"Gower and Bell" for short.[15]

The date approached. Everything seemed to be in order except the fare up to Canada. Gregg loaned the team thirty dollars, and they were off.[16] Gower and Bell opened in Montreal on April 25, 1947. They went on to play the Bradford Roof in Boston. Again, they had two shows a day, but because it was midsummer, they played the first show at 6:30 in the evening, in broad daylight.[17] It had been scheduled early to catch the theatre crowd that dined at the Bradford before walking across Tremont Street to the Shubert Theatre to see Dorothy Stone and Charlie Collins in *The Red Mill*.[18]

In Montreal, Champion had conceived and choreographed a story ballet for the team. He called it "Marseille." It was the story of an American sailor who was on the dock at Marseille, thinking about his girlfriend back in the United States. Bell played a French girl, also longing for her lover. The number was the second in the act, because Champion conceived it as a melange of monologues, music and dancing, and placing it any later would have rendered the team too out of breath to talk. He searched for the right French-sounding music—something wistful—and thought he had found it, only to discover that it had become popular as a Jewish wedding song. He scuttled that idea. Finally, Dolores Pallet, his friend from Radio City Music Hall, was able to supply music that seemed to work and would tie together the bits of monologue that Champion had written.

The number began with Champion at the microphone, talking about his girl while Bell moved in front of him. The choreography was not really dance steps, merely free-form movement that had been carefully timed to echo the phrasing of the monologue. There were slow turns, a couple of quick steps, a stop, a thought. Then the two changed places. Finally they danced at the same time, but not together: each was deep in thought, and while the movements related visually, they did not relate the two characters to each other dramatically. At certain points Bell and Champion were side by side, facing front, but not facing each other. For an instant at the end of the number, their eyes met, as if each had been able to conjure up the absent lover and imagined that the other was that person. They parted sadly and walked to opposite sides of the floor.[19]

This kind of concept was not typical of standard nightclub fare at the time. Champion was alone in his faith that a nightclub audience would have enough patience to sit through a story rather than merely a series of spins and lifts. He and Bell enjoyed doing the number tremendously, and the audiences appreciated it. When they performed it later in the summer in St. Louis, Ray Hunt, critic for the *Daily News*, thought that the number was "as poignant and full of pathos as if it had been written by a master of the short story. It's so powerful and so beautifully done that it dwarfs any other single routine."[20]

Suddenly news came that Bell had been called back for the third time to audition for the lead in Rodgers and Hammerstein's *Allegro*. This was the chance she had been waiting for, and the role was almost assuredly hers. But if she were cast in the show, it would mean breaking up the team, to say nothing of straining the personal relationship that had developed between Champion and herself. Champion proposed that he find another partner and fulfill the engagement they had been offered at the Municipal Opera in St. Louis. Bell could go on to New York to begin rehearsals for *Allegro*. Champion would join her after the summer was over. Everything would be fine, he explained, because they would be married. It was the first time that Champion had mentioned marriage, much less proposed. Bell made her decision: she would stay with Champion and refuse the role.[21]

By May of 1947 they were settled into a three-month run at the Palmer House in Chicago, with a good prospect of an even longer run in St. Louis. Champion was looking forward to the real test: opening in New York. He rehearsed every day, either refining numbers that were already being tried out in the act, or creating new ones. And after a couple of months of performing together, they could already see things in the act that had to be corrected.

First of all, the act needed a number during which the couple could relax. At this point, they were still using "The Missionary and the Maiden" and "Vaudeville 1910." They were exhausting numbers. The pair had added another called "Showing the Town" to their repertoire. It was a series of imitations, Champion doing Ray Bolger and Bell doing a quintessential Agnes de Mille dream ballet, full of up-turned, circling palms. "Showing the Town," which was added to the novelty number "Three Blind Mice" and the others, made for an exhausting act.

Champion devised a new number to the popular song "Margie." Bell was seated in the middle of the dance floor on a plain chair or stool. The lighting was subdued, concentrated on a small circle around her. Champion stood behind her. He began an easy, very intimate chorus of the song, with much interplay between the two dancers: not much real movement, but a lot of looks, smiles, nods. He began to move around again, very easily, using broad, precise sweeps of his arms with the palms downward and a couple of soft shoe steps. At the end of the chorus, he slid into the chair while Bell got up to do her version of the same routine. She returned to the chair, Champion arose, and they ended the number in an embrace—very, very quiet and simple. The audience loved it.[22]

Perhaps it was with this number that Champion began to discover that the more emotion that can be shown, the more an audience responds to it. Fancy or difficult steps do not always bring an audience to its feet; seeing a loving relationship, a decision made, or a person excited after a long period of grief—that makes an audience's heart swell. The quintessence of this, of course, would be the "Hello, Dolly!" number, where the waiters welcome Dolly Levi back to the Harmonia Gardens Restaurant after a long absence. The number would consist of nothing more than walking around, waving the arms, and a couple of modest kicks at the end, but it was packed with emotion.

Another reason for inserting "Margie" late in the act was that Bell perspired. By the end of a thirty to forty-five minute dance act, she was dripping wet. Champion could put her in the chair, mop her off, and, after wrapping her up in a Don Loper satin coat, begin the extremely low-activity number so that Bell could catch her breath.[23]

On June 5, 1947, Ivor Novello's *The Dancing Years* opened at the St. Louis Municipal Opera. It was produced by the Shubert Brothers, one of the top producing organizations in New York. Apparently, they were trying out the show in St. Louis with hopes that a Broadway run would eventually materialize. Novello was an English composer who was virtually a one-man show. He wrote not only the music but the lyrics and the book, directed, and starred in most of his own vehicles. His work was sentimental and romantic, more operetta than musical comedy. Bell played the soubrette, "Grete," and Gower was her lover "Franzel."[24] Although the show got decent reviews in St. Louis, the Shuberts did not bring it into New York. Perhaps it was too coy for the late 1940s.

The Park Plaza Hotel in St. Louis offered the team a contract for the balance of the summer. The St. Louis critics received the team rapturously. Robert Goddard of the *St. Louis Globe Democrat* noted the striking difference between Gower and Bell and the other dance teams making the rounds. "Most ballroom dancers," he said "do the same old thing that ballroom dancers have been doing for years on end. They glide, spin and in general look like people from another planet. Gower and Bell are definitely from this planet and their act is as modern as radar. . . . We have an idea that Gower and Bell are pretty much in love with each other."[25]

The act moved on to an engagement at the Empire Room in Chicago's Palmer House, probably booked through Merriell Abbott, a friend of Gower's from his Gower and Jeanne days. Their Chicago act was typical. An orthodox opening, with some standard ballroom turns and lifts, a waltz. "Marseille" followed. It had to be done early because of the need to speak—the team would be out of breath were the number to be scheduled later in the act. Alternately, they would perform a revision of "Showing the Town" called "Three to Make Ready." Champion substituted a very good imitation of Paul Draper for his less than stunning impersonation of Ray Bolger.[26] The third number in each show was either "Three Blind Mice" or "Vaudeville 1910."

The entire time that Gower and Marge stayed at the Palmer House—through July, August, and September of 1947—they rehearsed every day, often to exhaustion. Gower completely lost track of time and his appetite. A typical rehearsal would start about 9:30 in the morning and continue until 2:00 or 3:00 in the afternoon without a break, even for a snack. Gower was acutely aware that their New York debut was looming: it had been scheduled for early October at the Persian Room of the Plaza. The team needed more than the numbers that had served them well in St. Louis and Chicago. In New York, there often would be "holdovers": customers who saw the first show, went out to dinner, and then caught the second show as they enjoyed their after-dinner drinks. The team needed at least six numbers so that they would not have to repeat one in the course of two shows. And Gower was aware that the act needed two of each *kind* of number; that is, two openers, two middle numbers, and two closing numbers. They could then mix the numbers up as the days progressed to give themselves some variety, but each show had to maintain structural integrity as well.

One of the numbers they rehearsed in Chicago was a replacement for "Marseille" called "Remember," which could be put together using a number of different sections, which themselves could then be varied. One of the sections included Gower dancing to Bell reciting Lewis Carroll's "Jabberwocky," which they both thought was pretty sophisticated material for a nightclub act in 1947.[27]

Gower and Marge decided to be married on October 5 in Los Angeles, sandwiching the ceremony between their engagement in Chicago and their opening in New York. And so, at a late show in 1946, Marjorie Bell and Christopher Gower performed for the last time. They had discussed, long and hard, what to call the team after they were married. Champion did not want to perform indefinitely as a dance team, and he was already planning another career as a musical comedy director. They decided to call the team "Marge and Gower Champion" so that the name "Gower Champion" would be in the public consciousness.

On Sunday morning they caught the early flight out of Chicago for Los Angeles. All arrangements had been made, and they were met at the airport and whisked directly to the home of Mr. and Mrs. O. W. March, Marge's aunt and uncle, whose garden they had chosen for the wedding.[28] That night they caught the night flight to New York.[29] After appearing live on television with Milton Berle on October 7, they opened their act at the Persian Room the next day. Champion had decided to use material with which they were both extremely comfortable, and the act consisted of three numbers: their opening ballroom turn, followed by the new version of "Showing the Town." They ended with the by-now-standard "Vaudeville 1910."[30]

One of the highlights of the evening was a new section of "Showing the Town," a satire of Tony and Sally DeMarco, the *ne plus ultra* of dance teams since Veloz and Yolanda had retired. The DeMarcos specialized in the quick step, a standard ballroom combination that every team that attains any level of competence eventually learns. It is danced with the partners close together to very quick music and consists of very tiny steps. The DeMarcos' version was danced to "Holiday for Strings," which the Champions used for their spoof. Gower was intent and firm, Marge, all smiles, greeting people in the audience and throwing kisses at every opportunity. With Marge's special knack for instant audience contact, the satire worked—and audiences loved it.[31]

Marge and Gower Champion's style had found itself. They were not really a dance team as much as a pair of actor/entertainers who danced. Their act did not so much consist of dance numbers, one after another, as it was a minuscule review, with snips of dance, song, little dramas, and a bit of spectacle. Champion endlessly refined what material they did use so that each moment contributed to the whole. In an interview a couple of days after they opened, he said, "Our work is as near creative theatre as we dare make it. It's always nip and tuck. When we tried out our present show in Chicago, we went too far and had to substitute some commercial stuff. Here, we're hoping it will go as is."[32]

In November they were playing at the Mayflower Hotel in Washington, DC.[33] Their audience was full of politicians who were in Washington for weeks at a time. So many couples saw their show night after night that by the end of their engagement, they found that not only could the audience repeat their introductions and dialogue along with the act, but they often did.[34] Marge and Gower were so well received by the crowd that Pearl Mesta, that quintessential Washington hostess, asked them to dance at one of her parties.[35]

Engagement followed engagement: January at the Statler in Boston and Cleveland, February at the Terrace Room in the Detroit Statler.[36] They looked forward to returning to St. Louis, where they had worked the summer before. The show they were contracted for was Cole Porter's *Jubilee*, with rehearsals beginning in June.[37] But there was to be a change. While the Champions were touring the midwest, Bert Shevelove and George Nichols 3rd were attempting to mount an intimate revue called *Small Wonder*.[38] *Small Wonder* was capitalized at $150,000, and by February of 1948 Shevelove and Nichols had raised two-thirds of that amount.

They had engaged Anna Sokolow, who was later to gain fame as an important modern dance choreographer, but problems developed and she withdrew from the assignment shortly before rehearsals were to begin.[39] In haste, Shevelove asked Champion if he would step in as choreographer. He leapt at the offer, his first for a Broadway show. There was the problem, however, of the long-standing contract with the St. Louis Municipal Opera. After some negotiations, the opera released him from his contract provided that Marge would fulfill hers and that he was announced as the choreographer.[40]

As the Champions made their tour of midwest hotel nightclubs, however, Marge began to experience pain in her right knee. At first dismissing it, she was unable to ignore it until finally in Chicago, at the

Palmer House once again, the pain was so great that she could only perform their show and then retire to bed. When Merriell Abbott heard of Marge's difficulty, she referred the case immediately to her husband, Dr. Philip Lewen, an orthopedic surgeon, who diagnosed the trouble as a cyst on her kneecap.

With this development, engagements had to be cancelled. The young couple, although their careers were gaining momentum, had no savings. Marge was able to spend some convalescent time in Chicago staying with Gower's father, and then drove to California where they stayed with Mrs. Champion. Champion was again on his home territory, with time on his hands. There was not enough available material from the upcoming *Small Wonder* to keep him occupied, and he was too nervous about the impending show to spend time around the house nursing Marge.[41] George Bauer, with whom Champion had performed in *Tars and Spars*, asked him to come to a couple of rehearsals of a revue he was working on called *Lend An Ear*. With nothing better on the horizon, Champion began attending rehearsals regularly.

Lend An Ear had started out as a revue commissioned by Frederick Burleigh. After it premiered in Pittsburgh in April of 1941, plans to take the revue to New York were shelved. After the war, there was continuing interest, and by May of 1948 rehearsals were under way in Los Angeles.[42]

As Champion became more and more involved with the production readying itself for an opening at the Las Palmas Theatre in Los Angeles, he progressed from an advisor to choreographer to a listing in the opening program that announced "Dances and Musical Numbers staged by Gower Champion."[43] In actuality, he was responsible for much of the actual direction.[44]

In the cast was Carol Channing. Champion realized her potential and worked with her to develop a daffy, wide-eyed and innocently conniving character that Channing has used since. The show consisted of songs and skits—but most more inventive than regulation revue fare.[45] In one segment, the cast relived "Friday Dancing Class" with all its incipient romances and embarrassing situations; in another skit, the authors portrayed "Words Without Song," a satire on the ridiculousness of opera libretti: the words of the libretto were spoken instead of sung.[46] The absurdity of bad opera librettos—particularly with Channing playing the diva—was made all too apparent.

The hit of the show, however, was a satire of 1920s musicals called "The Gladiola Girl." The premise of the skit was that "The Messrs.

Lou and Z. Z. Sherbert'' had sent out a road company of *The Gladiola Girl* in 1928 and it had gotten lost.[47] We see it now, in 1948 after it has been touring in the midwest for the past twenty years. The book was intact and included such musical numbers as ''Where Is the She for Me?'' ''Doin' the Old Yahoo Step,'' and ''In Our Teeny Little Weeny Nest for Two.''

Lend An Ear premiered at the Las Palmas Theatre on June 14, 1948, to ecstatic reviews. Plans were immediately begun for a New York opening. Champion had no idea that it was his work on *Lend An Ear* rather than his ''big chance'' in *Small Wonder* that would establish his reputation as a choreographer. But he had concocted some imaginative, and occasionally strange, ways of staging problem numbers in the Las Palmas revue. For instance, in a rather prosaic and conventional song, ''I'm Not in Love,'' sung by William Eythe as a boss to Linda Ware as his secretary, Champion choreographed Gene Nelson and Bob Sheerer as the boss's alter egos, leaping enthusiastically over the desk. Champion was doing more than simply choreographing or staging numbers, he was influencing the very tenor of the piece, giving it a style that was beyond the material. In short, he was taking chances. He felt relaxed about the project and worked in what he perceived to be a non-pressured environment.

Not so with *Small Wonder*. Rehearsals for the show began on July 26, 1948, at the Coronet Theatre in New York.[48] Champion did not have the directorial or creative freedom that he had been afforded with *Lend an Ear*. He had been hired as a choreographer, nothing more. Although the producers had hired Champion to choreograph, Shevelove, as director, was responsible for the overall character of the revue. He was definitely in charge of the proceedings and kept a tight rein on Champion's creativity. Thus, he felt free to edit what the ambitious choreographer had created. The rehearsal period for *Small Wonder* was not a happy one: Champion felt that whatever choreography of his appeared on stage did so only after monumental struggle and defense on his part.[49]

During the rehearsal period, however, he met Richard Priborsky, who had been hired as a rehearsal pianist. Champion and Priborsky found that they were kindred spirits, or at least kindred workers. The two were mutually meticulous and willing to explore, often *ad nauseam*, every possibility in choreography and music. As Champion would choreograph, Priborsky would sit at the piano and improvise. Thus, the choreography and the dance arrangements would be created at the same time. This close collaboration, first experienced while choreographing

Small Wonder, was to become Champion's preferred way of working.[50] He felt that he had discovered a true creative partner with whom he could explore, both choreographically and musically, the boundaries of his art. Thus, Shevelove's editing of the fruits of their labors was all the more frustrating.[51]

The revue opened in Boston at the Majestic Theatre on August 30, 1948. The reviews suggested that the show needed work and placed the blame on Shevelove. Two weeks later, when the show debuted in New York at the Coronet Theatre on September 15, Champion garnered some fine notices, but Shevelove was again faulted for the show's lackluster effect. Although Champion was never one to pay much attention to renviews, it is not impossible that the reviewers' comments made an impression—as a director, Champion was always acutely aware of the overall pace and effect of a show, often deleting spectacular numbers for what he felt was the good of the production as a whole.[52]

Following the opening of *Small Wonder* the Champions appeared at the Persian Room once again, an anniversary of the team's opening there a year before.[53] The program suggests that Champion was beginning to explore the structure of an expanded evening's entertainment. By this point Marge and Gower had gained a reputation, and so they were headlining instead of opening the act.

By the time the engagement at the Persian Room had ended, plans to bring *Lend An Ear* to Broadway had materialized. Champion went right into rehearsal. The reviews that greeted the opening on December 16 were ecstatic. Any cloud that *Small Wonder* had cast over Champion's burgeoning career was quickly and completely dispelled. Walter Terry speculated that Champion was "saving his best stuff for Broadway on the choreography line in this show," and that *Small Wonder* was "just a second thought which he cared too little about."[54]

George Freedley observed that Champion's work on *Lend An Ear* seemed much more accomplished than on the previous revue: "The dances," Freedley said, "have more substance, while the dynamics and phrasing of movements are clearer and sharper. In addition, the patterns are fresh, novel, often complex, yet remain completely in character with the themes."[55]

The endorsements of *Lend An Ear* were not the only validation of the show. The success of Champion's most fanciful choreography over his most considered and hard-won work in *Small Wonder* gave him confidence, determination, and affirmation. In his subsequent work, Champion's already fanatic discipline redoubled, and he would become not only a choreographer of style but of character as well.

NOTES

1. Interviews with Marge Champion Sagal, New York, January 6, 1984; Great Barrington, MA, May 25, July 5, and October 10, 1985.

2. Sagal, Interviews.

3. Sagal, Interviews.

4. His fellow seamen, despite his protestations to the opposite, thought that he was scion of the Champion Automotive Parts fortune, so they called him "Spark Plug."

5. *Playgoer* (Los Angeles), June, 1948.

6. Howard Dietz, *Dancing in the Dark* (New York: Random House, 1975), p. 128.

7. Sagal, Interviews.

8. Sagal, Interviews.

9. Rex Reed, "A Champion—Almost Always," *New York Times*, July 15, 1975.

10. Reed, "Champion." Ironically, when Charisse had moved to California from her hometown, Amarillo, TX, she had studied at the Belcher school in classes conducted by Marjorie Belcher.

11. Reed, "Champion."

12. Sagal, Interviews.

13. Sagal, Interviews.

14. Sagal, Interviews.

15. Sagal, Interviews, and Interview with Jess Gregg, New York, January 14, 1985.

16. Gregg, Interview.

17. Sagal, Interviews.

18. Sagal, Interviews.

19. Sagal, Interviews.

20. J. Ray Hunt, "Night Life Notebook," *St. Louis Daily News*, July 12, 1947.

21. Sagal, Interviews.

22. Sagal, Interviews.

23. Sagal, Interviews.

24. *St. Louis Post Dispatch*, June 1, 1947.

25. Robert Goddard, "New Deal in Dancers," *St. Louis Globe Democrat*, June 29, 1947.

26. Sagal, Interviews.

27. Sagal, Interviews.

28. "October 5 Wedding Plans Announced," *Los Angeles Examiner*, September 11, 1947.

29. Sagal, Interviews.

30. Abel, *Variety*, October 8, 1947.

31. Sagal, Interviews. Also, see the Abel review.

32. Frances Herridge, "Champions Charm at Persian Room," *New York Star*, October 12, 1947.

33. "The Night Owl: Gower Champion Brings New Partner to Mayflower Lounge," *Washington Times-Herald*, November 20, 1947.

34. Sagal, Interviews.

35. "Chief Justice and Mrs. Vinson Feted at Dinner Last Evening," *Washington Evening Star*, December 13, 1947.

36. George W. Clarke, "Tops in Their Field," *Boston Record*, January 7, 1948; Winsor French, n.t., *Cleveland Press*, January 28, 1948; *Detroit Free Press*, February 17, 1948.

37. Sagal, Interviews.

38. Rowland Field, "Along Broadway," *Newark Daily News*, September 16, 1948.

39. "Anna Sokolow to Direct Dances," *New York Herald Tribune*, February 5, 1948.

40. "Champion to Direct Dances," *New York Herald Tribune*, June 18, 1948.

41. Sagal, Interviews.

42. Sagal, Interviews.

43. *Lend An Ear*, Souvenir Program, New York, 1948.

44. Sagal, Interviews, and Interview with Max Showalter, Los Angeles, March 13, 1985.

45. Charles Gaynor, *Lend An Ear* (New York: Samuel French, 1971).

46. Sagal, Interviews.

47. A jibe at Sam and J. J. Shubert, who had produced scores of like entertainments during the 1920s.

48. " 'Small Wonder' in Rehearsal," *New York Herald Tribune*, July 26, 1948.

49. Sagal, Interviews.

50. Interview with Richard Priborsky, Los Angeles, March 23, 1985.

51. Sagal, Interviews.

52. The most notorious example was Champion's decision to replace "Penny in My Pocket," the original first-act closing number of *Hello, Dolly!* "Penny" was an enormous number: literally thousands of props, the entire cast, costumes, scenery, arrangements—and it played to overwhelming audience response. It was replaced by the now famous "Before the Parade Passes By."

53. Jean and Robert Boardman, "About People," *New York Herald Tribune*, August 4, 1948.

54. Walter Terry, "Dance: Operatic, Ethnologic, and for Night Club Patrons," *New York Herald Tribune*, November 14, 1948.

55. George Freedley, " 'Lend an Ear' Is Amusing, Tuneful, Not to Be Missed," *New York Morning Telegraph*, December 18, 1948.

Chapter 4

MGM
(1948–1953)

At the end of 1948, Max Liebman was in the final stages of negotiation with NBC to present a ninety-minute variety show, *The Admiral Broadway Revue*, sponsored by the Admiral Television Company.[1] For years Liebman had produced a weekly musical revue at a resort in Pennsylvania's Pocono Mountains called Camp Tamiment. This summer camp for adults had gained a reputation for nurturing talent, and one of these weekly shows had even been taken to Broadway as *The Straw Hat Revue*.

Liebman had worked with Champion on *Tars and Spars*, and after their success at the Persian Room, asked the Champions whether they would be interested in a contract.[2] They agreed, and were signed to dance in sixteen shows. The first *Admiral Broadway Revue* was televised on January 28, 1949. The Champions danced in two numbers. The first was as visual complement to Estelle Loring and Loren Welch singing "The Night Has a Thousand Eyes." The second was the opening number from their nightclub act, "Dance With Me." They were not the only act on the show to use numbers they had performed before—as a matter of fact, that was the basis of the Admiral revue. It was television's presentation of the best of Broadway, or at least those parts of Broadway that Liebman could get under contract. Among them were Sid Caesar performing the hamburger scene from his recent Broadway hit *Make Mine Manhattan*, and Mary McCarthy in "Flaming Youth" from *Small Wonder*.[3]

The revue had been scheduled originally for a nineteen-week run, from January through May, televised simultaneously on NBC and the combined East-West Dumont Networks.[4] The team used up their entire repertoire of nightclub numbers in the first three or four weeks. As the weeks wore on, Champion became more and more aware that it was virtually impossible to choreograph and perform two new routines each week, at least to his standards. The regulars on the show observed a grueling schedule, but the Champions worked even longer hours, usually from nine in the morning to six or seven in the evening.[5]

Since *The Admiral Broadway Revue* was television's first attempt at a variety show with genuine Broadway talent and a Broadway flair, the press coverage was extensive. The television magazines published stories, and *Life* sent a team of photographers and writers to cover rehearsals. In April, the Champions were invited to Washington, DC, to perform at the White House Correspondents' dinner. Facing the prospect of brand new television routines for many weeks to come, Champion decided that he and Marge should simply pull something out of their repertoire for the dinner. They presented their old standby, "Vaudeville 1910."[6]

As it happened, President Truman paid a visit to the dinner and stayed to see the performance. Truman was a frustrated musician and freely admitted it.[7] Something about the flavor of the Champions' number inspired him, and in his comments he extolled the young dancers as an example of all that was good in America. With that endorsement, it was Marge and Gower Champion who appeared on the cover of *Life* instead of the stars of the *Revue*, Sid Caesar and Imogene Coca.[8] The editors of *Life* had, at first, rejected the idea of using the Champions as a focal point for the article. But Henry Luce, the publisher, had been in the dinner audience. Because of Truman's endorsement, the Champions were deluged with publicity and their national reputation was established.[9] Up to that time, they had been well known and well respected—but only in cabaret circles. With the *Life* cover, they became national figures, and their career prospects began to seem very bright, indeed.

The Admiral Broadway Revue was a tremendous success. It was so successful, in fact, that the show was cancelled. Before it appeared the company was selling five to eight hundred television sets a week. After it became a hit they had orders for five thousand sets a week. The company simply did not have the capital to produce the quantity of sets ordered *and* to sponsor a major television show.[10]

From his experience on the show Champion learned techniques of choreographing for television, a medium he had not experienced before. Up to this point in his career, he had choreographed only for the stage. And, with one exception, he had worked only with non-narrative shows; that is, although his dances were *in themselves* narrative ("The Missionary and the Maiden" or "Marseille," for example), they were performed not in a book show but in a nightclub act or revue. Champion was now

beginning to consider the larger circumstances surrounding his choreography: whether it would appear on a television screen or a nightclub
dance floor; whether it would take place by itself (and therefore need its
own infrastructure) or have to depend on and therefore interact with a
larger structure or narrative. Champion came to feel that if a dancing
couple were more than five feet apart, the camera would have to pull so
far back that it would render the shot ineffective. Thus for the first time
he was beginning to consider a focus that was not only movement-
related, but medium-related.[11]

Champion also came to believe that in order for group movement to
register on camera, the group should be limited to four to six dancers,
unless all the dancers were performing the same movement. But as his
choreographic style eventually developed, he came to rely on unison
chorus movement less and less. Very seldom would a Champion chorus
move up to the footlights and kick. Two notable exceptions to this in
later years were his "Grande Imperial Cirque de Paris" from *Carnival!*
and his "Hello, Dolly!" In both numbers, however, the formation of a
kick line was achieved only after a build-up, a layering of many smaller
units fitted together to create a climax. He used such unison movement,
however, only as an ultimate payoff at the end of a number rather than
as a basic building block, and in both instances he used the "show
business" quality of a kick line to make a comment on a particular
situation in the narrative.

Champion also became increasingly aware of the camera's ability to
magnify small movement by coming in for a close-up. This is one of a
number of camera-related devices that Champion was able to adapt for
the stage. In the "Hello, Dolly!" sequence, for example, he would use
both the position of the male chorus and a dramatic shift in lighting to
bring the audience in for a "close-up" on Carol Channing during the
verse of the song.

After their success on *The Admiral Broadway Revue*, other possible
projects were offered to the Champions, but financially they were not
able to wait for just the right one to appear. They accepted an engagement to play at the Riviera, a nightclub in Fort Lee, New Jersey, beginning on June 8, 1949.[12] Meanwhile, Walt Disney—perhaps remembering
the success Marge had in *Snow White*—offered the couple a contract as
models for a full-length cartoon.[13] In addition, George Abbott offered
them a spot in his new review, *Thank You, Just Looking*. But appearing
in a review, they felt, would not be much different from performing a
nightclub routine every night.[14] The offer that Champion leapt at was

precisely the one for which he had been grooming himself—his ultimate goal: a Broadway show.[15]

Early in June of 1949, Oliver Smith, the scene designer and producer, approached Champion with an offer to direct and choreograph the show. Champion was ecstatic. The euphoria proved to be short-lived, however. Late in the same month, Agnes de Mille, who had been offered the show but turned it down because of prior commitments, once again became free and claimed her option to direct and choreograph. A gentleman, even in a difficult situation, Smith called on the Champions in person to tell them the news.[16] The press was told that Champion had declined because of prior commitments and that de Mille had rearranged her work schedule to fit in the show.[17]

In July, whatever unhappiness Champion might have felt over the *Gentlemen Prefer Blondes* disappointment was dissipated by an important honor. He was presented the Donaldson Award for his choreography of *Lend An Ear*.[18] The award, established in 1943, was named after William H. Donaldson, the founder of *Billboard*, the show business trade paper. The Donaldson winners were chosen by ballot by members from all levels of show business, stagehands to producers.[19] Champion's award was made all the more impressive by the competition in 1949; the legendary Jack Cole had been nominated for his Brazilian-inspired dances for *Magdalena* and Hanya Holm for *Kiss Me Kate*.[20] That year Champion also received the *Dance Magazine* award.[21]

On the debit side, however, while performing at the Riviera, Champion got a bad review from Lee Mortimer, a columnist for the *New York Daily News*.[22] Mortimer found Champion's imitation of Paul Draper to be offensive. The columnist had no quarrel with the accuracy of the imitation but with its very existence. In the midst of the then-rampant McCarthyism, Champion was criticized for having imitated an allegedly communist dancer.[23]

Once again the Champions were coming to the end of their contract. They were held over at the Riviera for four weeks, ending late in July.[24] On the strong recommendation of Walter Winchell and Louis Sobol, the newspaper columnists, Charles Morrison hired the couple to appear at his nightclub, The Mocambo, in Los Angeles.[25] Despite their relatively high earnings at this point, they had not developed a financial plan, and they continued to pour everything they made back into the act—new costumes, hiring more musicians, and the like.[26]

The Champions were in an odd position. They were fresh from a success on television, but had found that the medium was not right for them. Gower simply did not work quickly enough to supply the voracious appetite for choreography of a weekly variety show. His working methods were too painstaking. And, in any case, he preferred to have the time to choreograph dances he thought were worth his while rather than to earn the more-than-comfortable salaries that television personalities could command. Because the Champions had never earned high salaries, they simply lived from engagement to engagement, always seeming somehow to make ends meet.[27]

The Mocambo was far from a perfect venue. The club was small and crowded, and the view of the dance floor was obstructed by pillars—all in all, not an ideal place to perform.[28] While at the Riviera, however, Marge had become a good friend of Sophie Tucker (whom Gower had known from his days with Jeanne), who advised them to take the engagement in spite of the drawbacks. Tucker told Marge that the act was still new, and that recovering from a less than ideal date was just a matter of time.[29] And so, the Champions accepted the offer from Morrison to appear in Los Angeles.

They opened at the club on August 14, 1949, and were a sensation. As Champion later put it, "Like a B movie, we were an immediate smash and it was New Year's Eve every night. The act had a lot of hokey stuff in it, but it had class too."[30] The Los Angeles critics acclaimed them, and the cramped surroundings only made their act look better. In Hollywood it became the thing to do to go to the Mocambo to see Marge and Gower Champion.[31] As their contract neared completion, Morrison publicly begged them in a newspaper advertisement to extend—his business had never been so good: "Dear Marge and Gower, Will you please, please stay over at Mocambo another two weeks. Business is so wonderful that I just won't let you leave. Love, Charlie."[32]

At this point, however, the Champions could afford to be choosy. Their dressing room had become a whirl of offers and negotiations, and they had signed a contract to make a motion picture with Bing Crosby called *Mr. Music* for Paramount late in 1949.[33] It was MGM, however, that offered the best opportunity, and they eventually signed a two-year, two-films-a-year contract to take effect after the completion of *Mr. Music*.

They gave Morrison only one more week, and then flew to New York to make an appearance at the Harvest Moon Ball on September 14.[34] During his time with Jeanne, Champion had made a point of visiting ballroom contests and supporting ballroom dancing, and he had got his own start winning a contest much like this one.

Back on the West Coast again, the Champions filmed their sequences for *Mr. Music* late in 1949. Champion had been hired not only to perform but to stage the film's dance sequences. Three extended dances were planned, two duets and a large-scale production number, although only one of them appeared in the final cut. The film was an adaptation of Samson Raphaelson's play *Accent on Youth*; it was directed by Richard Haydn. In the cast, along with the Champions, were Bing Crosby, Peggy Lee, Groucho Marx, and Dorothy Kirsten.[35] But the dance team did not figure in the narrative of the picture, which was about a song writer (played by Crosby) who is jolted out of a writing block by a young co-ed (played by Nancy Olsen) from his alma mater who is hired by his producer to make him work. The Champions appeared in just two sequences, the more notable at a party given by Crosby to celebrate his completion of a new score. In it Crosby and Peggy Lee sing "Life Is So Peculiar," by Johnny Burke and Jimmy Van Heusen, while sitting on a piano, ostensibly accompanied by Champion.

The choreography suggests that Champion had spent long hours in movie theatres, watching both Gene Kelly and Fred Astaire. In fact, Champion idolized Astaire's work, and in *Mr. Music* his use of space (the dance begins in a crowded room and proceeds out onto a terrace overlooking Manhattan) and properties (much of the furniture in the room) testify to his debt.[36] Champion's first move is a grand leap from the piano bench up to the top of the piano. The dance continues, using every chair within camera range, with the Champions bouncing and bounding off them. The couple continues out onto the balcony, where we see the first filmed evidence of what was to become a Champion staple: the pair swing around the poles which hold up the awnings. Champion had first been introduced to the possibilities of such a movement when he visited Marge on the set of *Beggar's Holiday*, and he used it over and over again—it even appears in his last work, *42nd Street*.[37]

Olsen the co-ed is finally able to coerce Crosby into writing, and she produces his show at the college. An extended number involving a wedding was choreographed and filmed for this sequence, but was cut from the final version.[38] The number also contained yet another device that was used by the choreographer time and time again: a train.

With their first film completed, the Champions awaited the call to begin their contract with MGM. The studio could not decide on a suitable vehicle and released the team until a script could be secured.[39] They accepted four weeks' work in the Peacock Court at the Mark Hopkins Hotel in San Francisco, where they opened on February 7, 1950.[40] By this point their repertoire was ample and they had a national reputation. On the night of February 22, for example, their act consisted of six numbers, with "Marseille" and "Margie" among the dances.[41] They were at their peak as a team, and one review typifies to their impact: "The Champions don't wrap their audiences around their respective fingers. They do much more. They simply entwine themselves around the spectators' hearts and with but a delicate gesture make those hearts sing, laugh, sob—or maybe skip a beat."[42]

RKO, at the time owned by Howard Hughes, now offered them a unique opportunity. Hughes had planned a musical with Janet Leigh called *Two Tickets to Broadway*. But Leigh had minimal experience as a singer and none as a dancer. As a result, Hughes approached the Champions with an offer to coach and choreograph his star in preparation for her musical film debut. With their own studio not offering any work, they accepted. Hughes built a dance studio, and for the next six months the Champions and Leigh worked together eight hours a day, experimenting and rehearsing.[43] The experience was invaluable. Champion was given the opportunity to mold a talented performer and to develop not only his choreographic but his directorial skills. He had not yet had time to really hone his craft. All of his choreography to date—whether for nightclub acts, revues or films—had been done under pressure. His work during the summer of 1950, however, was leisurely and without a deadline.

It was also the first time Marge and Gower had stayed in one place— and earned enough money to buy a house, on Woodrow Wilson Drive in Los Angeles. Champion always called it "the house that Howard Hughes built."[44] The film, *Two Tickets to Broadway*, was completed, but not with Marge and Gower.

Meanwhile MGM had found a vehicle: a remake of *Show Boat*. After the long summer coaching Janet Leigh, the Champions were only too happy to be collaborating on a project that had some prospects of actually being seen. There had been two previous versions of the evergreen classic, the first a silent picture to which sound was later added—but, oddly enough, not the Kern score. The first film was adapted directly from the Edna Ferber novel in 1929 and released even before the Broadway run of the original musical had ended.[45] The second movie was made in 1936 with Irene Dunne as Magnolia and Allan Jones as Ravenal.[46]

This third screen version was directed by George Sidney and choreographed by Robert Alton, with whom Champion had worked twice before. Marge and Gower appeared in two full-length numbers, as well as in an extended teaser at the beginning of the picture in which the show boat docks. The choreography was the result of a happy collaboration between Alton and Champion. Their first number, "I Might Fall Back On You," takes place on the show boat stage. The Hollywood penchant for building numbers around scenery provided Champion and Alton with a loveseat around which to choreograph. Champion used it much the way he had previously used poles—as an axis around which to build the choreographic expression of a relationship. The number ends with an extended cakewalk, including eighty-seven hitch kicks. Although there is a cut in the middle of the sequence, bringing the camera in closer to the couple, each time the kicks were filmed, all of them were performed.[47]

There is a dialogue scene directly after this number, which took place just off stage. While the sheriff comes to arrest Julie (Ava Gardner) and her husband for miscegenation, the stage show continues in the background. Because of technical difficulties, the dialogue needed to be recorded in the foreground while the scene was being filmed, but the music (to which the Champions are dancing in the background) had to be added afterwards. They were fitted with transistor radios, hidden under Gower's coat and Marge's bustle. Through earphones they were able to keep the tempo to which the underscoring would later be recorded. It was allegedly the first time that the technique—now replaced by far more sophisticated devices—was used in a film.[48]

The other number which used the team was "Life Upon the Wicked Stage." Although it is choreographed from top to bottom, it is not really danced, but is an example of Champion's staging, with points being made through placement and timing rather than virtuosity.

When the film was released during the summer of 1951, the Champions probably won the highest praise for their performance: "And at welcome intervals during its uneven story," wrote *Time,* "*Show Boat* brings on the dancing of Broadway's Marge and Gower Champion, whose bounce and grace (most ably in 'Life Upon the Wicked Stage') give the production its smoothest sailing."[49] MGM felt that it had chosen wisely, and featured the team in most of the film's publicity. A pose struck during the opening tease sequence became the advertising logo for the film. Both MGM and the Champions looked forward to the next films, for the team seemed to be box-office gold.

But with no immediate possibilities at MGM, Champion accepted an offer to choreograph another Broadway show, an adaptation of Ferenc Molnar's *The Good Fairy.*[50] When the production, called *Make A Wish,* opened in Philadelphia on March 12, 1951, it was obvious that major revisions were needed. *Variety* reported that Nanette Fabray's three best numbers came in the last half hour of the show, which was overly long to begin with—the final curtain came down at 11:25 P.M. The score was referred to as "serviceable, but not distinguished," with a "Cole Porter flavor, but only a flavor."[51] George Abbott was called in to doctor the show, and he told the cast: "The book we have here is useless. We'll forget it. I want you all to go home now and think things over and come back with suggestions."[52]

Despite Abbott's efforts, Abe Burrows was at length engaged to help with the production. Although the original author and director retained billing, Burrows was never credited for his work. The New York opening was postponed from April 5 to 13, and finally further. Parts were reduced, then finally cut; the score was rearranged and a song added. Burrows' revision of the first act was played in Philadelphia, but his revision of the second act opened with the show in New York, on April 18, 1951.[53]

Fabray and Champion emerged from *Make A Wish* as stars. Although the show was thought by *Life* to be "harmlessly undistinguished in other respects, it rattle[d] the floorboards with good dancing."[54] One number from the show became a legend as Champion's first Broadway choreographic triumph. The second act "Sale Ballet" was criticized at the time as being a pale imitation of Charles Weidman's work, but the distinguished dance critic Walter Terry leaped to Champion's defense with an extended article detailing the differences between it and "Weidman's great Bargain Counter episode in his 'Atavism,' " pointing out that "where the Weidman piece is frightening, ferocious in its humor, the Champion piece represents satire of a gay and bouncy sort. The shop lifter, the girl with the head scarves, and the other invaders charge about the scene with a fine disregard for courtesy. Acrobats—the Sylvia Manon Trio—are also integrated into the proceedings as contributors to a funny, rousing and altogether delightful number."[55]

Champion had successfully transferred his idea of a two-person story ballet onto the Broadway stage. The "Sale Ballet" in *Make A Wish* was a precursor of such later extended narrative dance sequences as "the Shriners' Ballet" in *Bye Bye Birdie* and "the Waiters' Gallop" in *Hello, Dolly!*. Moreover, his influence on the texture of *Make A Wish* went far beyond a mere second-act showstopper. Building on his work in *Small Wonder* and *Lend An Ear*, he had been able to function within the confines of an extended book show, and to vitalize the characters through dance. Champion was clearly beginning to use narrative situations as springboards for his choreography, an ability that he was to perfect in his motion picture work.

Three films for MGM followed in rapid succession: *Everything I Have Is Yours* (1952), *Lovely to Look At* (1952), and *Give a Girl a Break* (1953). Each is an invaluable visual record of the Champions' craft and art. Together they document Champion's growing mastery, not only of choreography, but of the very conception of what a musical number can do.

Everything I Have Is Yours was the Champion's first starring vehicle. They played Pamela and Chuck Hubbard, a husband and wife dance team much like themselves. Pamela becomes pregnant, and the couple decides that she should retire from show business to care for the baby while Chuck finds a new partner (Monica Lewis) and continues performing. Pamela has the baby while Chuck suffers psychosomatic pains—thus the title. Chuck continues to be successful with his new partner. Rather predictably, Pamela becomes bored and the marriage comes perilously close to divorce. A final reconciliation provides a happy ending.

When Champion read the script, he noticed that no musical numbers were actually part of the story; instead, all of the numbers were to take place in the context of performance—either onstage or at gatherings of friends. He approached Nick Castle, with whom he was collaborating on the musical sequences, and suggested a dance number in the opening moments of the picture, to be shot as Chuck and Pamela walk home after a rehearsal.[56] With the approval of George Wells, the producer, and Robert Z. Leonard, the director, a song was commissioned for the situation and Champion and Castle went to work on a staging concept. Typical of Champion's modus operandi, he and Castle explored a multitude of ideas before settling on one they thought would work. They were searching for an incident with which to begin the sequence. After rejecting the device of the couple being chased by a squad car, being lifted by a freight elevator, knocking over trash cans, and being squirted by a janitor hosing down a sidewalk, they finally settled on the simplest possible solution—they simply walked.[57]

Champion and Castle envisioned a number that would take the couple out the stage door of a theatre, down an alley, and out onto a street. In true Hollywood fashion, the alley and the street would be filled with levels and properties off which Champion could bounce the choreography. The old song, "Like Monday Follows Sunday," by Johnny Green, Rex Newman, and Douglas Furber, was purchased, a section of the back-

lot was prepared, and shooting was scheduled. Because of the complicated choreography, the shooting was scheduled over a number of days.

The finished number is an example of Champion's use of narrative
situations and actions as the basis for choreography. As envisioned by
Champion and Castle, it begins ever so gradually with Pamela and Chuck
walking out the stage door. The couple walk down the alley, Marge
keeping a brisk pace while Gower accompanies her, now behind, now
in front. The walking action turns into small jetés, and the jetés into
turns and lifts. When Gower leaps onto a loading dock, the number has
grown from walking to full-fledged dancing.

Champion's rationale for the number was an attempt to open up the
script. He wanted to dissolve, cinematically—but with staging—into a
musical sequence and then back out of it, so that the number could
become part of the fabric of the narrative rather than being separated
from it. Eventually he mastered this device, and many of his later numbers in Broadway musicals began almost imperceptibly, growing to enormous climaxes. "When Mabel Comes in the Room" from *Mack and
Mabel* (1974), for example, began intimately, with two people sharing
coffee and doughnuts in a deserted movie studio, but it ultimately included the entire cast in an extended production number. Another manifestation of this device was Champion's attention to boundaries—not
only the boundaries of musical numbers, but of scenes and acts as well.
Increasingly, he became as concerned with the flow of a production as
a whole as he was with the internal cohesion of the choreography in a
particular number.

The Champions' MGM films were made in the final days of the ex-
pensive Hollywood musical. The cost of MGM productions of the day
was remarkable; for example, Champion and Castle had choreographed
a solo dance number, "Serenade for a New Baby," for Champion to
perform to a crib. The choreography was set and the collaborators reported early one morning to the sound studio where the accompaniment
was to be recorded by a particularly large orchestra. When the recording
was finished, Champion and Castle returned to the film studio to shoot
the sequence that afternoon. To their consternation they discovered that,
although Champion had danced while the orchestra recorded in the sound
studio, they had not taken into consideration all the intricate moves that
involved such properties as dolls and toys. The entire number had been
recorded much too fast. They sheepishly returned to John Green, the
musical director, with the news that the take was unusable. Rather than
insist that the number be re-choreographed to the music, Green issued

an emergency call to the musicians to return the same day to the studio for another take.[58]

Lovely to Look At, another film, contains a dance duet that shows a different aspect of Champion's ability to create seamless transitions. The picture was a remake of Jerome Kern's *Roberta*, which was originally filmed with Fred Astaire and Ginger Rogers in 1935.[59] The 1952 version, produced by Jack Cummings and directed by Mervyn LeRoy, split the role Astaire had played in two, dividing it between Red Skelton and Champion. The Rogers part was also split.[60] In the revised story, Skelton has inherited half of a couture house in Paris, now being managed by two sisters (Kathryn Grayson and Marge). Champion and Howard Keel play two friends who go to Paris with Skelton in hopes that by selling his business they can finance a show in the United States. The sisters at first resist, of course. The men, on the other hand, relent and stage a fashion show that puts the house, Gowns by Roberta, back in business. Finally Skelton and Marge fall in love. Besides doing all the basic choreography for the sequences involving Marge and himself, Champion was also given the opportunity to work on refinements with one of his idols, Hermes Pan, who had choreographed Astaire in the original film.

The Champions' duet was danced to an arrangement of Kern's "Smoke Gets in Your Eyes." It starts as Clarisse and Jerry are just beginning to realize that they are in love. They have finished dinner at a bistro and get up to dance. As the camera slowly moves in for a close-up, it catches the couple in front of an open window. The frame contains only the two dancers and, through the window, the starry sky over Paris. As the camera pulls back for the dance sequence, the bistro has disappeared and the duet takes place against the stars surrounding the couple. Besides the visual splendor of the Champions' dancing to the Kern music among the stars, the transition had been magical, catching the viewer totally unprepared. It foreshadowed many such *coups de theatre* yet to come.

The happy collaboration between Pan and Champion produced not only the "Smoke" duet, but another number—when Clarisse and Jerry meet—choreographed to the famous "I Won't Dance." In constructing it, nearly every property in the scene was used. The two masters inspired each other, and the experience was one of the Champions' happiest during the MGM period.[61] The final sequence, featuring gowns designed by the legendary Adrian, contained only one section featuring the Champions. The filming took place in November of 1951 and the press had been told that the gowns were smuggled into the studio under armed guard, since they were from Adrian's spring 1952 collection, not yet released.[62] In fact, LeRoy had simply asked Adrian to design what he thought might be in fashion eighteen months from the shooting date. Vincent Minelli and Marge conceived and directed the number at LeRoy's invitation. Champion danced a vaguely satanic role, dressed in black with red gloves. It may have served as inspiration for the gangster in the ballet from his final work, *42nd Street*.[63]

Their next film for MGM was *Give a Girl a Break* (1953), again produced by Cummings, but this time directed by Stanley Donen, with a score by Burton Lane and Ira Gershwin. The story concerned the casting of a star for a Broadway show. Each of the staff—the composer, played by Kurt Kasznar; the director played by Champion; and the dance assistant, played by Bob Fosse—had his favorite. At one time or another each of the contenders, played by Helen Wood, Marge Champion and Debbie Reynolds, is offered the role. The musical sequences include the dreams of each man about the woman he hopes will play the lead, together with the usual romantic duets, and the finale of the show being rehearsed.

The dream sequence is actually a series of three discrete numbers, each highlighting the performing strengths of one of the three women in contention for the role. Fosse dreams about Reynolds, and they dance an especially interesting duet that intercuts footage running forward and backward. The second number portrays Kasznar conducting Wood as a ballerina, and the third involves Champion dreaming about casting Marge, who plays his ex-wife and an established Broadway star. The three numbers are in three distinctly different styles. The Reynolds-Fosse segment is a straightforward tap dance, the Wood-Kasznar segment a classical ballet, and the Champion section is presented in their own lyrical manner. What is notable about the sequence as a whole—indeed about all of the numbers in the film—is the elements they have in common. Champion, now exercising more creative control than he had been allowed previously, requested very plain backdrops in a poster style, of a sort which he later used in most of his Broadway work. No part of the sequence is in darkness or not readily discernible—it is uncomplicated and totally comprehensible.

In addition, each number is a study of the ambitions of the male dancer or of the relationship between the members of each couple. Fosse dreams of being both a director and a star, and the style used is naive and optimistic, much like that used by Gene Kelly with Reynolds in *Singin' in the Rain*, released the same year. Kasznar is at first shown conducting

Wood *en pointe* in a classical tutu. But subsequently she is transformed
into a wild and sexy jazz dancer, oozing animal magnetism.

The number with the Champions is the apotheosis of his taste for
choreography built around poles. The set consists of endless rows of
black poles set against a medium ochre background. One long segment
uses a row of the poles as frames. The two dancers move in opposition,
mirror images of one another. The two then break the plane and swing
around the poles. The middle section of the dance shows Champion's
lyricism at its finest—an endless legato line, interweaving the two bodies
around the poles. The finale illustrates the temptations facing a choreographer—a chorus of women sweeps around Champion while Marge
disappears. In desperation, he leaps off a platform onto a pole, and in a
languid spiral, descends the pole to Marge, waiting below. A final pose
finds the two dancers face to face, each questioning, but not touching,
as inconclusive as the situation in which they find themselves.

Their final film for MGM was *Jupiter's Darling* (1955). Their MGM
films are a record of Champion's awakening experimentation with the
functions that a musical number can serve in a film. Champion's first,
tentative steps were taken in *Everything I Have Is Yours* in his insertion
of a narrative dance sequence. The development from *Lovely to Look At*
through *Give a Girl a Break* is on two levels. In *Everything I Have Is
Yours*, the narrative sequence merely heightens a simple walk home,
stylizing the moment so that what the couple feels is expressed through
dancing. In *Give a Girl a Break*, however, a dramatic situation is resolved *by* dancing, rather than merely *through* it. Champion, playing the
director, comes to the apartment of his ex-wife in order to taunt her into
auditioning for the role. He dares her to dance, and, gradually, a duet
develops. He is using dance in a far more integrated way than before—it
had become one with the plot. Moreover, while Champion had earlier
used the action of walking as the basis of his choreography, here the
seed is far more dramatic. Champion confronts Marge, and she demurs,
turning away. He counters, and she again turns to avoid him. This motif
of stepping-to-confront and turning-to-escape becomes the basic movement pattern of the duet that follows.

Instead of using movement as a building block, Champion had discovered that a simple action—one full of both dramatic content and
intensity—served his choreographic and directorial purposes even better.
What is significant here, and what becomes yet another hallmark of his
style, is Champion's discovery of a telling simplicity—movement that
is at once easy and uncomplicated but full of meaning.

NOTES

1. For a full account of the genesis of *The Admiral Broadway Revue* and its successor, *Your Show of Shows*, see Ted Sennett, *Your Show of Shows* (New York: Collier Books, 1977).

2. Interviews with Marge Champion Sagal, New York, January 6, 1984; Great Barrington, MA, May 25, July 5, and October 10, 1985.

3. "Admiral Bows Sock Revue With Top Artists, Yocks, Sizzling Pace Comparable to Best Broadway Hits," *Billboard*, January 29, 1949.

4. Sennett, *Show*, p. 13.

5. Sagal, Interviews.

6. Irv Kupcinet, "Kup's Column," *Chicago Times*, April 17, 1949.

7. See, for instance: Merle Miller, *Plain Speaking* (New York: Scribner's, 1973).

8. "Broadway's Dancingest Show," *Life*, May 14, 1951, p. 137.

9. Kupcinet, "Column."

10. Revlon later was in the same predicament: it had to eliminate a large part of television advertising because it could not keep enough stock on the shelf to keep up with the demands following the success of *The $64,000 Question*. Sid Caesar and Bill Davidson, *Where Have I Been? An Autobiography*. (New York: Crown, 1982), pp. 89–90.

11. Arthur Altshul, "Television Dancing: A Different Approach," *New York Times*, n.d., Fugitive clipping from the private collection of Marge Champion Sagal, Great Barrington, MA.

12. Walter Winchell, "In New York," *New York Post*, June 30, 1949.

13. Louis Sobol, "Snapshots at Random," *New York Journal American*, June 20, 1949.

14. *New York Daily Mirror*, June 17, 1949.

15. Earl Wilson, "The Midnight Earl," *New York Post*, June 10, 1949.

16. Sagal, Interviews.

17. "Agnes DeMille to Do Dances," *New York Herald Tribune*, June 24, 1949.

18. "Ex-Musical Director Comes Back With Meller," *New York Daily Mirror*, July 26, 1949.

19. *Billboard*, July 16, 1949, p. 46.

20. Ibid.

21. *Dance Magazine*, December 1949.

22. Lee Mortimer. "New Show, Gowns—Same Wonderful Sophie," *New York Daily News*, July 8, 1949.

23. Sagal, Interviews.

24. Mortimer, "New Show."

25. "Rambling Reporter," *Hollywood Reporter*, July 27, 1949.

26. Sagal, Interviews.

27. Sagal, Interviews.

28. Rex Reed, "A Champion—Almost Always," *New York Times*, February 19, 1967, Section D, pp. 1, 3.

29. Sagal, Interviews.

30. Champion in Reed, "Champion."

31. Sagal, Interviews.

32. Advertisement placed by Charles Morrison, *Hollywood Reporter*, September 6, 1949.

33. Louella O. Parsons, "Hollywood," *Los Angeles Examiner*, August 12, 1953.

34. Jack Smith, "1800 at Harvest Ball Thrill to Stars and Dance," *New York Daily News*, September 15, 1949.

35. Clive Hirschorn, *The Hollywood Musical* (New York: Crown, 1981), p. 316.

36. Sagal, Interviews.

37. Sagal, Interviews, and Paramount Pictures, *Mr. Music*, released 1950.

38. Sagal, Interviews.

39. Sagal, Interviews.

40. *New York Herald Tribune*, February 22, 1940.

41. Ted, "Peacock Court, San Francisco," *Variety*, February 22, 1940.

42. Maggi, "The Champions Capture Hearts of Alameda Group," *Alameda Times-Star*, February 14, 1950.

43. Sidney Skolsky, "Watching Them Make Pictures," n.d.; Dick Williams, "Howard Hughes Creates a Dancer," August 14, 1950.

44. Sagal, Interviews.

45. Miles Krueger, *Show Boat: The Story of a Classic American Musical* (New York: Oxford University Press, 1977), passim.; Lawrence B. Thomas, *The MGM Years* (New York: Columbia House, 1972), p. 74.

46. Stanley Green, *Encyclopedia of the Musical Film* (New York: Oxford University Press, 1981), p. 257.

47. Sagal, Interviews.

48. Sagal, Interviews.

49. *Time*, July 2, 1951.

50. *New York Herald Tribune*, January 4, 1951.

51. Waters, "Plays Out of Town: 'Make A Wish,' " *Variety*, March 14, 1951.

52. Arthur Pollock, *Brooklyn Daily Eagle*, March 26, 1951.

53. "Inside Stuff—Legit," *Variety*, April 1, 1951.

54. *Life*, April 25, 1951.

55. Walter Terry, "Dance: 'Make A Wish'; The City Ballet," *New York Herald Tribune*, June 3, 1951.

56. Sagal, Interviews.

57. Robert Cahn, "A Dance Is Born," *Collier's Magazine*, July 12, 1952.

58. Sagal, Interviews.

59. Green, *Encyclopedia*, p. 240.

60. John Mueller, *Astaire Dancing* (New York: Knopf, 1985), p. 211.

61. Hermes Pan, Letter to the author, June 12, 1985.

62. Sagal, Interviews.

63. Champion confided to his scene designer Robin Wagner during the rehearsals for *42nd Street* that he was choreographing a compendium of dances he had performed and dreamed. Interview with Robin Wagner, New York, September 14, 1984.

Chapter 5

The Later Movies and *3 for Tonight*
(1953–1959)

With their two-year MGM contract completed, the Champions were faced with deciding whether or not to renew. They were unable to come to terms with the studio over the rights on television appearances, so they allowed their contract to expire on April 1, 1953.[1] Four weeks later they opened at the Flamingo in Las Vegas and broke all records. From there, engagements followed at the Fairmont in San Francisco, the Coconut Grove in Los Angeles, and with Vic Damone at Bill Miller's Riviera in Fort Lee, New Jersey.[2]

In May they returned to Hollywood to negotiate further motion picture work. They agreed to appear in and choreograph one picture each with MGM and Columbia. Their work with Janet Leigh had so impressed Howard Hughes that he was prepared to have RKO remake each of the Astaire-Rogers films with the Champions.[3] The discussions advanced as far as a few tentative decisions about the order in which to make them. The Champions viewed all of the Astaire-Rogers pictures and decided that *Follow the Fleet* would be the most likely candidate with which to start.[4] In the end, however, they decided that it was simply too soon to begin remaking the films—the memory of Astaire was too much alive. Champion would not compete with his idol—and they regretfully refused.[5] He did, however, agree to direct a film for the studio.

Ed Sullivan, the New York columnist, who hosted a Sunday evening variety show on CBS-TV called "Toast of the Town," offered to devote an entire show to their career.[6] He had been a fan of Gower and Jeanne, and had followed Champion's work closely when he teamed up with Marge.[7] The segment was aired on June 7, 1953. It included "County Fair," "The Clock," and "Great Day" from Marge and Gower's nightclub act, interspersed with three clips from their motion pictures: "I Won't Dance" from *Lovely to Look At*, and the two numbers from *Show Boat*. Up to that time, only three persons had been honored with a full hour on the Ed Sullivan Show—Robert E. Sherwood, Richard Rogers, and Joshua Logan.[8] As a result, the Champions' television career began to blossom, and they appeared as guests with Milton Berle, Perry Como, Steve Allen, and Dinah Shore, sometimes using material directly from their nightclub act, at other times tailoring a sketch or a dance to the person with whom they were appearing.[9]

Back in California once again, they began work on the films for which they had signed contracts. The first—for MGM again—was *Jupiter's Darling* (1955), Esther Williams' final film. George Sidney directed, Burton Lane composed the music, and Hermes Pan choreographed the dances. The Champions played a pair of Roman slaves, Meta and Varius. They were in only two numbers, one of which bears some discussion.

The number was conceived as a dance with elephants—a kind of duet with elephant accompaniment. Pan and Champion auditioned elephants from the Cole Brothers Circus and, in addition, hired two baby elephants from local nightclubs in Los Angeles.[10] They did not have a routine in mind, but instead requested a trainer to show them what steps the elephants could perform. After they had been shown such elephant moves as the three-legged hop, a waltz, both a long mount oblique and walking long mount, a merry-go-round, and a shimmy, they had enough material from which to design the movements of their pachyderm chorus.[11] Significantly, this is the first instance of Champion's surrendering strict choreography in favor of more general staging—an approach which, by the time of his final shows, became his standard working method. Champion began to become more interested in overall effects and in larger movement patterns, rather than in the steps themselves.

The film for Columbia was *Three for the Show* (also 1955), Betty Grable's last picture. But the choreographic styles in the picture are so diverse that it is plain that the work is not all from the same hand. Jack Cole, in fact, is listed as the choreographer. In any case, Champion found it perfect torture to work with Cole, as did many dancers.[12] Cole did not like choreographing for film and, moreover, was an extremely demanding and punctilious person. His style was the opposite of Champion's, full of intricate hand gestures, wide stances, and knee drops—what dancers call "into the floor." Champion's style, on the other hand, was lifted up and lyrical, with extensions and very controlled hand motions.

The film was moderately successful, but by the late 1950s, movie musicals were losing more money than they made. The Champions had a dubious distinction: as Marge would point out later, ''We finished off Esther Williams and Betty Grable.''[13] With no immediate offers, ''it was back to the closet for the old act again. We didn't care because we never thought of ourselves as movie stars anyway.'' Although they had never really attained stardom, their films had made them well enough known to be celebrities in their own right. They were no longer just a nightclub act—albeit the best.

The Champions' next project was one that took them to New York— and their only appearance together on Broadway. Paul Gregory, *wunderkind* producer, had been hired by Music Corporation of America, Gower and Jeanne's agents. Gregory approached the Champions with an idea for a lighter sort of entertainment, one employing minimal scenery, props, and changes of costumes, but with an emphasis on music and dance and whimsy. The Champions were teamed with Harry Belafonte and The Voices of Walter Schumann, a vocal ensemble conducted by the producing team's musical director. The result, called *3 for Tonight*, was not really a concert, not really a revue. Basically, it was a succession of acts strung together with a commentary by Don Beddoe, who was replaced with Hiram Sherman just before the production opened in New York.[14] The theme of the evening was not a subject or a period, or in fact anything else that was clearly defined. Each participant did a specialty—Belafonte offered Caribbean folk songs, the Champions did story ballets, and the Voices of Walter Schumann presented their intricate harmonizing. The unifying factor was not a narrative or an abstract conceit, but simply the fact of spending an evening with these talented people.

3 for Tonight opened in New York at the Plymouth Theatre on April 6, 1955. The show had made a rigorous four-month, cross-country tour, playing in fifty-seven cities during those months. By the time New York audiences saw the company, it was honed to within inches of perfection, and the critics were dazzled. After an eleven-week run in New York, the company returned to Los Angeles and played the Greek Theatre for an additional week.[15] On Wednesday, June 22, 1955, Gower's thirty-fifth birthday, an hour-long version of the show was televised, and again praise was heaped on it.

3 for Tonight demonstrated once and for all that Champion was a director of many resources. The contrast with his direction of *Lend An Ear* in 1948 is worth some discussion. By the time Champion took over as director of *Ear*, the show had been through a rather protracted try-out period, first in Pittsburgh and later in Los Angeles. What Champion was able to give the show was a particular sparkle and style—what worked, worked fabulously. Not so with *3 for Tonight*, and the differences give clues to his future contributions to musical theatre.

3 for Tonight had nothing to make it seem integrated except its cast and its fundamental rhythms. The intermixing of the acts (Belafonte, the Champions, and the Voices) did give it a sort of cohesiveness, but it was not a piece with a conventional beginning, middle, and end. This unity— or the appearance of it—was precisely Champion's contribution and achievement. He was able to fashion the show so that the progression of numbers *seemed* cohesive.

A dramaturgical sensibility was at the base of his talent, and it continued to inform both his choreography and his direction. *3 for Tonight* was the first time that he had been called upon to exercise so many of his skills, learned from such disparate sources as piano study as a child, work in vaudeville, and his years as a ballroom dancer. After *3 for Tonight* Champion's sights were set resolutely on directing—he decided that he would no longer even accept choreographic jobs simply to build a reputation. Accordingly, in 1955 he would turn down an offer to choreograph *My Fair Lady* in the hope that directing work would materialize.[16]

Meanwhile, the Champions continued their nightclub appearances, most notably in Las Vegas at the New Frontier, becoming the only dance team that a casino, as *Billboard* said, "would dare to headline."[17] Champion had choreographed a new finale for their act, "The Happy Clown," a routine that demonstrated his particular ability to invest, choreographically, meaning in unlikely theatrical situations. The number began with the cliché of the two making up as clowns at tables and mostly performing slapstick moves. But those movements, wrote *Daily Variety*, "contain the nobility of fine dance-theatre."[18] Champion was beginning not only to control his material but to transcend it.

Other engagements followed, at the Coconut Grove, the Fairmont in San Francisco and the Fontainbleau in Miami. In March, however, it was apparent that Marge was pregnant and would be unable to continue performing for a number of months.[19] With perfect timing, Champion was offered membership in the Screen Directors' Guild, which also included television directors among its members.[20] In 1956 television was still considered a second-class arena, and competent directors were difficult to find. It happened that George Sidney, the president of the Screen Directors' Guild, who had directed the Champions in *Show Boat*, was a moving force behind a television series called *Screen Directors Play-*

house. Sidney asked Champion if he would be interested in starring in and directing a half-hour segment, built around the "Happy Clown" number.[21]

Jean Holloway had written the teleplay, a story of battling clowns, inserting three musical numbers into the slight script: "Yankee Doodle Dandy" and "Mary's a Grand Old Name" by George M. Cohan, and the song that the Champions used in their act, "When You're a Clown," by Jeff Bailey and Jack Latimer.[22] The segment aired on June 5, 1956, retitled "What Day Is This?" The next day a full-page advertisement appeared in the *Hollywood Reporter*, featuring a figure in a director's chair in silhouette. The only text was "What Day Is This?" set in medium type above the figure with "DIRECTED BY GOWER CHAMPION" below.[23] Champion was not about to let the opportunity to publicize his new and long-dreamed-of career pass him by.[24]

Champion also fulfilled his contract with RKO for a musical. *The Girl Most Likely* (1957), was designed originally to co-star Jane Powell and Carol Channing and to use material left over from *Lend An Ear*. But the cast was changed before shooting began, and Powell was paired with Kay Ballard.[25] The men in the cast included Cliff Robertson, Tommy Noonan and Keith Andes.[26]

The director, Mitch Leisen, allowed Champion free rein in devising and shooting the musical sequences, which have a style completely different from the rest of the film.[27] In comparison with *Mr. Music, The Girl Most Likely* shows such a clear line of artistic development that one can only lament the fact that Champion never made another musical film. Although he was offered a further assignment by RKO, he had already accepted a television series.[28]

J&M Enterprises, which produced *The Jack Benny Show*, was looking for a replacement for Ann Sothern's long-running series, *Private Secretary*.[29] The agreement was for six shows, one on film and five of them live. Soon after the contract was signed, Gregg Ernest Champion was born, named after the Champions' good friend Jess Gregg and Marge's father, Ernest Belcher.[30] To commemorate the event, it was planned that Champion would perform a number called "Ballet of the Expectant Father" on the first television show.[31] But the dance was not to take place.

The first episode of the series was to be filmed, so that the next two could be broadcast live with plenty of preparation, work starting on Wednesday, March 13, 1957. Marge had reported to the studio early for extensive makeup, and Champion was to join her later in the morning.

On the way, winding through Laurel Canyon, Champion lost control of his car and crashed.[32] Paul Harrison, the director of the first episode, happened to be driving the same route shortly after Champion's accident. To his amazement, he saw his star sitting on the ground outside an overturned car, holding his bloodied face in his hands. Harrison rushed him to Mount Sinai Hospital, where the badly shaken but not seriously injured Champion was treated and released. The director phoned Marge at the studio and she rushed to the hospital in makeup.[33]

The first episode was scheduled to air in two weeks, on March 31.[34] There was time for Champion to heal well enough to appear, but not really enough time to film, so the decision was made to broadcast live. Champion had mostly sustained injuries to his face not his body—but his swollen face negated the possibility of close-up shots. The result was that a new story was devised for the episode with Champion in a wheelchair and Marge and Jack Whiting, who played her father, doing the dancing.

With Champion barely participating and with the technical vagaries of early television, the first "Marge and Gower Champion Show" was not a success.[35] On successive segments the pair hosted guest stars—including Mary McCarthy, with whom Champion had worked on *Small Wonder*—each episode having a slight plot line on which to hang some musical numbers. The episode with McCarthy found the Champions starving in a Greenwich Village flat and appearing in a musical produced by a mobster. In another episode, Champion was supposedly chosen to direct the community talent show. The show's producers found that he made an amiable television host, and, on Jack Benny's advice, they scheduled him for a monologue at the top of each segment.

Marge had developed a fine comic sense, and was given a bubble-headed quality that Gower always had to keep under control.[36] Her character was another example of a type popular in the early days of television—Lucille Ball and Gracie Allen played similar roles. Although a number of writers and directors attempted to find the right combination to make a long-running show, the Champions decided to let the series die after six episodes. "We wanted to do a musical show, MCA [their agency] wanted a straight situation comedy, and Jack Benny, who packaged [the show], wanted a comedy. Split it three ways and we didn't know what we were doing. The sponsor also wanted a situation comedy, but we didn't want to become 'Ozzie and Harriet' . . . Everybody was pulling in a different direction. We changed directors and writers. The experience embittered me . . . it left scars.''[37] By the end of July, the series was dead.[38]

Negotiations began for Marge and Gower to appear in the London production of *Bells Are Ringing*; but the show had no substantial dancing in it and Jule Styne, the composer, did not want to do the kind of rewriting that would be necessary to star a dance team.[39] By mid-August, the Champions were back at the Coconut Grove, doing what they perhaps did best: entertaining in person in intimate surroundings.[40]

Marge and Gower continued to perform as a dance team and, to a limited extent, on television, while he looked for directing work. On television, they would appear both on variety shows as dancers and in straight dramas as actors. Mostly Champion directed the shows. For example, on October 13, 1957, they danced on the "Standard Oil 75th Anniversary Show" and dominated it.

Publicity was a particularly tricky problem at this time because, for the most part, Marge and Gower were simply continuing to do what they had done before. They seemed unable to find usable new material. While continuing their television appearances, Champion began to look for a stage play to direct. The news reached William Tregoe, who operated a tent theatre at the Avondale Playhouse-in-the-Meadows in Indianapolis, Indiana.[41] In the spring of 1957, he approached Champion with a play by William Mercer, *Hemingway and All Those People*. It seemed ideal— Champion could direct, and Marge could play the lead.[42]

Champion took charge of the proceedings and, perhaps, directed with a bit too firm a hand. The Avondale Playhouse was not only a tent theatre, but also an arena, and for an inexperienced stage director both represent formidable obstacles. He did not allow his actors much improvisation or much freedom, and as the super-disciplined style of rehearsal that Champion had evolved for himself met the looser style of the acting profession, some tensions developed.[43] He later commented on what he was to learn about the very real differences between rehearsing dancers and actors. "The choreographer," he said, "is more dictatorial than the director. The very nature of his work requires him to tell dancers exactly what to do. Yes, you *tell* the dancer. As a director, you *point* the actor in a direction and let him carry it from there and if it doesn't work, you start again or revise or adapt.''[44]

On July 29, 1958, Champion made his legitimate directing debut. Although he had wanted to take the play to Broadway, the notices quashed his plans for a New York debut: "Like all of his colleagues," wrote the

Indianapolis News, "he [Champion] worked hard to make a play. The material isn't there."[45] This experience was not to repeat itself—from that time Champion insisted on having control over the script, and he was invariably involved not only with the production but the writing of his projects.

In March of 1959, CBS aired a special called *Accent on Love*, directed by Champion. It was a musical revue with Marge and Gower, Jaye P. Morgan, Louis Jordan, Ginger Rogers, and Mike Nichols and Elaine May.[46] Champion's experience with *Hemingway* had moved his attention away from complex choreography, and the staging of *Accent on Love* was simple in the extreme. He used stools and chairs, and very direct camera angles.

The revue resulted in an offer from NBC for Champion to produce and direct six specials for the 1959–1960 television season.[47] The possibility of directing on Broadway prevented Champion from making a commitment—Ed Padula had given him a script for a teenage musical called *Let's Go Steady*. Although he did not like the script at all, Champion accepted.[48] It would be his first Broadway assignment as both director and choreographer.

In the meantime, the Champions heard that their friend Ed Sullivan was planning a tour of Russia, and Marge called and asked him if the tour needed a dance team.[49] Sullivan made the commitment immediately on the telephone. They took two numbers from their nightclub act, "Let's Dance," their signature, and "The Clock."[50] Because the latter involved narration, Champion went to Berlitz to learn the part phonetically in Russian. His pronunciation became so good that after the show opened, Russians assumed he spoke the language fluently and often began conversations with him.[51] The "tour" was restricted to two cities, Leningrad and Moscow, for a total of fourteen performances in the middle of August, 1959.[52] Directly after the tour the Champions, along with Richard Priborsky, their musical director, chartered a yacht and spent a much-needed two weeks sailing among the Greek islands.[53] They returned to Los Angeles in late September. Although he was not at all enthusiastic, Gower Champion now immersed himself in the preparations for what was to become *Bye Bye Birdie*.[54]

NOTES

1. Sidney Skolsky, "Hollywood Is My Beat," *Hollywood Citizen-News*, February 27, 1953, p. 17.

2. *Hollywood Reporter*, February 18, 1953; Hedda Hopper, "Glynis Johns, Richard Todd to Be Co-Stars in 'Rob Roy,' " *Chicago Daily Tribune*, February 18, 1953; *New York Daily News*, May 19, 1953.

3. *Los Angeles Times*, May 1, 1953.

4. Interviews with Marge Champion Sagal, New York, January 6, 1984; Great Barrington, MA, May 25, July 5, and October 10, 1985.

5. Sagal, Interviews.

6. Mario Torre, "Only in Their 20's but Life Story Will Be on Television," *Hollywood Reporter*, June 19, 1950.

7. Interviews with Jeanne Tyler Estridge, San Bernadino, California, March 20 and June 5, 1985.

8. John Crosby, "Radio and Television," *New York Herald Tribune*, June 19, 1950.

9. The Television and Film Archives of the University of California at Los Angeles hold copies of most of the Champions' television appearances.

10. *Syracuse Herald Journal*, January 25, 1955.

11. Ibid.

12. Sagal, Interviews; Glenn Loney, *Unsung Genius: The Passion of Dancer-Choreographer Jack Cole* (New York: Franklin Watts, 1984).

13. Rex Reed, "A Champion—Almost Always," *New York Times*, February 19, 1967.

14. Hobe Morrison, "3 for Tonight," *Variety*, April 13, 1955.

15. Dick Williams, "Near-Capacity Crowd Sees Greek Theater Summer Bow," *Los Angeles Daily Mirror News*, June 28, 1955, Part I, p. 2.

16. Reed, "Champion."

17. "Marge and Gower Champs at Vegas," *Billboard*, December 3, 1955.

18. "Nitery Reviews." *Daily Variety*, November 17, 1955.

19. Sagal, Interviews.

20. "Gower Champion in Debut as TV Director," *Variety*, March 20, 1956.

21. "Hollywood Newsreel," *Showmen's Trade Review*, October 15, 1955; Sagal, Interviews.

22. Kove, "What Day Is This?" *Daily Variety*, June 8, 1956.

23. *Motion Picture Herald*, September 3, 1955, and *Hollywood Reporter*, June 6, 1956.

24. Sagal, Interviews.

25. Mike Connolly, "Rambling Reporter," *Hollywood Reporter*, August 20, 1956; Edward Schallert, "Cinemiracle Director Elected; 'Guard of Honor' Okayed; Big West Bwy," *Los Angeles Times*, July 17, 1956.

26. Clive Hirschorn, *The RKO Story* (New York: Crown, 1982), p. 363.

27. Sagal, Interviews.

28. Edwin Schallert, "Comedy Lawyer Role Sighted for Cotten, Champion in 'Tempo,' " *Los Angeles Times*, December 26, 1956.

29. Walter F. Kerr, "Belafonte and His Supersongs," *New York Herald Trib-*

une, April 17, 1955, sec. 4, pp. 1, 3; "Champion's, Jack Benny Vidpix Prod'n Partners," *Daily Variety*, August 13, 1956; "Champion Vidpix Series to Supplant Sothern's 'Sec' as Benny Alternate," *Daily Variety*, November 13, 1956.

30. Sagal, Interviews.

31. Danton Walker, "Broadway," *New York Daily News*, February 14, 1957.

32. Louella O. Parsons, "Gower Champion, TV Actor, Hurt in Crash," *Los Angeles Examiner*, March 14, 1957.

33. Champion quoted in Reed, "Champion."

34. Hank Grant, "Marge and Gower Champion Show," *Hollywood Reporter*, April 2, 1957.

35. Sagal, Interviews; Kap, "Marge and Gower," *Daily Variety*, April 1, 1957.

36. Sagal, Interviews.

37. Champion quoted in Dave Kaufman, "On All Channels," *Daily Variety*, December 23, 1958.

38. Charles Mercer, "Happy TV Ending," *San Diego Union*, July 28, 1957.

39. Mike Connolly, "Rambling Reporter," *Hollywood Reporter*, June 12, 1957.

40. "Champions at Grove Tonight," *Los Angeles Herald and Express*, August 14, 1957, p. A–19.

41. "World Premiere for Avondale," *The Indianapolis Star Magazine*, July 20, 1958, p. 24.

42. "Champions Buy Play for Broadway Stint," *Los Angeles Times*, May 12, 1958.

43. Sagal, Interviews.

44. "Television Feature," *Newark Star-Ledger*, May 31, 1953; Champion quoted by Walter Terry, "Broadway Choreographer," *New York Herald Tribune*, March 1, 1964.

45. Walter Whitworth, "What Gives in Avondale Fantasy?" *Indianapolis News*, July 30, 1958.

46. *Hollywood Reporter*, January 14, 1959.

47. Atra Baer, "Giselle's Show a Merry Bit of Entertainment," *New York Journal American*, February 2, 1959; "The TV Scene," *Los Angeles Times*, March 13, 1959; "On the Air," *Hollywood Reporter*, June 1, 1959.

48. Sagal, Interviews.

49. Sagal, Interviews.

50. John L. Scott, "Gower, Marge Breaking Up Dance Act," *Los Angeles Times*, August 2, 1959, part V, pp. 1–2.

51. Sagal, Interviews.

52. "Critic Hits Modern Dance in Sullivan's Moscow Show," *Oakland Tribune*, August 7, 1959.

53. Sagal, Interviews.

54. Sagal, Interviews.

Chapter 6

Bye Bye Birdie and *Carnival!*
(1958–1961)

Ed Padula had been the production manager of the national company of
No Time for Sergeants.[1] His dream, however, had been to produce a
musical of his own.[2] Padula's experience in show business had been
wide. He had directed the first Lerner and Loewe musical, *The Day
Before Spring*, on Broadway in 1945. Thereafter, he turned to production
management, and it was this experience that led him to conceive of a
kind of musical which would encourage and employ new talent. Padula
was enamored of *West Side Story* (1957) but was not at all fond of the
image that it projected of American youth. Although he had been born
in Newark, New Jersey, he did not connect with the romantic image of
modern urban savages that Jerome Robbins and Leonard Bernstein had
fashioned in the show. Padula thought that a musical ought to be used
to portray the joy of adolescence.

Champion was not his first choice to direct what turned out to be *Bye
Bye Birdie*. Padula and his co-producers wanted Fred Astaire.[3] Unfortunately, Astaire did not like the material, either. Champion, however,
could not afford to be picky at this point: he needed a show to direct as
well as to choreograph.

Padula gathered his team. He asked Charles Strouse and Lee Adams
to write the music and lyrics. They had worked previously on several
Shoestring Revues and had composed music at Green Mansions, a summer camp in the Poconos.[4] Padula also engaged Warren Miller and Raphael Millian to write the book. An announcement was made that the
show—then called *Let's Go Steady*—would open on Broadway on
October 20, 1958, a year and a month after *West Side Story*.[5] When
Padula's writers came to him with the script, that date was pushed back.

Padula fired Miller and Millian and asked his composer and lyricist if they could suggest anyone. They suggested Michael Stewart, with whom they had worked at Green Mansions.[6]

Stewart, a native New Yorker, had earned his MFA at the Yale School of Drama. He had written a number of one-act and full-length plays and had contributed material to *The Shoestring Revue*, along with Strouse and Adams. His major work to date, however, had been in television, writing for *The Sid Caesar Show*, along with Carl Reiner and Neil Simon.[7] When Strouse and Adams contacted Stewart, he was preparing to depart for London to be Lillian Hellman's assistant on the English production of *Candide*, but he lacked enough cash to pay his way across the Atlantic. He looked at the script and found it impossible. Stewart agreed, however, to write the first draft of a completely new script, using the songs that had already been composed. The stipulation was that he be paid $1000 at once by certified bank check. Padula agreed and Stewart went to work on the Miller and Millian script after cashing the check and buying his passage to England.

Let's Go Steady was a story of a couple about to get a divorce who are convinced to stay together by their teenage children.[8] It was set in a department store where the couple was about to buy a yacht. Stewart's task was to write a new book around an already existing set of songs. The first thing he did was to forget the divorce. And the department store. In their place he conceived a story about a rock and roll singer who was being drafted into the Army and a publicity stunt thought up by his agent that involved sending him to his home town in New Jersey to be given a last kiss by a teenage girl. (Although Elvis Presley had recently been inducted into the Army, Stewart did not consciously set out to produce a parody or satire of that situation, only to enlarge upon it.[9]) His mind was on the London *Candide*, and he really did not think that his script would actually ever be produced.

Stewart worked quickly, and within about two weeks he handed the first draft, called *Love and Kisses*, to Padula, and sailed for Europe that afternoon. By the time he got to London, however, he discovered he had been fired by Hellman's director, Robert Lewis. Too humiliated to return to the United States immediately, he stayed in Europe for two months until the remainder of the money he had received from Padula ran out. When Stewart got back to New York, he discovered to his great surprise that his script was going into production. He also discovered that there was major work to do on his script, and that Champion, whom Padula had hired to direct the show, intended to have a full role in the revision.[10]

Champion had received the script on June 25, 1959.[11] In it, it is dawn of the day on which Birdie, a rock and roll singer, is to leave for the army. A newspaper boy pedals past Kim's house singing of the "Great Events" of the day. Kim's father bemoans the "Younger Generation." Rosie returns, to find that Birdie has bolted. Albert tries to convince her, in another projected song, that everything he has written for Birdie to sing was really meant for her. She does not buy it, and connives to make her boyfriend Hugo a rock and roll star. She composes "Thief of Love" for him on the spot—that spot being Maud's Roadside Retreat, one of the places where Albert has left a message. That night some beatniks show up at the high school dance, proclaim Hugo their new-found guru, and sing of his philosophy, "Nothingness." Rosie repents, is reconciled with Albert, and finds Birdie. All is well. Albert sings of his love for her. They retire from show business to Iowa, where Albert's mother bakes muffins for them every day.

Champion thought the story was distasteful—not because of the event, but because of the rock and roll premise. The Champions had never included any rock and roll in their act, and, in fact, Champion hated it.[12] Moreover, he thought the score was over-composed and mostly came out of nowhere. In other words, he believed that the score was not integrated into the plot. In addition, he felt that ten musical numbers in a second act were a lot. When Champion first read the script, he really did not want to do the show, but Marge reminded him that this was the break they had been waiting for—choreographing *and* directing a Broadway show. He went to work.[13]

One of the first things Champion did was to list each song in order and note his initial reactions to it.[14] Using the score as a sort of barometer as Champion did—taking into consideration whether a number was up or down, fast or slow, if it came at a crucial moment in the plot, or simply musicalized an unimportant moment—revealed the weaknesses of the show. In addition to the problems with the score, Champion thought that the two plot lines—Birdie's effect on a small town in Ohio (changed from New Jersey), and the trouble between Albert and Rosie—were unrelated. They existed side by side, he believed, rather than intertwining, and because of that, staging and directorial opportunities would be missed.

Champion was scrupulous about the division of labor in all of his shows. The writer was to write, the composer was to compose, and the actor was to act. His job was directing, and that is what he did. He did not rewrite one word of *Bye Bye Birdie*. What he did was, in conference after conference, to discuss the plot and the score with Stewart, Strouse and Adams. Not one word or note was left unexamined. In those days, Champion's favorite phrase was "let's find the soft underbelly of this scene." In seemingly endless meetings, he and Michael Stewart plotted and replotted their script until they were satisfied that the show was going to work.[15]

The first revision written under his direction drastically simplified the show. Champion had succeeded in clearing out the dross, but along with it he removed some of the complications and excitement that a varied score offers. He then devised a sort of compromise. There would be complications, but with a gradual and logical build and release of excitement in place of the emotional rollercoaster that the first version had offered.

Champion had so far been unable to work up a lot of enthusiasm for the production, mostly because of his perception that the story line was silly. But an idea for the staging of the "Telephone Hour" occurred to him and it became a trigger.[16] Up to this point, Champion had been attempting to make sense of the story, to motivate it, to integrate the score into the plot—an approach that was much the fashion in musical comedy during the late fifties. With his idea of a radically nonrepresentational staging of "The Telephone Hour" in the first act, he began to realize that a coherent plot was not necessary to the show. Only theatricality was. He began to envision a dramatic convention not unlike that found in the variety shows in which he had toured for years. Champion began to consider the score as the show's principal structural device. He began to play with the order of the numbers, arranging them much as the numbers in a fast-paced variety show would be arranged. The plot could somehow be worked around the order of the musical numbers he wanted to use.[17]

Champion had previously been able to take time with his choreography, both developing story ballets with Marge and devising and perfecting the revues and the choreography for *Make A Wish*. He had worked beautifully with Richard Priborsky, his musical director, and had been doing so for almost ten years. Champion and Priborsky were much the same type. Each liked to explore to the utmost before making a decision. They would, as they said "noodle" for hours.[18] Champion was afraid that due to the pressures of a Broadway rehearsal schedule they would simply not have enough time to work in the manner to which they had become accustomed. He came to the painful decision that, since the post of musical director was so central to his work, Priborsky should not join the *Birdie* team.[19] He hired John Morris after one interview.[20] Champion seemed to intuit that a partnership with Morris would hurry him along—Morris would improvise along with Champion (the same modus operandi as with Priborsky), but the new musical director seemed to be able to settle in quicker. And Champion, always a fierce editor of his own work, was thus able to produce presentable choreography faster.

Dick Van Dyke was cast as Albert Peterson, the rock and roll song-writer. In late 1959 Van Dyke was fresh from the flop revue *The Boys Against the Girls* with Bert Lahr and Nancy Walker.[21] Chita Rivera, cast as Rose Grant (which changed the role from Polish to Spanish) was fresh from London, having appeared as Anita in the London company of her New York hit, *West Side Story*. As Albert's mother, Champion had cast Kay Medford. When Stewart heard what Medford was doing with the four-line part he had written, the role of Mae Peterson was quickly enlarged.[22]

Rehearsals with the principals started during the week of January 25, 1960, after a week of final chorus auditions at the Winter Garden Theatre in New York.[23] Padula had secured the Anderson Theatre, an old Yiddish house on Third Avenue, since Champion wanted to rehearse in a theater rather than a rehearsal hall.[24] Champion had hired Gene Bayliss, who had danced for him in *Make A Wish*, to be his associate choreographer, and Tony Mordente to be his personal assistant.[25] This being his first show, Champion was determined to be as thorough as he possibly could. Every morning he held a warm-up session for the chorus from 10:00 to 10:30 with Morris at the piano.[26] Each session would end with the entire chorus tearing through the house, running as fast as they could around the perimeter of the auditorium.

Champion was fiendishly methodical, from insisting on a leather binding for the script to wearing the same uniform each day: black T-shirt and slacks and white tennis shoes.[27] Perhaps because of his nervousness about the rehearsal schedule, Champion gave three numbers to Bayliss to choreograph, one of them, "Honestly Sincere," in the first act.[28] Following the lead of his mentor, Bayliss rehearsed the number for hours, meticulously arranging each movement. "Honestly Sincere" is the introduction of Birdie, the rock and roll singer, to Sweet Apple, Ohio. It is the first moment in the show where we hear Birdie sing, and his song devastates the town, from the youngest teenage girl to the mayor, who has shown up with the key to the city. Bayliss had worked out some rather intricate choreography for the number. After a couple of days' rehearsal, Champion took a look at it. The director thought that the number was all wrong, in feeling and in technique. In a couple of hours, using the cast's own ability to improvise within a framework, a new "Honestly Sincere" was staged to Champion's satisfaction.[29]

For all of his nervousness over a Broadway debut, Champion had the presence to delegate authority and to let others do what there was simply not time for him to accomplish. He also recognized when something was wrong and could correct it, often on the spot. Champion maintained his own vision while encouraging his fellow artists to contribute what they had to offer. He would not, for instance, teach an already finished number, choreographed by Bayliss and other assistants, to the whole chorus. Champion wanted the freedom of the full creative resources of an entire company and the control of the choreographing directly on those who would perform it.

One musical number in the first act bears some examination, mainly because Champion's staging of it prefigured a device that he was to use time and time again. The setting is Pennsylvania Station in New York. Birdie is departing for Sweet Apple, Ohio, where he will kiss Kim MacAfee goodbye as a publicity stunt. Reporters are covering the event, and they deluge Birdie with questions. Rosie and Albert interrupt, answering for the gauche singer. Their answers develop into a musical number: "A Healthy, Normal, American Boy."[30] As the number draws to a close, the scene shifts to the train's arrival in Sweet Apple, with the teens and adults singing their welcome, "Penn Station to Sweet Apple."[31]

Champion conceived the shift cinematically, that is, as a dissolve. He wanted no blackout with "cover music" while the scenery was shifted and the performers quickly changed costumes. His solution was what came to be called a "brown out."[32] As the applause started, the lights dimmed slightly. Billows of steam from the departing train filled the stage while the performers downstage turned their backs on the audience and stripped off the topcoats that concealed their Sweet Apple costumes. At the same time, the Penn Station set was being winched off stage as the Sweet Apple set was brought on. As this took place, the additional members of the company (most prominently the Mayor of Sweet Apple and his wife) maneuvered through this melee into position. The lights came to full again on a completely transformed scenic picture, one that had literally dissolved into another.[33]

The second act shaped up to Champion's satisfaction, and when the show was run through for an invited audience on Friday, March 11, 1960, the reaction was electric. The audience of "gypsies" went crazy and the elated cast was sent off, confident of a smash hit, to Philadelphia that evening for a tryout.[34] The second night out of town, however, was horrible. The cast had become too cocky. Champion called them into a dressing room one by one and read the riot act.[35]

At that time he also realized that as a result of putting the second-act ballet so far back in the act, he lacked a solid eleven o'clock spot. Chita Rivera simply was not getting the exposure she needed, and the act seemed to lack sparkle. "Spanish Rose" was written, staged, and performed in less than two days.[36] In an eleven o'clock spot with Rivera swishing her skirt and stomping her way into the hearts of the audience, the song fit perfectly into the plan. The second act was complete.

Bye Bye Birdie opened at the Martin Beck Theatre in New York on April 14, 1960, to rave reviews. Champion had successfully resurrected a form that no longer really existed: musical comedy as it was presented in the 1920s and 1930s. The major structural device was that of a variety show. As Walter Kerr noted in his review, even though " 'Bye Bye Birdie' does not in every instance nail down its claim to having justified a freer, almost forgotten, form," Champion had been astute enough to use these conventions to his—and the show's—advantage.[37]

What Champion had done was, at base, simply scholarship. He had been able to analyze and apply principles that he had learned from sources as disparate as classical music and vaudeville, classical ballet and ballroom dancing. Although he was not at all aware of it, Champion's mind was remarkably wide ranging. When asked once what his choreographic impetus was, however, he replied that he was simply looking for applause.[38]

In mid-September of 1960, Champion called Michael Stewart, with whom he had so successfully worked on *Bye Bye Birdie*, and asked him to take over writing the book for his current project. Although Stewart felt that he was not particularly well equipped to treat the romantic, European subject matter of *Carnival!* as thoroughly as Champion might want, he agreed.[39] *Bye Bye Birdie* had been open barely five months.

Two years earlier, in December of 1958, David Merrick had announced that he was beginning work on a musical version of the film *Lili*, which had starred Leslie Caron.[40] The screenwriter Helen Deutsch was engaged to prepare a "plot," and Gerard Calvi, who had written *La Plume de Ma Tante*, a successful musical revue currently running on Broadway, was to compose the music. Merrick had first achieved Broadway success with his production of *Fanny* in 1954. His genius for publicity had parlayed the middling reviews of the show into a two-year, 888-performance run.

When he saw *Bye Bye Birdie*, Merrick immediately wanted Champion. Among Merrick's abilities was vision; he could often imagine a person capable of things far beyond what they were currently doing. The imagination evidenced by Champion in *Birdie* prompted Merrick to offer him his latest script. Champion was only too happy to accept.[41] Meanwhile Calvi withdrew from the project and Merrick considered Harold Rome, who had composed *Fanny*. Deutsch, however, suggested Robert Merrill, a young composer and lyricist whose work she admired and whom she had convinced MGM to hire.[42] Merrill had composed for Broadway before, making a specialty of adapting Eugene O'Neill plays as musicals.

Deutsch had condensed the screenplay of *Lili* so that the show was located mostly within the carnival compound. But Champion was not satisfied and knew that many, many revisions lay in the future. He felt that he needed to work with a writer who could speak the same language he did, and who would ruthlessly explore all options. Stewart seemed a likely candidate, and he replaced Deutsch.[43] He immediately saw that the puppets were the "exotic" element in the show, and began to expand their role and to integrate the numbers that had already been written for them more clearly. In close discussion with Champion, Stewart also began condensing and simplifying the scenic presentation.

A month after Stewart handed in his first draft, Merrick exercised his contractual right and fired him. At the time it seemed like a minor skirmish, for Stewart was rehired thirty-six hours later. But neither Champion nor Stewart realized at the time that the action was typical of Merrick, whose method of dealing with a production company was a barrage of threats. Because Stewart had been hired under duress (a script badly in need of help and an author unwilling to work with the director), the playwright had been able to elicit very favorable conditions in his contract.[44] Merrick now was showing him who had the upper hand.

The Deutsch script that Stewart first saw was fairly tight. Although some songs were only suggested, the general shape of the show, as well as that of the score, had been determined. Still, the script was not yet simplified enough, and Champion needed Stewart to complete the task. It was the task of sifting and condensing, making each line absolutely integral to the story, with each scene as succinct and logical as it could be, that occupied Stewart and Champion for the next two months. They met daily, in the afternoon. Stewart would then return to his apartment, rewrite at night, and type the revisions in the morning, ready for the next meeting.[45]

The new script was ingenious and tight. At the top of the show, Jacquot, a puppeteer, plays the concertina as the carnival is assembled. The parade leaves. Lili enters and is hired and fired by Grobert, and just as promptly hired by Marco (changed from "Marcus"). That evening she totally destroys his act and, in despair, tries to commit suicide by climbing up to the top of the "Leap for Life." She is talked down by Carrot Top and Horrible Henry, puppets manipulated by Paul Berthalet, a bitter ex-dancer and Jacquot's partner, whose poetic soul emerges only through the puppets. At length Lili and the puppets, with whom she had fallen in love, become the toast of the carnival. Meanwhile, Lili and Paul clash mightily. She is repelled by his unswerving severity and he is, much against his will, attracted by her simplicity and naivete. He kisses her and she bolts. In a daringly unconventional and heart-rending final scene, Lili discovers that inside the puppets, figuratively as well as literally, is Paul.

The last words spoken, only part way through the scene, are "Now, get out!" The resolution of the plot is worked out in action underscored by music rather than through dialogue. In *Carnival!* Champion was able to create a simple but effective final reconciliation solely through what was quickly becoming his forte—staging. In *Carnival!* Champion made great strides, but perhaps the greatest was the galvanizing of all his capabilities into such a simple statement as the reconciliation scene. He later told one of his assistants, Larry Carpenter, that he did not—and had never—considered himself either a director or a choreographer, but rather as a person who "did shows."[46]

The role of Lili was, of course, of prime importance. Champion auditioned countless hopeful young sopranos, but could find no one who had the right combination of innocence and vocal authority. He originally considered giving the role to someone who was primarily a dancer, and accordingly he attempted to sign Leslie Caron (who had made the film of *Lili*) and her husband Dean Jones to play Paul.[47] By November of 1960, singer-dancer Carol Lawrence (who had played Maria in *West Side Story*) had become the front runner, but she did not end up with the part.[48] Meanwhile, Champion was auditioning the other parts. Late in January 1961, James Mitchell, a dancer turned actor, was hired to play Marco.[49] In February, Champion and John Morris, who had done the dance music for *Bye Bye Birdie*, went to see *The Fantasticks* in Greenwich Village.[50] Jerry Orbach, who originated the role of El Gallo, was offered the role of Paul and accepted.[51]

Kaye Ballard, with whom Champion had worked on *The Girl Most Likely*, auditioned for the part of Rosalie and was hired on the spot, turning down the national tour of *Gypsy* to do the role.[52] Ballard had appeared on Broadway before, in the much-acclaimed *The Golden Apple* (1954), and had replaced Bea Lillie in the *Ziegfeld Follies of 1954.*[53]

Anna Maria Alberghetti, an Italian lyric soprano who had sung the lead in the film of Gian Carlo Menotti's *The Medium*, had also read for the role. In January Champion went to Philadelphia to see her nightclub act. When he saw how she handled the audience, he knew that he had his Lili.[54]

Champion had a much firmer grip on the overall structure of *Carnival!* at the beginning of the rehearsal period than he had had on *Bye Bye Birdie*. The general shape of the piece was evident—what remained was to determine and control how the staging of each particular number would modify that structure. Champion used the experience of *Bye Bye Birdie* to his advantage, and it is clear that in the preproduction work for *Carnival!* he employed a much surer hand in guiding the dramatic structure. Moreover, Champion scheduled a much longer pre-rehearsal period of *Carnival!*. For *Bye Bye Birdie* he had given himself approximately nine mornings in which to "plot" the dances, as he called it, with assistants.[55] For *Carnival!* he set aside two full weeks.[56]

When he began rehearsing with the full chorus, which he did on Monday, February 6, he had already worked approximately eight hours with James Mitchell, in addition to the time spent plotting.[57] The presence of Mitchell, himself an accomplished dancer, gave Champion the opportunity to explore an aspect of musical theatre which he thought almost extinct—the individual male dancer. Champion felt that the last important male dancing lead had been played by Gene Kelly in *Pal Joey* in 1940. The female dancer, notably Gwen Verdon and Carol Haney, had dominated Broadway in recent seasons, while the male dancer had simply been ignored.[58] In reformulating and casting *Carnival!* for the stage, Champion had shifted the dancing emphasis from the female lead, Lili, to the male lead, Marco, played by Mitchell.[59]

Champion was firm that no one, including the stage manager, be present during the preliminary, exploratory stages of rehearsal. He promoted an atmosphere of trust and freedom, actively encouraged the cast, and elicited suggestions from his principals. His tact in incorporating or dismissing those suggestions left no one feeling demeaned or excluded.

Moreover, Champion explicitly acknowledged the blame for anything that he perceived did not work; he never made the actors feel that they were inadequate.[60]

Yet Champion demanded complete control, and he spent hours in rehearsal with Alberghetti, minutely choreographing and staging each twitch, shudder, and sigh.[61] Ballard's comic style was brought to the test because of this insistence on absolute consistency. Since the character of Rosalie had relatively little stage time in which to develop, Champion wanted each moment on stage to count. Ballard, however, was a comedienne who needed room to improvise and play with the audience. The balance between the two needs was difficult to find.[62]

With the book scenes, Champion had an even more secretive approach. Rehearsals took place in odd corners or out-of-the-way rooms in the theatre basement.[63] He was not comfortable with dialogue, and consequently he relied on the actors for creative suggestions. He never offered a line reading or even attempted to explain the motivation of a character. Rather, he would take the first intuitions of the actors and begin refining them. He was careful not to choreograph the scenes, but spatial relationships were all-important. Moreover, as in the case of the dance numbers, he would often edit not only blocking, but the flow and the very form of each scene as it was being rehearsed.[64]

Having experienced upheavals with the book in *Bye Bye Birdie*, Champion began rehearsing the big dance numbers first in an attempt to judge how the balance and flow would turn out. As rehearsals progressed, he realized that the big second-act dance number needed to be comic; therefore "Grand Imperial Cirque de Paris" would come to feature Pierre Olaf as Jacquot rather than Mitchell, the lead male dancer. Before he began rehearsing the number, he spoke to Mitchell privately and apologized.[65] The dance was very simply staged, with one of the oldest gimmicks known to the musical stage as the highlight: the chorus lined up for a kick line and the music modulated up a half-tone. As loath as Champion was to use this ancient formula, he knew when it would work, and the number became a showstopper.

The eleven o'clock spot, however, remained with Ballard and Mitchell. "It Was Always, Always You" was a love song, sung with Rosalie trapped in a magician's box and Marco sliding swords through it at carefully timed intervals. Once again Champion experimented with Mitchell alone, with himself in the box, finding out what sort of agony the number should suggest on Rosalie's part.[66] When something hazardous or strange was involved in a number, Champion would always play with the device in private before asking the cast to attempt to use it. More than once, in later shows, he was discovered wearing butterfly wings or sliding down corkscrew slides.[67]

Carnival! opened Thursday, March 9, 1961, at the National Theatre in Washington, DC, with President and Mrs. Kennedy in the newly-renovated presidential box.[68] The show was an instant success, and all the Washington critics—with Richard Coe leading the pack—predicted that it would be a smash in New York. But Champion, never satisfied, began to tinker with it. "There are spots in the show that bug me, but I am afraid to fool with them very much. I mustn't disturb the balance of the delicate mechanism, which somehow works in its present form. Yet there are changes I would like to make."[69] By the time the company reached the Forrest Theatre in Philadelphia on March 28, his tinkering had elicited negative reviews. Merrick cornered Champion and demanded that he restore what had been changed, which he did.[70]

Carnival! opened at the Imperial Theatre in New York on Thursday night, April 13, 1961, to rapturous reviews. It had cost $226,624 to mount and had earned $25,620 out of town.[71] By mid-July, 1961, *Carnival!*, its name slightly altered, had paid back its investment.

NOTES

1. Barbara Wilson, "New Producer Flying High with 'Birdie,' " *Philadelphia Inquirer*, February 28, 1960.

2. Ed Padula quoted in Don Ross, " 'Bye Bye Birdie' Clicking," *New York Herald Tribune*, April 10, 1960.

3. *New York Journal American*, August 17, 1958.

4. Reuben Rabinovitch, news release, June 5, 1958, Billy Rose Theatre Collection, New York Public Library at Lincoln Center.

5. *New York Journal American*, August 17, 1958.

6. Interviews with Michael Stewart, New York, May 5 and 17, 1984; June 25, July 20, August 27, and September 3, 1985.

7. Stewart, Interviews.

8. Warren Miller and Raphael Millian, *Let's Go Steady* (Act Two only), Wisconsin Center for Theatre Research, Madison; and Stewart, Interviews.

9. Stewart, Interviews.

10. Stewart, Interviews.

11. Gower Champion, Notes for the newly titled *Goodbye Birdie Goodbye*, Los Angeles: University of California at Los Angeles Research Library, #305.

12. Interviews with Marge Champion Sagal, New York, January 6, 1984; Great Barrington, MA, May 25, July 5, and October 10, 1985; February 13, and March 28, 1986.

13. Sagal, Interviews.

14. Champion, Notes. Champion always worked on Eureka legal pads using #2 Black Eagle pencils. From *Bye Bye Birdie* to *Sayonara*, a project he had planned to work on after *42nd Street*, his last show, all of his notes appear in this form.

15. Stewart, Interviews.

16. Sagal, Interviews.

17. Champion, Notes.

18. Sagal, Interviews, and Interview with Richard Priborsky, Los Angeles, March 23, 1985.

19. Priborsky, Interview.

20. Interview with John Morris, New York, February 13, 1985.

21. *Playbill*, April 18, 1960, p. 26.

22. Interview with Ed Kresley, New York, October 27, 1984. It is interesting to note that Champion had originally offered the role to an old friend, Bibi Osterwald. Miss Osterwald's agent advised against it—pointing out that none had heard of Champion except as a ballroom dancer at that point. She declined the stage role to accept the film *Shane*.

23. Champion, Notes.

24. Kresley, Interview.

25. Champion, Notes.

26. Champion, Notes; Kresley, Interview; Morris, Interview. In Champion's personal calendar for this day, 10:00–10:30 A.M. is double underlined and marked *Barre*.

27. Kresley, Interview.

28. Kresley, Interview; Interviews with Pat McEnnis, Dallas, TX, October 18, 1984; Princeton, NJ, October 25, 1985.

29. McEnnis, Interviews.

30. Charles Strouse and Lee Adams, *Bye Bye Birdie*, Vocal Score (New York: Edwin H. Morris, 1960), p. 46.

31. Strouse and Adams, *Bye Bye Birdie*, p. 55.

32. Kresley, Interview, and McEnnis, Interview.

33. Kresley, Interview, and McEnnis, Interview. Needless to say the rehearsals of the technical aspects of this feat were long and tiresome. While Champion was working on the number he often became perplexed about what to do next. He would stand in the midst of the cast and come to a particularly knotty place and say "... and then we go to black." He never did.

34. Champion, Notes; Kresley, Interview, and McEnnis, Interview. "Gypsies" are dancers who "travel" from show to show. At this time, most Broadway shows, before leaving town for a tryout tour, would have a dress rehearsal for all of the other dancers working in New York.

35. Interview with Marijane Maricle, New York, November 14, 1983.

36. Champion, Notes; Kresley, Interview.

37. Walter Kerr, " 'Bye Bye Birdie' Flies Above Plot," *New York Herald Tribune*, April 24, 1960, pp. 1, 4.

38. Sagal, Interviews.

39. Interviews with Michael Stewart, New York, May 5 and 17, 1984; June 25, July 20, August 27, and September 3, 1985. The title frequently waffled between having and not having an exclamation point. In general, it was named *Carnival!* until it opened, April 13, 1961. Thereafter, David Merrick removed the exclamation point and it ran in New York as *Carnival*. After it closed, the exclamation point was again added, and today it is known as *Carnival!*.

40. Sam Zolotow, "Stage News" (Press Release), December 12, 1958, Billy Rose Theatre Collection, New York Public Library at Lincoln Center.

41. Interviews with Marge Champion Sagal, New York, January 6, 1984; Great Barrington, MA, May 25, July 5, and October 10, 1985. Interview with Lucia Victor, New York, April 11 and 18, 1984; April 4 and 11, 1985.

42. *Hollywood Reporter*, January 26, 1960. Merrick had produced Rome's *Fanny* and *Destry Rides Again*.

43. Deutsch did, however, retain billing. On each poster and program for *Carnival!* the line "based on material by Helen Deutsch" appears.

44. Stewart, Interviews.

45. Stewart, Interviews.

46. Interview with Larry Carpenter, New York, November 4, 1984.

47. *New York Daily Mirror*, March 21, 1960.

48. *New York Post*, November 9, 1960.

49. *New York Herald Tribune*, January 28, 1961.

50. Interview with John Morris, New York, February 13, 1985.

51. *New York Post*, February 10, 1961.

52. Interviews with James Mitchell, New York, September 26 and October 3, 1985.

53. Harvey Sabinson, news release, August 11, 1960, Billy Rose Theatre Collection, New York Public Library at Lincoln Center.

54. Sagal, Interviews.

55. Gower Champion, Notes for *Bye Bye Birdie*, manuscript, Research Library of the University of California at Los Angeles. He had once again hired Gene Bayliss to be the associate choreographer.

56. Gower Champion, Notes for *Carnival!*, manuscript, Research Library of the University of California at Los Angeles.

57. Champion, Notes for *Carnival!*.

58. Champion quoted in *New York Herald Tribune*, September 30, 1960.

59. Mitchell, Interviews.

60. Mitchell, Interviews.

61. Sagal, Interviews.

62. Mitchell, Interviews.

63. Mitchell, Interviews.

64. Mitchell, Interviews.

65. Mitchell, Interviews.

66. Mitchell, Interviews.

67. Interview with Pat Trott, Boston, August 18, 1984. The butterfly wings were in *Hello, Dolly!* in a number that was deleted after a year on Broadway. The slide was used in *Mack and Mabel* for the entrance of the bathing beauties.

68. Harvey Sabinson, news release, March 9, 1961, Billy Rose Theatre Collection, New York Public Library at Lincoln Center.

69. Les Carpenter, "Hopes for 'Perfect' Musical," *Variety*, March 29, 1961.

70. Interview with Kaye Ballard, New York, October 10, 1985.

71. *Variety*, July 25, 1961.

Gower and Jeanne Tyler in an early snapshot. From the collection of David Payne-Carter. Reproduced by permission of Elizabeth D'Angelo.

Gower and Jeanne in a studio photograph by Bruno of Hollywood. From the collection of David Payne-Carter. Reproduced by permission of Elizabeth D'Angelo.

Studio photograph of Gower and Jeanne. From the collection of David Payne-Carter. Reproduced by permission of Elizabeth D'Angelo.

Carol Channing and William Eythe in *Lend An Ear*. Photography by Wilson Millar. From the collection of David Payne-Carter. Reproduced by permission of Elizabeth D'Angelo.

Gower and Marge Champion in the film of *Show Boat*. From the collection of David Payne-Carter. Reproduced by permission of Elizabeth D'Angelo.

Ernest Belcher, Marge and Gower on the set of *Lovely to Look At*. Reproduced by permission of Marge Champion.

The Plymouth Theatre

Select Operating Corporation

THE · PLAYBILL · A · WEEKLY · PUBLICATION · OF · PLAYBILL · INCORPORATED

Beginning Wednesday Evening, April 6, 1955   ●   Matinees Wednesday and Saturday

OPENING NIGHT, APRIL 6, 1955

PAUL GREGORY

presents

MARGE & GOWER CHAMPION   HARRY BELAFONTE

The VOICES of WALTER SCHUMANN

in

3 FOR TONIGHT

A Diversion in Song & Dance

with

HIRAM SHERMAN

and

BETTY BENSON

Staged and Directed by

GOWER CHAMPION

Lyrics and special material by Robert Wells

Original Music by Walter Schumann

Arrangements by Nathan Scott

Conducted by Richard Pribor

Guitarist for Mr. Belafonte: Millard Thomas

Woodwinds: Sherwin Lichtenfeld   Percussion: Bob Morrison

Bass: Milton Nadel

Pianist: John Williams

CHORUS—John Bennett, Robert Brink, Andrew Case, Gina Christen, Diane Doxee, Elaine Drew, Joyce L. Foss, Dorothy Gill, Nancy Harp, Jimmy Harris, Mark Karl, Jerry Madison, Robert Miller, Ned Romero, Jack Steele, Brad Thomas, Robert Trevis, Karen Vonne, Richard Wessler

A Paul Gregory-Charles Laughton Production

Chita Rivera and Dick Van Dyke on the playbill cover for *Bye Bye Birdie*. PLAYBILL®
is a registered trademark of Playbill Incorporated, N.Y.C. All rights reserved. Used by
permission.

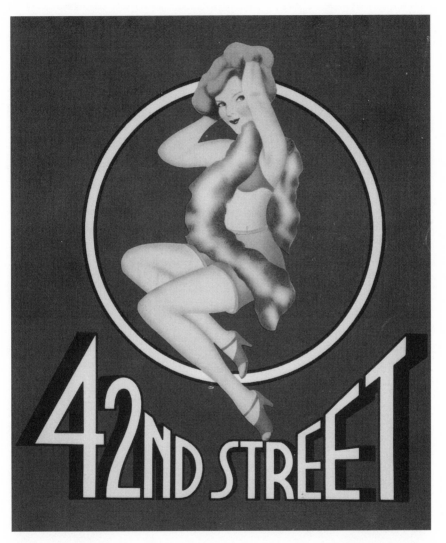

Souvenir program for *42nd Street*. Reproduced from the collection of Brooks McNamara.

Marge Champion. Reproduced by permission of Marge Champion.

Gower Champion. Reproduced by permission of Marge Champion.

Chapter 7

Hello, Dolly!
(1961–1965)

When David Merrick secured the rights to Thornton Wilder's *The Matchmaker*, itself a revision of Wilder's earlier work *The Merchant of Yonkers*, he immediately thought of Champion. Merrick had experienced a marvelous working relationship with Champion during *Carnival!*, and had been sure that he had a hit even before the show opened.[1] The press would later report that Champion had turned down Merrick's offer to direct a musicalized version of *The Matchmaker* seven times before finally assenting. But he really only turned it down the first time it was offered, sometime in late 1961.[2] Perhaps Champion had some reservations about the project itself, but his reason for hesitation was much more pragmatic. He was already working on two projects, *My Mother, My Father and Me*, a farce by Lillian Hellman, and a Richard Rodgers–Alan J. Lerner project, then tentatively entitled *I Picked a Daisy*.[3]

Michael Stewart, who had been hired by Merrick, left for a vacation, taking along a copy of *The Matchmaker*. He fell in love with it and wrote the first draft of the script on board a ship to France.[4] Champion, meanwhile, had not even waited in New York for the reviews of *Carnival!* He hated parties, particularly opening night parties where he was forced to appear optimistic and to put his reaction to the reviews on display. He hated and distrusted reviews even more than parties; and although Champion claimed never to read them, he always seemed to know exactly what each critic had said.[5] On the night of *Carnival!*'s opening, he had lurked in the wings of the Imperial Theatre until the final curtain and had congratulated the cast on their seventeen curtain calls. But he had a limousine waiting to take him to La Guardia Airport, where he caught the night flight to San Francisco where the national company of *Bye Bye Birdie* was in the final stages of rehearsal for its opening.

At this point—April 1961—Champion was at the top of his career. As he flew across the country he had two acclaimed hits running on Broadway and was about to open the national company of one of them on the West Coast, his home territory. The day after he arrived in San Francisco he threw himself into the rehearsals with undiminished vigor, working long hours to put the Champion polish on a company that would show his fellow Californians his triumph—a Broadway hit that every critic had pronounced successful largely because of *him*.

As he had throughout the rehearsals of *Carnival!*, Champion worked from early morning to late at night with hardly a break for food. His nerves were supplying the energy. On the morning of April 21, Champion collapsed at rehearsal and was taken to Cedars of Lebanon Hospital. The diagnosis was exhaustion, and the cure was complete rest.[6] Champion, with Marge and Gregg, spent a solid month of recuperation at their house in Balboa.[7]

A London company of *Carnival!* had been proposed, and Champion's assistant, Lucia Victor, was dispatched to direct it. So implicit was Champion's trust in Victor that he did not conduct even one rehearsal.[8] The production elicited uniformly unfavorable reviews from the London critics, but the real fault is hard to pinpoint. The critics found the writing, both book and score, to be the culprit.[9] Yet it was the same show that had triumphed in New York. Could transatlantic taste be that different? One possible reason could have been the casting. Champion hired very carefully, usually only after exhaustive auditions and callbacks. He cast not only according to type and ability, but according to the energy a performer was able to pour out into the audience.[10] For this very reason, revivals, or even replacement casts, could, and still can, make Champion shows seem lopsided. Perhaps this is what happened to the London *Carnival!*

Stewart, meanwhile, returned to New York from France with a first draft of a musicalized *Matchmaker*. Tentatively called *Dolly*, the book was a distillation of what Stewart perceived as the main themes of the play. Since *Dolly* was to contain a full musical score (which in performance consumes about an hour of playing time), the four-act *Matchmaker* had to be drastically cut.[11]

The first act of *The Matchmaker* introduces Horace Vandergelder, "half a millionaire," who is a hay and feed merchant in Yonkers, New York. He has hired Dolly Gallagher Levi, an Irish widow who has taken up marriage brokering, to find a suitable wife. Mrs. Levi, however, has intentions of marrying Vandergelder herself and is secretly helping Ermengarde, Vandergelder's ward, to marry Ambrose Kemper, an artist. One day, when Vandergelder goes into New York to visit Mrs. Levi's latest prospect, Irene Molloy, his clerks, Cornelius Hackl and Barnaby Tucker, slip away for a lark in the city themselves.

In the second act, as the day well spent proceeds, Vandergelder discovers his clerks in Mrs. Molloy's hat shop. Mrs. Levi appears and diverts Vandergelder's attention with the promise of a much better prospect in an heiress. At the same time she matches Cornelius with Irene, and Barnaby with Irene's assistant, Minnie Fay. In the third act, Mrs. Levi has arranged to meet Vandergelder for dinner in the same restaurant she has recommended to Cornelius and Irene, and Barnaby and Minnie, as well as to Ermengarde and Ambrose. When Vandergelder discovers his two clerks at the "informal and rustic" Harmonia Gardens restaurant, he fires them on the spot and threatens to have Ambrose arrested. The young people bolt, and while Vandergelder searches for his coin purse, which he has dropped and Barnaby has recovered, Mrs. Levi pressures him to propose. Vandergelder refuses.

The fourth act takes place in the house of Flora van Huysen, a friend of Vandergelder's first wife. Vandergelder's soulful henchman, Malachi, mistaking Cornelius and Irene for Ambrose and Minnie, delivers all of the young people to Miss van Huysen following Vandergelder's instructions. Soon, Mrs. Levi and Vandergelder arrive and the merchant of Yonkers, convinced that he has been a fool, reinstates his clerks, gives Ermengarde's hand in marriage to Ambrose, and finally proposes to Mrs. Levi after she returns his purse. Barnaby, as the youngest cast member, steps forward to give the moral: "We all hope that in your lives you have just the right amount of—adventure!"[12]

Stewart assessed the play and, although unaware of the changes Wilder had made between the earlier *The Merchant of Yonkers* (1938) and *The Matchmaker* (1944), came to the same decision that Wilder had: Dolly Levi, rather than Horace Vandergelder, was to be the central character, and whatever else changed, the focus had to remain on her.[13] With this in mind he completed a first draft of a revised script. A note gave an idea of what this initial effort was meant to be: "This is a first draft. Rough and somewhat overlong, yet a good general indication of overall feeling of script. The lyrics contained herein are just hasty improvisations to give a sense of flow."[14]

In the first draft, Stewart began his trimming of *The Matchmaker* by shifting the fourth act from the interior of Flora Huysen's parlor to the interior of an elevated railway car, on the way back to Yonkers after the events of the riotous third act (which stayed more or less intact). This done, Stewart was able to completely cut two characters, Miss Huysen and her cook, who appear only in that fourth act of the original. He was also able to trim Malachi from the plot, as well as a number of other even more minor characters.[15]

Stewart and Merrick began thinking about composers. After a number of discussions, and some unsuccessful offers to well-known Broadway figures, the name of Jerry Herman came up, and Merrick called him in.[16] Herman had a hit running on Broadway called *Milk and Honey*. The show was set in Israel, but it mostly involved Americans visiting that country. The score of *Milk and Honey* had been a marvelous blend of Israeli rhythms and Oriental modes, in a more or less conventional Broadway style.[17] Merrick, however, thought that Herman's approach was too operatic, too classical. In point of fact, *Milk and Honey* was a departure for Herman, whose work up to that point had been very much in a popular Broadway style.[18]

In any event, Merrick was not convinced that Herman was capable of writing the kind of songs that *The Matchmaker* demanded, with music and lyrics in a thoroughly American idiom. When Herman realized that Merrick was seriously considering him as the composer, he told him that he would return after the weekend with a number of old songs that would demonstrate his versatility. In fact, what he intended was to write a clutch of new songs as a sample of what could be done. Herman and Merrick shook hands on a Thursday afternoon. Over the weekend, Herman cloistered himself in his Greenwich Village apartment with Stewart's first draft and his piano. On Monday morning he appeared at the Merrick office with four songs. Three of the four remain in *Hello, Dolly!* to this day: "I Put My Hand In," "Call On Dolly," and "Put On Your Sunday Clothes." Herman was hired on the spot.[19]

Stewart and Herman began working together, refining the script and composing songs. From time to time they would take their work to Merrick for an outside opinion. The producer, never at a loss for words, would tell the team what he liked. Before substantial work could be done, however, the actress who was going to play Mrs. Levi would have to be cast. A different actress would influence not only the score in terms of vocal range, but also the script in terms of personality. At this point the team expected that they would be able to get Ethel Merman to play Mrs. Levi. She was under contract with Merrick at the time, still playing

Mama Rose in the national tour of *Gypsy*. As a result, Herman composed with Merman's famous trumpet-like voice in mind. In September of 1961, the team was invited to Merrick's office for the official phone call offering her the role.

At the time, *Gypsy* was playing in San Francisco. Although Merrick was unaware of it, Merman was suffering from a herniated disk; she had been advised to withdraw from the show, but she had insisted that if any way could be found to do it, she would like to continue performing. Each evening at 5:00, she would receive an injection, dulling the pain until about 11:15—after the performance. She would then be put in traction until the following evening.[20]

Merrick assumed that Merman would be interested in her next show. He was excited and positive about the project; and when he called her, he informed the legendary star that her next vehicle was waiting. Merrick listened in deadly silence. At the end of what seemed to be an interminable period, he reluctantly hung up. Merrick explained to Herman and Stewart that Merman had decided never to do another Broadway show. She still had not told Merrick that she was seriously injured; she had simply declined the role, explaining that she thought that it was time for her to live for something other than eight performances a week.[21]

Merman's refusal to even consider the role was a severe blow to the hopes of the team. Parts in musicals are often written with specific performers in mind. The part of Mrs. Dolly Levi had been tailored to Merman, and Stewart was now left without a clear idea of what Dolly Levi should be. Another actress would bring completely different qualities, and some of what he wrote—some of the Irish brashness that was beginning to become one with the character—might have to be substantially altered if another person were to play the role.

But Herman's work was, probably, on even shakier ground. He had composed for Merman's vocal timbre, to say nothing of her range, which was remarkably wide for a character woman. If another actress were to be hired, the range could change dramatically. In setting Mrs. Levi's opening song, for example, Herman had characterized Dolly's exuberance by writing a melody that ranged from the bottom of Merman's register to the very top.[22] If an actress with a considerably different range were hired, the lyrics could perhaps be set to a different tune. On the other hand, the entire number might have to be scrapped in favor of a completely different concept. So it was with the rest of the score.

But Merrick knew that, even without a star, now was the time to hire a director. He began the search, offering the show to everyone he could think of, including Joe Layton and Hal Prince—as well as Gower Champion. They all turned it down for one reason or another: Prince thought the show was ridiculous, while Champion was simply otherwise occupied.[23] Herman and Stewart continued working, even in a casting limbo.

Plans for the rehearsals of a show on which Champion was working with Lerner and Lane were nearing completion. But *Dolly*'s producer insisted that Champion begin rehearsing after he finished directing his current project, the Lillian Hellman play *My Mother, My Father and Me*, based on the novel *How Much?* by Burt Blechman.[24] After his collapse in San Francisco, however, Champion knew his rehearsal habits well enough to be certain that he would be physically exhausted by the time any of his shows opened. He would need at least two weeks, if not a month, between opening one show and beginning rehearsal for another. Without a vacation he would simply not be able to do it. The producers were adamant, however, and Champion backed out of the Lerner-Lane show, leaving him free to pursue the *Matchmaker* adaptation.[25] The three collaborators began work at once. Champion reviewed the script and score and began making notes about his first impressions on his ubiquitous legal pads.

Stewart describes himself as an ''easy settler,'' that is, someone who will settle for a version of a scene as long as it works.[26] But Champion was precisely the opposite: he would labor over a scene until every possibility was exhausted before picking the option he would begin to stage. He reserved finality for opening night—and on this show, beyond. Herman was a meticulous craftsman who liked to lay out the architecture of an entire show before really writing.[27] Because Stewart and Champion had worked on two previous shows together, they had arrived at a modus operandi. Herman was amenable to the method, and the three set to examining the script and the score line by line, note by note. They would meet for about two hours every day and discuss intensely whatever they, as Champion put it, found ''iffy.''[28]

At the same time Champion was fulfilling his contract to direct the Hellman play. The experience was not at all affirming for the newly-established director. This was Champion's first non-musical Broadway work, and he felt that if he could be successful as a director of straight plays as well as musicals, then his reputation would be solid. Hellman had requested Champion after having seen *Bye Bye Birdie*. Champion was flattered beyond measure. She thought that he would be able to bring to her work the sense of madcap farce that he was able to find in *Birdie*. But she was not interested in a creative partner, only in someone who would stage what she wrote with precision. At this point in his career, Champion was no match for the legendary Hellman, and he worked on the project with little enthusiasm. A week before opening, she insisted that Arthur Penn take over the direction, and Champion slunk into the background, discouraged and disheartened.[29] The show opened in New York on March 21, 1963, at the Plymouth Theatre and played for six performances. Free from his obligation, Champion returned to Los Angeles and threw himself into work on the *Matchmaker* adaptation.

The first item to settle, before any work on the book or the score could really proceed, was the casting of the leading role. Champion suggested Carol Channing, with whom he had worked in *Lend An Ear* and narrowly missed choreographing in *Gentlemen Prefer Blondes*. The others were incredulous. Channing was not at all what anyone had imagined. Herman, in particular, was devastated. He had written the score, which by this point (mid-1963) was eighty percent finished, for the voice of Ethel Merman. Channing's contra-bass was no replacement for Merman's baroque trumpet. As discussions continued, Herman fell into a depression.[30]

At the moment Channing was playing the lead in Bernard Shaw's *The Millionairess* in stock on Long Island.[31] Champion flew to New York from California, and the three collaborators went to see her. Stewart was skeptical, but Herman was beyond skepticism and sulking. He could not imagine why they were going to see Carol Channing play Shaw in order to consider her for a part in a Thornton Wilder musical. As the curtain went up in Mineola, New York, Gower Champion sat between Stewart and Herman. Stewart was open to the experience, although less open to Channing playing the role than he had told Champion. Herman was resolutely determined *not* to enjoy the show *or* Channing.

As the evening progressed, Herman, almost in spite of himself, began to enjoy Channing's portrayal of the madcap millionairess. And he began to understand what Champion had seen in Channing: a larger than life, almost cartoon-like quality. It was not the Dolly he had imagined, but by the time the three went backstage to meet Channing, Herman's mind was spinning. The three agreed that Channing was a definite possibility; the next task was to convince David Merrick.[32]

Champion worked with Channing for hours the next night, with Lucia Victor, his assistant, reading the part of Vandergelder. An audition was arranged on the stage of the Imperial Theatre at noon the following day. Carol Channing emerged from the theatre cast as Dolly Levi.[33] The next task was to find a Horace Vandergelder. With his usual thoroughness, Champion considered actors from Nelson Eddy to Broderick Crawford, from Martyn Green to Art Carney.[34] The role fell to David Burns, an actor and consummate comedian who had served his apprenticeship in vaudeville and who had the ability to make irascibility seem funny.

Most of Champion's preproduction work on *Dolly* was done in Los Angeles. Toward the end of the summer of 1963, Stewart and Herman flew to the west coast and spent a week working separately in their hotel rooms and together with Champion at his home in the Hollywood hills. The revisions on the script and score were legion, and by the time the composer and author left for New York, the rehearsal version of *Dolly, A Damned Exasperating Woman* was more or less settled.[35] Much to Stewart's regret, the extended comedy scene in the second act in which Barnaby dressed as a girl had to be cut. As the book had developed, there was simply not enough time to spend on a gratuitous comedy scene. By that point the plot was hurtling towards its finish—to stop for anything not integral to the narrative would have been theatrical suicide.[36] The rest of the changes were not as drastic—rearranging, transferring, substituting, rather than outright chopping.

The opening sterioption sequence remained, but the fate of "Call On Dolly" was not yet decided. The place of "I Put My Hand In," however, was firm. Herman had attempted to write a song for Vandergelder: a song that would introduce him and explain his mindset. In *The Matchmaker* Vandergelder has an extended monologue about foolishness which had been considered a possibility for musicalizing. Herman had written a lyric, but as yet no melody had been written.[37] At length, the idea had been discarded. Herman had written another song which was a musicalizing of Vandergelder's explanation to Cornelius and Barnaby about his economic theories. Champion felt that it was not a personal enough musical subject, but he thought that the song had great possibilities as a production number. Herman wrote yet another song, "This Time," in which Vandergelder expressed his nonchalance about remarriage.[38] The song was rehearsed, but it simply was not right for the irascible yet lovable character that Burns was developing.[39]

The three collaborators agreed that when Dolly appeared on stage with Vandergelder for the first time, a song was absolutely necessary—an audience would simply expect two great comedians to have a scene if not a song together. Herman, at Stewart's suggestion, had written "Ernestina" for the first draft, in which Mrs. Levi extols the virtues of the marriage prospects with which she intends to divert Vandergelder from Irene Molloy.

A particularly difficult spot in the show was the first act finale. Herman had written a song for Merman called "World Take Me Back," but, with Channing now playing Mrs. Levi, the song was impossible. It had been written for a belter. They faced a gaping hole at the end of the act.[40] Herman's second attempt at a song for Vandergelder was reconsidered and settled upon. If the song were transferred to New York rather than Yonkers, and set in a store owned by one of Vandergelder's colleagues going bankrupt, it would give Champion an opportunity for a gigantic production number. Champion loved to choreograph around props. It was a technique with which he had become familiar through his film work at MGM, and especially through his friendship with Hermes Pan, who had choreographed many numbers using props for Fred Astaire. Champion's concept was to have Mrs. Levi follow behind Vandergelder, charging much of the merchandise being sold to his account— including a red dress she would wear in the second act. The lyrics were revised, a tune was written, and "Penny in My Pocket" became the first act finale.[41]

The second act opened in front of the Harmonia Gardens with the title number, "Damned Exasperating Woman," a comedy quartet with Vandergelder being hounded by tradesmen wanting to collect the bills charged by Mrs. Levi in the first act closing number. Inside the restaurant, after Mrs. Levi had entered (with "Hello, Dolly!" sung to her by the waiters), another comedy duet with Vandergelder ensued, in which she steadfastly refused to marry him, over his refusals to marry: "No, No, No."[42]

As entertainment at the restaurant, Herman suggested a song he had in his trunk, called "The Man In the Moon." Champion liked it at first, but a few days after Herman gave him the song's lyrics, Champion returned them. Herman defended the song and tried to convince Champion to test it. But the director's mind was made up, and he refused even to consider the song further. Once Champion had decided against a number, convincing him that he was wrong was next to impossible.[43] Herman, once again, wrote an alternate which Champion liked much better, "Come and Be My Butterfly."[44] The only number which was now left totally undecided was a ballad for Cornelius to sing to Mrs. Molloy in the second act.

Early in September 1963, the Champions moved into the Dorset Hotel in New York. While Marge searched for an apartment, Gower began pre-rehearsal meetings in earnest on Monday morning, September 16, 1963.[45] During the next two weeks Champion had meetings with his staff. Lowell Purvis was interviewed and hired to be his dance assistant;

Ed Kresley, who had worked in the chorus of *Bye Bye Birdie*, was hired to be Champion's personal assistant. Champion had meetings with Herman and Phil Lang, who was orchestrating the music, as well as with the music assistants and rehearsal pianists—among them Peter Howard who was to become an important Broadway conductor. He met with his designers—Freddy Wittop, the costume designer who had worked with Champion on *Carnival!*, and Oliver Smith, the famous scenic designer. Smith's assistant on the show was Robin Wagner, who was later to design *Sugar* and *42nd Street* for Champion. Also, Champion auditioned countless gypsies for the chorus. Among the people he cast during those two weeks was the young David Hartman—also hired to be an assistant stage manager—to play Rudolf, the head waiter at the Harmonia Gardens.[46]

With *Dolly!*, Champion's directorial style matured. He had learned from *Carnival!* that a central vision was essential to the unity of a piece of work. He had discovered that if a unifying technique could be found, then wildly different kinds of entertainment could be combined and still remain of a piece. With *Carnival!* that unification was brought about chiefly through the scenery. For *Dolly!*, that straightforward kind of unity would be impossible; there were simply too many locales even to consider staging the show on a unit set. Champion searched for a unifying technique and found it by focusing on a central concept. For *Dolly!*, his concept was a cinematic dissolve and pan shot from Yonkers into New York.[47] Champion was not simply conceptualizing the two cities, but creating a seamless transition *between* the locales. He was particularly concerned that the transition have its own lift and style.[48]

In other words, Champion was attentive not only to scenes and musical numbers, but to those theatrical moments that are usually dead time between one scene and the next. He recognized them for what they are: small, sometimes tiny, theatrical crises. And like most crises, they offer not only danger but opportunity. The plot of *Dolly!* was filled with such moments, and Champion seems to have seized upon them to give the story his particular style. An example might be the staging of the transition from "Dancing," a number in which the stage was filled with performers, to Dolly's soliloquy in which she asks her dead husband's permission to marry Horace. In lesser hands, the stage would have simply emptied after the applause for the dance number. Instead, Champion tapered the choreography of the number so that there was no button for applause. As Dolly moved downstage, the dancing couples, now all paired and in love, interacted in silence with her, providing her with added impetus for the soliloquy.

Any show, of course, needs a unique style. And Champion's pre-production notes for *Dolly!* indicate that the overall concept of the production was well-established in his mind before rehearsals began. Evidence of his directorial growth are Champion's comments to himself concerning the function that each number should perform in terms of the overall concept. For instance, in his notes for "I Put My Hand In," the opening number, he wrote, "*MOST IMPORTANT*: This number and its staging and whole approach must set the tone and style for entire show. Must be far out—for one thing, the 'people' painted on the traveler is good device. But who else—And what else—and *how*."[49] At the very first rehearsals of the number Champion began, not by blocking general movement, but by giving the performers specific steps in particular patterns. The concept was clear in Champion's mind from the start, both in general terms and in its specific realization.

On Wednesday, October 2, 1963, on the stage of the Mark Hellinger Theatre, he began to block the waiters for the title number, "Hello, Dolly!"[50] Champion wanted both the opening number, "Call On Dolly," and the one that he felt would be the highlight of the show, on their feet before working on the rest of the choreography. He was establishing his choreographic vocabulary at this point, and his work on the rest of the show would be in the style of this number.[51] He had conceived of a "pasarelle," a ramp built out from the apron of the stage around the orchestra pit, ringed with footlights to give a turn-of-the-century feel to the scenery. At this point he felt that the "pass around" should be actually used only once, during "Hello, Dolly!"[52] For the next three weeks he worked on the number every day, approximately two to three hours per day. As he worked, he discovered that the simpler he made the steps, the more emotion the number was able to contain. As he had done with the script, he explored multitudes of possibilities—various walks, kicks, struts, all in the search for the "perfect step."[53]

When the number was in good enough shape to begin working with Carol Channing, she was called for rehearsal. She stood at the top of a makeshift stairway, ready to descend, but Herman had not written her entrance music. Herman told Peter Howard, who was at the piano, to improvise something, that he would write the entrance music as soon as possible. As Channing descended the stairway, Howard broke into burlesque music. Its very incongruity—racy music accompanying a middle-aged widow descending stairs into an elegant restaurant—seemed to add a dimension of which Herman and Champion had never dreamed. The idea was kept, orchestrated, and the music accompanied Channing down the stairs on opening night.[54]

As it progressed, the choreography for the number became an exercise in group movement and dynamics rather than simply a display of fancy footwork. Champion used unison movement for the waiters, often having them move, as a unit, in the opposite direction from Mrs. Levi, then reverse themselves. The counterpoint between Mrs. Levi and the waiters became the communicative edge that Champion wanted. He had the waiters surround Dolly, exuding affection. She passed among them, greeting each one. When she came back to the center—a single red-dressed figure moving amidst stationary black-and-white-suited waiters—the waiters began to sway. They had come under Dolly's spell. She was, as the lyrics put it, back where she belonged.[55] The waiters' swaying developed into a gentle soft shoe and then into a kick line. Dolly led them out onto the "pass around" and back onto the stage proper. Finally, Dolly was left alone center stage on the pasarelle, the waiters in back of her on the stage. Champion was stumped. He could not finish. He had choreographed approximately three-quarters of the number and could not continue. Each day he would run the number up to that point and sit in the house, musing. The finale would not come to him.[56]

Finally he discovered a solution. The waiters leapt from the stage, right over the orchestra, onto the pass around, surrounding Dolly and leading into a final, high-kick line. Although high-kicking chorus lines are rare in Champion's work, this solution was typical of his choreography in a multitude of other ways. First of all, it was simple—a single movement packed with great meaning—the waiters *choreographically* joining Mrs. Levi as she had returned to join them. Second, it expressed the emotion of the moment: Mrs. Levi had taken the leap to rejoin life at the Harmonia Gardens, and so the waiters were leaping to join her, welcoming her back to life. Third, the movement was in contrast to the rest of the staging: Champion had been working in basically crosswise movements, either with the waiters themselves crossing and counter-crossing, or with Mrs. Levi's staging juxtaposing their movement. When Champion felt a choreographic motif was beginning to be taken for granted, he cut across the audience's expectations with the reverse (or the inverse). Finally, it was as close to the audience as it could get. One step forward and the company would have literally been dancing in the laps of the first row patrons.[57]

Champion had spent approximately thirty-five hours working on the staging of "Hello, Dolly!"[58] Members of the company not directly involved with the staging had not been permitted to observe any rehearsals of the number. When it was finished, Champion ran the sequence for the cast. Many of them wept at seeing the number, which was so simple and so emotional.[59]

During the early rehearsals, the actors had needed to follow blindly the patterns given to them from the outset. Although Champion would often describe the overall picture of a number to the cast, it was generally so complex that they could not get an idea of how it would look when finished.[60] He would assemble numbers person by person, movement by movement, working like a painter who first applies a color and then stands back, looks at his work, and applies another color. While Champion was doing this, the other "colors" simply had to stand around and wait.[61] The cast, of course, would get restless and start to talk. But Champion demanded complete silence whenever he worked. When noise would start, he would click his tongue, which became the signal for order. The room would fall silent and the work would go on.[62]

At times his mania for silence could reach comic proportions. During rehearsals for *Dolly!*, Marge would often observe rehearsals from the house and knit. Following her lead, the women of the chorus also took up knitting, and when they were not being used by Champion in a number they would sit in the wings with their needles and yarn—it was something to fill up the silent waiting. During one particularly protracted silence, the clatter of knitting needles filled the stage. Champion exploded, and turned in the direction of the noise. When he realized that his demands for patience and concentration were getting out of hand, he agreed to the knitting—with the proviso that the chorus use plastic needles.[63]

Rehearsals were always a time of particular concentration for Champion; but before the company left for Detroit, where the show was to start its tryout tour, he confided to Victor that he felt that the real work would not begin until *Dolly!* was in previews.[64] But as the company made its way to Detroit, Champion had no idea that the show that was to open there would bear little resemblance to the one that would finally open in New York two months later.

While still in Detroit, Champion realized that the most direct way to make the audience love Dolly was something at which Dolly herself was a master, merchandizing. He opened with the chorus expressing their love for Dolly rather than having Dolly herself try to engender it from the audience. The overture and the first scene were cut; Dolly entered on a streetcar, reading a newspaper, hidden behind it. The chorus sang "Call On Dolly," describing exactly what she does, creating a dramatic need (i.e., setting up the plot), and at the same time creating a *theatrical* need (i.e., setting up the audience's sympathy and interest in Dolly). What could be simpler?[65]

This very spare transition, wasting no time, getting directly to the point, is what Champion's direction was all about. As *directly* as he moved, however, that motion was often at an oblique angle. Although the point was to introduce Dolly, it was not the character herself who did the task; it was the chorus. Oblique, but direct. As a choreographer, Champion's medium was movement in time. So he approached a piece of theatre the same way—moving it through time. Thus *Dolly!*, after the excision of the opening scenes, began the way musicals had opened for years—with a chorus. But that chorus was at the same time describing itself and the central character by describing an *action*. The chorus did not sing "we *are* so-and-so," as a Gilbert and Sullivan opening chorus would. On the contrary, they were on their way to "Call on Dolly." She materialized; the show was off and running.

Champion's concept resulted in a production in which character was communicated almost completely in terms of movement style. Although a homogeneity of style was certainly imposed, within those boundaries the relationships between characters were clearly shown.

When the production premiered at the Fisher Theatre in Detroit on November 18, 1963, as *Dolly—A Damned Exasperating Woman*, the first act was the major problem, because it did not set up the story or characters—but most of all because it did not set the show in motion. For a director/choreographer this was a disaster. A particular difficulty was transitions. Champion thought that *Dolly!* had "four numbers with pizzazz and the rest of the show died around them."[66]

Merrick was fully aware of the difficulties the show was undergoing. Earlier he had flown to Detroit and attempted to stir up the creative juices. As a result, Champion felt that his authority as a director was being compromised.[67] Champion informed Merrick that he would not tolerate Merrick's presence at rehearsals, and stated that until the producer left town, he would remain incommunicado. Only Marge knew that in reality he had taken a bus to Ypsilanti and had gone to see a movie.[68]

Merrick, however, decided that intervention was needed. Champion had at the same time asked Bob Merrill to write a number.[69] Their presence was a major pressure on Herman. Champion realized that nothing more had been made of Vandergelder's mention that he was marching in the 14th Street Parade. A parade number was the perfect solution. The four went to work separately.[70] Three different versions of a parade finale were presented, and eventually Herman's was chosen. There was a controversy as to whose idea the parade motif was and a lawsuit was begun.

But Champion would not open in New York with an unknown quantity—"Before the Parade Passes By" needed to be tried out in front of an audience. The show ended its run in Detroit and moved on to the National Theatre in Washington, DC. While the "Detroit version" was played at night, Champion rehearsed a new ending.

During the rehearsals Champion was the soul of calm—his insistence on silence brought about an intense concentration, not only in him but in members of the company as well. Eventually, however, the pressure resulted in an atypical episode that demonstrates just how tense the situation had become.

In Washington, during a run-through of the new number, Champion stopped the proceedings and bounded up on the stage. He called the entire cast out from the wings and insisted that they tell him why they were not giving their hearts to the number. He wanted to know why the number was simply not working. He grabbed one of the props and began to stalk around the stage like a cat, taking swipes at the scenery. At length one of Champion's most trusted dancers, Nicole Barth (who had worked with him previously in *Carnival!* and who was to continue working for him), walked up to him and offered him a stick of gum. He stared at her incredulously, but the sheer senselessness of the action dissipated his rage, and he began to laugh. The rehearsal continued.[71]

Hello, Dolly! opened at the St. James Theatre in New York on January 16, 1964. In spite of all the work in Washington, Champion held one last rehearsal to add one small something—something inconspicuous—right before opening, just to keep the cast on its toes for the all-important night.[72] The cast was then dismissed and Champion sat in the darkened house with his assistant, Ed Kresley. He confided to Kresley that for him this was the saddest moment of any show—when the house, just before opening, was as empty and still as it had been before any of the work was done. He confessed to Kresley that he had been thinking about how naïve he had been, how much he had learned over the course of the last few months, and about how he wished that he had handled many situations better. The two left the theatre in silence.[73]

The reviews for the show could not have been better. At 9:00 the next morning, 185 people were counted in the line at the box office, and at least 400 were in line at 11:00. The receipts at the box office that day totalled $25,000; $7,000 more than the day after *My Fair Lady* opened.[74] Merrick released a statement: "I love the drama critics today. I can just lean back and enjoy this success. I had no idea it would be like this. I always run scared."[75]

NOTES

1. Interviews with Lucia Victor, New York, December 4, 1983, April 11 and 18, 1984; April 4 and 11, 1985.

2. William Glover, Review teletype (September 9, 1970), Billy Rose Theatre Collection, New York Public Library at Lincoln Center. Interviews with Michael Stewart, New York, May 5 and 17, 1984; June 25, July 20, August 27, and September 3, 1985.

3. This Rodgers-Lerner project ended up as the Burton Lane–Alan J. Lerner musical *On a Clear Day You Can See Forever*.

4. Stewart, Interviews.

5. Victor, Interviews.

6. Interviews with Marge Champion Sagal, New York, January 6, 1984; Great Barrington, MA, May 25, July 5, and October 10, 1985.

7. Sagal, Interviews.

8. Victor, Interviews.

9. "London Critics Clobber 'Carnival' Though Several Predict Long Run," *Variety*, February 20, 1963.

10. Various interviews.

11. Stewart, Interviews.

12. Thornton Wilder, *Three Plays: Our Town, The Skin of Our Teeth, The Matchmaker* (New York: Harper & Brothers, 1957), p. 401.

13. Stewart, Interviews.

14. Michael Stewart, *Dolly* (manuscript), n.p.

15. Stewart, Interviews.

16. Stewart, Interviews.

17. See Lehman Engel, *American Musical Theatre: A Consideration* (New York: CBS Books, 1968), p. 136.

18. Interview with Jerry Herman, New York, April 2, 1985.

19. Herman, Interview.

20. Ethel Merman with George Eells, *Merman* (New York: Simon and Schuster, 1978), p. 218.

21. Herman, Interview.

22. Michael Stewart, *Dolly*, typescript, Private Collection of Michael Stewart, p. I-1–3; Herman, Interview.

23. Stewart, Interviews.

24. Lillian Hellman, *My Mother, My Father and Me* (New York: Random House, 1963).

25. Sagal, Interviews.

26. Stewart, Interviews.

27. Herman, Interview.

28. Stewart, Interviews.

29. Sagal, Interviews.

30. Herman, Interview.

31. John S. Wilson, ''Carol Channing as 'Dolly,' '' *New York Times*, January 12, 1964, sec. II, p. 3.

32. Herman, Interview, and Stewart, Interviews.

33. Victor, Interviews.

34. Gower Champion, manuscript notes for *Hello Dolly!*, University of California at Los Angeles Research Library, Special Collections, Number 346.

35. Herman, Interview, and Stewart, Interviews.

36. Stewart, Interviews.

37. Herman, Interview.

38. Michael Stewart, *Dolly, A Damned Exasperating Woman*, Typescript, Private Collection of Michael Stewart.

39. Herman, Interview.

40. Herman, Interview.

41. Champion, Notes; Herman, Interview; Stewart, Interviews.

42. Champion, Notes.

43. Sagal, Interviews; corroborated by Herman and Stewart.

44. Herman, Interview.

45. Champion, Manuscript notes for *Hello, Dolly!*, Research Library of the University of California at Los Angeles.

46. Champion, Notes.

47. Victor, Interviews.

48. Victor, Interviews.

49. Champion, Notes.

50. Champion, Notes.

51. Victor, Interviews.

52. Victor, Interviews.

53. Interview with Will Mead, New York, September 4 and 11, 1984.

54. Interview with Jerry Herman, April 2, 1985.

55. Herman, ''Hello, Dolly!'' Lyrics.

56. Interview with Ed Kresley, New York, October 27, 1984.

57. Following the success of this solution, Champion became insistent that his designers provide him with the possibility of playing a scene close to the audience. Ramps or aprons built out from the stage were common in later Champion shows, *Rockabye Hamlet* or *Mack and Mabel*, for example.

58. Computation from Champion's manuscript rehearsal schedule.

59. Various interviews.

60. Interview with Igors Gavon, Washington, DC, April 14, 1984.

61. Victor, Interviews.

62. Various interviews.

63. Interview with Pat Trott, Boston, June 1, 1985.

64. Victor, Interviews.

65. Michael Stewart, *Hello, Dolly!*, Mimeographed Script, Private Collection of Michael Stewart, p. 1–1–1.

66. Rex Reed, "A Champion—Almost Always," *New York Times*, February 19, 1967.

67. Interviews with Marge Champion Sagal, New York, January 6, 1984; Great Barrington, MA, May 25, July 5, and October 10, 1985.

68. Sagal, Interviews.

69. The theatre lore about this particular situation is most elaborate, with conflicting stories abounding. What is presented here is no more than an educated guess. Another, though different, educated guess is given by Steven Suskin in his *Showtunes: 1905–1985* (New York: Dodd, Mead, 1986), pp. 445, 471. Suskin's research has led him to believe that Merrick engaged Merrill and that Champion contacted Strouse and Adams. While this is possible, it is inconsistent with Champion's action in dealing with the book during the development of the opening of Act One. At least one other author actually submitted a version and Champion rejected it categorically: Stewart was the author and he would find the solution. Stewart, Interviews.

70. Herman, Interview.

71. Trott, Interview.

72. Kresley, Interview.

73. Kresley, Interview.

74. Albin Krebs, "A Hit Is Born on Broadway," *New York Herald Tribune*, January 18, 1964.

75. Merrick quoted by Krebs, "Hit."

Chapter 8

I Do! I Do!
(1964–1968)

When Merrick realized that, in *Hello, Dolly!*, Champion had taken a show that could very well have been a disaster and had won a record number of Tonys, the producer began looking for another property for him to direct. The relationship between the two men has evoked much speculation. The two had clashed, and clashed mightily, but each has a fascination for the other that made them both love and hate to work together.

It was a strange creative dynamic that produced an enviable record. Champion directed seven Merrick productions: *Carnival!* in 1961, *Hello, Dolly!* in 1964, *I Do! I Do!* in 1966, *The Happy Time* in 1968, *Sugar* in 1972, *Mack and Mabel* in 1974, and *42nd Street* in 1980—an impressive list by any measure. The shows that Champion directed for Merrick (with the sole exception of *Carnival!*), he at first refused to consider and accepted only after being cajoled.[1] But after working on each production, Champion fell in love with the script, or at least developed a passion for solving its problems (with, again, the possible exception of *Sugar*).[2] Even after the stress involved with *Dolly!*, Champion had not closed the door on the possibility of another Merrick production—although at the time he swore he would never again speak to, much less work with, the producer.[3] In fact, they never had much to say to one another. Each saw himself as the center of precisely the same universe, but because they communicated so rarely and so poorly, neither entirely realized the other's perceptions or power.[4]

Merrick apparently felt that Champion was no more than an employee, an ex-ballroom dancer who had a gift for directing. The producer often considered many other directors before admitting that Champion was the best that he could find—and the only one who could possibly succeed with a particular show. If Merrick had been able to find someone else he thought would do a better—or even an equivalent—job, he might well have hired the person; loyalty was not an issue with him.

A lawyer and adversarial by nature, Merrick was instinctively suspicious of Champion. Originally from the midwest, Merrick had migrated east; Champion, also a native midwesterner, had come to love California. Merrick was dark and not particularly attractive; Champion was tall, fair, a film star. Merrick was instinctual where Champion was methodical; Merrick was choleric while Champion was sanguine. Merrick was interested in finance; Champion, in art. Merrick was a producer; Champion, a director. Champion was the epitome of the white, Anglo-Saxon Protestant; Merrick was Jewish.[5]

From the beginning of the relationship (in 1961 when he directed *Carnival!*), Champion insisted on the confidentiality of the rehearsal period. No one, not even a stage manager, was allowed to be present if he or she was not needed—particularly in the early, formative stages. When his performers were the most vulnerable, Champion attempted to protect them the most. He excluded Merrick from the very project he was producing, a decision that provoked intense ambivalence in him. Champion had become, to some extent at least, uncontrollable by the person who was supposed to control everything. By the time of *Hello, Dolly!*, Champion had become a master at handling Merrick's moods—he simply departed, returning only after the producer had either capitulated or left town. Champion was very much his own man, and even money was not a concern. But principle was. It was different with Merrick. Sly as a fox, the producer was adept at sidestepping issues and finagling deals, and garden-variety integrity was of no significance to him.[6] Not that Merrick was overtly dishonest; his principles were simply ad hoc rather than a priori.

Precisely whose idea it was to musicalize Jan de Hartog's two-person play *The Fourposter* is unclear, but it was probably Merrick, and, indeed, he has claimed the notion.[7] There was some speculation that de Hartog had submitted an outline for a musicalization of his play to Merrick, resulting in the initial idea. But it has never been proved.[8] Similarly, Martin Kalmanoff, composer and author of another adaptation entitled *No Bed of Roses*, which had played summer stock in 1963, claimed not only the idea but that he had played a tape of the first two musical numbers of his version for Merrick himself.[9] Both men sued and both suits were settled quietly, out of court.

If for no other reason than that there are only two characters, the project that resulted in *I Do! I Do!* does not resonate as a Champion idea, and Merrick was certainly the first person to take any action on the project. In any event, after he had secured the rights to *The Fourposter*, the first thing Merrick did was to sign Champion to a contract.[10]

Next the producer began looking for writers, and after a number of inquiries, called Tom Jones and Harvey Schmidt, who were spending the summer in Italy.[11] Although the team initially refused, they completed the first draft at Porto Santo Stefano, the villa they had rented for the summer, before they returned to the United States.[12] When the composer and lyricist had enough material, Merrick and Champion began searching for suitable stars. Although it was rumored that Mitzi Gaynor was being considered for the female role, Champion had naturally suggested Mary Martin, who was then playing *Hello, Dolly!* in London.[13] When the team auditioned the show for the star by playing the songs that were finished, she reportedly wept—and accepted on the spot.[14]

Finding a leading man to match the Martin charisma was not easy, and after considering Howard Keel of MGM fame (and announcing him to the press as having been cast) and Ray Middleton (who held his own against Ethel Merman in *Annie Get Your Gun*), the role finally went to Robert Preston, to whom Merrick offered the role eleven times.[15] Despite the fact that he was about to begin rehearsals for *The Lion in Winter* (which would turn out to be a triumph), Preston's agent was able to negotiate a schedule that would allow him to do both.[16] But Preston was concerned with the draft he read, for the role of HE, Michael, was diminutive in comparison with SHE, Agnes. He felt that without the proper material he could never hope to match the Martin charm. After a rewrite, he agreed, and their agents began to negotiate the billing of the two stars.[17]

Meanwhile Champion was considering several projects after the smashing success of *Hello, Dolly!* He had briefly agreed to direct a straight play by Michael Stewart, tentatively titled *He to Hecuba*, to be produced by Edward Padula, who had brought *Bye Bye Birdie* to the stage. As work began, however, the two felt that they needed a respite from one another, and Champion withdrew.[18] He considered an offer to direct Barbra Streisand in the film version of *Funny Girl*, as well as a musical movie version of *Goodbye, Mr. Chips*, to star Richard Burton and Samantha Eggar, with a score by Andre and Dory Previn.[19] Meanwhile, his second straight play on Broadway, *Three Bags Full*, opened at Henry Miller's Theatre on March 6, 1966 and closed three performances later, a resounding flop. The play, a domestic farce set in turn-of-the-century New York, was an adaptation by Jerome Chodorov of a French farce, *Oscar*, by Claude Magnier.

Champion's ability to stylize movement had seemed perfect for the play, and he filled the stage with the kinds of gestures that had made *Hello, Dolly!* so successful. But when *Three Bags Full* opened in Philadelphia, the critics blasted the director for simply repeating what he had done in *Dolly!*. Between the out-of-town tryout and the New York opening he redirected the piece, making the movement less arch. The New York critics, however, complained that the Champion style, as typified in *Hello, Dolly!*, was precisely what *Three Bags Full* needed. He called the cast together and publicly apologized for having followed the Philadelphia critics' instincts rather than his own.[20] Champion then turned to the task at hand—trying to fill up a Broadway stage with only two actors in *I Do! I Do!*.

Champion's concept was to make visible every possible theatrical device that was either implicit or explicit in *The Fourposter*. The play follows the history of a marriage completely through the conversations of a couple in their bedroom. In the first scene of *The Fourposter*, the couple arrive from their wedding; in the last scene, they depart for retirement after having raised two children. In the play, for instance, makeup changes indicate the passage of time on the actors' faces. In *I Do! I Do!*, the actors theatricalized that conceit by making up at dressing tables on either side of the stage. In the play, the actors allude to all the toys and clothes their children need; in the musical, all those toys and clothes actually appear. So, instead of a chorus, Champion filled up the stage with properties. Moving, dancing properties.

Over the months of preparation, Champion's concept grew and deepened. At first he conceptualized the piece as a strictly, though amply, representational show. That is, he intended to ''fill out'' an already basically realistic play about a particular marriage.[21] It was Oliver Smith's set design that triggered the basic change in his concept. Smith initially had submitted a design that was essentially a box set, complete with a ceiling piece. While working with the design, Champion realized that he did not think of the play as being about Agnes and Michael, but about the institution of marriage itself. He asked Smith if the set could be opened up, if it could become a theatrical *locus* rather than the representation of an actual place. Smith's solid walls transformed into curvilinear screens that suggested, rather than represented, the bedroom.

The characters, Agnes and Michael, now became simply the two people through whom Champion illustrated what every couple endures and enjoys. This fundamental change was really just a consequence of Champion's intention to theatricalize as much as possible. Instead of directing a play about particular people, which had a universal application, he would turn it into a universal musical.[22] *I Do! I Do!* became less and less about Agnes and Michael and more and more about the concept of marriage. It was becoming a "concept" musical, though the term had not yet been coined.

The rehearsal period for *I Do! I Do!* was extremely quiet. The two assistant stage managers, Pat Drylie and Robert Sheerer, were stationed on either side of the stage while Champion and Victor were out front. Champion wanted Victor not only to know what was going on, but why—he would fully explain each detail to his assistant, who was also the overall production supervisor.[23] The reason soon became apparent: Champion wanted to entrust Victor with the London company as well as maintaining the touring companies.

Champion later confessed that he approached the project as if it were "impossible."[24] He worked for weeks with Marge, planning and recording the movement vocabulary he would use in the production. In his script, he began to make diagrams, keeping track of who was where, and planning on paper what he would do.[25] As rehearsals progressed he became as precise as he had been during the rehearsals of *Hello, Dolly!* Working within the limitations imposed by blocking two people in a bedroom, each action and gesture became tied to a beat of music.[26] The production was as choreographed as the most complicated ballet Champion had ever made.

Even the offstage changes were set and choreographed in the finest detail. Ordinarily, wardrobe changes are underscored with a "safety," that is, a certain number of bars (usually in multiples of four) that can be repeated until the actors are ready to continue. All the changes in *I Do! I Do!*, however, were choreographed so that the music and stage action could be precisely controlled. The production was continually moving forward, and there was no time when the orchestra was simply filling in. The actors were reading dialogue through microphones as they were changing. In fact, Champion choreographed the changes himself. When it came time to arrange them, the director and his entourage would move backstage and Champion would direct them like any other part of the show.[27]

Champion made each aspect as theatrical and direct as he could. He decided, for example, to remove the major physical obstacle between the actors and the audience—the orchestra pit. The orchestra was placed behind an upstage scrim and was revealed to the audience only at the climax of several numbers.[28] John Lesko, the conductor, could not see the actors, so every musical cue that depended on sight was a problem. There was no closed-circuit television at the time, so Drylie and Bob Sheerer, the two assistant stage managers, were equipped with light switches hooked up to a lamp at Lesko's podium. The light would go on as a warning of an impending cue, and when the step was taken, or gesture made which would signal the cue, Drylie or Sheerer would turn off the light.[29]

The production opened in Boston on September 26, 1966, to lukewarm reviews. The book was generally blamed, although other concerns were also voiced. Because of the intricacy of the production—particularly the changes of costume and makeup—the two stars had not yet absorbed everything they needed to do. The production seemed rushed, and only after the audience became accustomed to the gimmicks did "the pace settle into the important matters of the play."[30] Moreover, the critics universally objected to a number late in the second act called "Thousands of Flowers."[31] The number, which involved ropes of artificial flowers strewn around the stage, was simply overdone. Merrick insisted that it be cut.[32]

Champion firmly believed that the real work on a production was done on the road, for only in front of an audience is the mettle of a show really tested.[33] The kinds of interactions he had with Martin and Preston during this crucial period attest to the director's growth from the fragmented direction of *Bye Bye Birdie* to the fully integrated style he had now achieved.[34] *Bye Bye Birdie*, while well constructed for its genre, was essentially a revue-with-story—an old-style musical comedy. The aspect of its structure most to the point was the mosaic-like way that disparate elements were joined. In such shows, songs were simply interspersed throughout a narrative, or, to put it differently, a story was told between different vaudeville-like turns. The book was directed discretely from the score.

In *Carnival!*, however, Champion had begun to let the intense style of his musical staging penetrate the book. The whole production began, ever so tentatively, to dance. The flow of scenes up and down, from enclosed caravan to open space, from solo to ensemble was, in itself, a piece of choreography. This tendency reached its apex in *Hello, Dolly!*, where the entire production was saturated with style. The interplay of archness with naivete, color with movement, actual dance with dance-like blocking patterns in *Dolly!* would have been difficult to exceed.

In *I Do! I Do!* this intense saturation was relaxed. Champion became more concerned with *what* was being expressed than with *how*. He was now less interested in a predetermined movement style than in an exploration of the varied and shifting moods of two people as they progressed through a relationship. Once those moods were identified, he concentrated on finding the gestures that would express them precisely, and then on making those gestures part of a carefully timed whole. Fully sixty percent of his notes to Martin and Preston on the road were concerned with gesture and timing.[35] To a much lesser degree were the notes about acting or about the precise execution of detail.

The production went on to Washington, DC, and stayed there through December 5. The book was still not satisfactory, and a quick engagement in Cincinnati was arranged to allow more tryout time. Betty Comden and Adolph Green, as well as N. Richard Nash (who had previously collaborated with Jones and Schmidt), were called in to help the ailing book.[36] The contributions of Comden, Green, and Nash, however, were minimal—Schmidt and Jones themselves were able to solve the problems. By the end of the Cincinnati run, both Merrick and Champion agreed that the production was ready to open on Broadway.[37] Merrick claimed that *I Do! I Do!* was "the least trouble of any show I've ever produced—one tenth the trouble of *Hello, Dolly!*"[38] His enthusiasm could well have been influenced by the fact that another show he was producing, *Holly Golightly*, a musical version of the Truman Capote novella *Breakfast at Tiffany's*, starring Mary Tyler Moore and Richard Chamberlain, had closed to devastating notices.[39]

I Do! I Do! opened at the 46th Street Theatre on December 5, 1966. Typical of the rapturous reviews it received was the one published by Hobe Morrison, the veteran critic for the show business trade paper *Variety*. Morrison summed up Champion's art: "*I Do! I Do!* is not really a dancing show, but the whole performance has a choreographic pattern that only a dancer-stager of Champion's demonstrated ability could design and carry out. The dancing, in other words, tends to be part of the action and dramatizes the situation and the ideas and emotions of the characters. In short, it's simple, but theatrically true."[40]

Because there were only two people in the cast, if one of them were taken ill, the show simply had to be cancelled. The regular Broadway schedule included eight performances a week, six evenings and two matinees, with Monday off. By the end of May 1967, that schedule had been reduced to only six performances per week, due to the strain on Martin's voice.[41]

Both Martin and Preston had contracted to stay together for the national tour. Mary Martin loved ''the road'' and would much rather have toured in a production than run for an extended period in New York. The last New York performance by the original cast was a benefit for the Actors' Fund on December 3, 1967.[42] A little over a month later, Champion opened his next show at the Broadway Theatre, *The Happy Time*. Martin and Preston took vacations and returned to New York to begin preparing the tour in April of 1968.[43] Gordon MacRae and Carol Lawrence had assumed the New York leads on December 4th, although they had been playing the matinees for some weeks.[44]

Champion, as this was his wont, had returned to California for a rest after the opening, but he came back to New York to brush up the show for the tour. He had had a frustrating year. Most difficult, however, was the beginning of an arduous personal journey which would include great failures and only modest successes, great personal doubt, the death of his mother, and his divorce and remarriage.

NOTES

1. Interview with Helen Nickerson, New York, April 8, 1986.

2. Nickerson, Interview: Interviews with Marge Champion Sagal, New York, January 6, 1984; Great Barrington, MA, May 25, July 5, and October 10, 1985; February 13, and March 28, 1986.

3. Sagal, Interviews.

4. The information about the relationship between Champion and David Merrick is distilled from countless sources, the most prominent (in alphabetical order) being: Interviews with Karla Champion, Los Angeles, March 19 and June 4, 1985; Interview with Tom Jones, Sharon, CT, October 15, 1985; Nickerson, Interview; Sagal, Interviews; Interviews with Michael Stewart, New York, May 5 and 17, 1984; June 25, July 20, August 27, and September 3, 1985; Interviews with Lucia Victor, New York, April 11 and 18, 1984; and April 4 and 11, 1985; Interviews with Robin Wagner, New York, September 19 and November 1, 1984.

5. Nickerson, Interview.

6. In negotiating the Los Angeles premiere of *42nd Street*, for instance, just before all contracts were signed, Merrick realized that the lobby refreshment arrangements were not included in the deal. The contract was voided and all negotiations started from the beginning. Champion, Interviews.

7. Sam Zolotow, "Show's Authors Sing for Buyers," *New York Times*, April 14, 1966.

8. "Tom Jones Never Saw De Hartog 'Do' Outline," *Variety*, February 8, 1967.

9. "Inside Stuff—Legit," *Variety*, December 14, 1966.

10. Record Corporation of America, " 'I Do! I Do!'—The conception and writing of a musical play," *Press and Information* [newsletter], n.d. [1966].

11. Sagal, Interviews.

12. Whitney Bolton, "Musical for 2 Persons By 2 Talented Texans," *New York Morning Telegraph*, September 12, 1966.

13. *New York Journal American*, June 30, 1965. The release could have been a private joke, for Gaynor had always symbolized a sort of empty Hollywood glamour to Champion.

14. Record Corporation of America, "Conception."

15. "Broadway Ballyhoo," *Hollywood Reporter*, June 16, 1966; *New York World Journal Tribune*, November 15, 1966; *Variety*, December 8, 1965.

16. *Variety*, December 8, 1965. Preston was signed by Merrick about December 8, 1965. Rehearsals for *Lion in Winter* began on January 10, 1966, and the play opened on March 3. Rehearsals for *I Do! I Do!* began in New York at the 46th Street Theatre on August 23, 1966, which gave Preston almost five full months to play.

17. Interview with Robert Preston, Santa Barbara, CA, July 22, 1985. A compromise had to be worked out, because each star's contract required top billing. Martin's contract stipulated that no one should be billed above her—so both names appeared above the title, with Martin's to the right.

18. Stewart, Interviews. The play eventually reached Broadway entitled *Those That Play the Fools* with Alfred Drake, but it was not successful.

19. Rex Reed, "A Champion—Almost Always," *New York Times*, February 19, 1967; Interview with Dory Previn, Great Barrington, MA, March 28, 1986; Sagal, Interviews.

20. Interview with John Hallow, New York, November 4, 1985.

21. Victor, Interviews.

22. Victor, Interviews.

23. Interview with Pat Drylie, New York, April 29, 1985; Victor, Interviews.

24. Samuel Hirsch, "Hirsch on Theatre," *Boston Herald*, September 25, 1966.

25. Gower Champion, Manuscript notes on *I Do! I Do!*, Research Library of the University of California at Los Angeles.

26. Preston, Interview.

27. Drylie, Interview.

28. An interesting note about Champion's perseverance to make each aspect of the production pay off: when the orchestra was revealed, it did not receive as much applause as Champion had hoped. After a great deal of consideration,

he discovered the touch it needed. In order to remain inconspicuous, the orchestra was attired completely in black and white, and the music stands were in tones of grey. But Champion brought in a red handkerchief and placed it in the conductor's breast pocket. It was just the touch he needed to give sparkle to the reveal.

29. Drylie, Interview.

30. Samuel Hirsch, "Musical 'I Do! I Do!' New Wrinkle on Matrimony," *Boston Herald*, September 27, 1966.

31. Elliot Norton, "New Mary Martin Show Co-Stars Robert Preston," *New York Post*, September 27, 1966; Kevin Kelly, "Enchanted Team in Sentimental Romp," *Boston Globe*, September 27, 1966, p. 27.

32. Nickerson, Interview.

33. Victor, Interviews.

34. Gower Champion, Notes to Mary Martin and Robert Preston for *I Do! I Do!*, typescript, Research Library of the University of California at Los Angeles.

35. Champion, Notes.

36. *New York World Journal Tribune*, November 15, 1966.

37. Merrick quoted in Record Corporation of America, "Recording . . . 'I Do! I Do!,' " *Press and Information* [newsletter], n.d. [1966], p. 3.

38. Record Corporation of America (RCA), "Recording."

39. *New York Daily News*, October 25, 1966.

40. Hobe Morrison, " 'I Do! I Do!,' " *Variety*, December 7, 1966.

41. Sam Zolotow, " 'I Do! I Do!' Drops a Saturday Show," *New York Times*, May 29, 1967.

42. Ben Washer, press release, November 16, 1967, Billy Rose Theatre Collection, New York Public Library at Lincoln Center.

43. Sam Zolotow, " 'I Do! I Do!' Will Add a Matinee Cast," *New York Times*, August 22, 1967.

44. Zolotow, " 'I Do! I Do!' "

Chapter 9

Difficulties and Decline
(1968–1972)

The period between the completion of *I Do! I Do!* and the beginning of production work on *42nd Street*, roughly ten years, was the low point of Champion's professional life. The work he produced during those years was decidedly inferior, in terms of both critical response and box office receipts, although some of it was honored with various awards, among them a Tony. None of his shows from this period, with the possible exception of his revival of *Annie Get Your Gun* (directed in April and May of 1977 for the Los Angeles Civic Light Opera), managed to become a unified statement—a quality that had characterized all of his earlier efforts and, indeed, had become a Champion hallmark.

The year 1967 had proved a particularly frustrating one, one in which he had begun preparing for a film production of *Goodbye, Mr. Chips*, a musical version of the James Hilton novel, which was to be filmed in England. Champion had previously turned down offers to direct movie versions of both *Bye Bye Birdie* and *Hello, Dolly!* After preparing one sample scene of *Birdie* for motion pictures, he felt that he simply had nothing more to say about his stage musicals—and, in any case, attempting to transfer stage conventions to the screen was not something he relished.[1] The score for *Mr. Chips* was to have been by Andre and Dory Previn, friends with whom Champion looked forward to working. By this point (late 1967), however, Rex Harrison was scheduled to play the retiring schoolmaster in place of Richard Burton. The star was unfamiliar with the Previns' work, and he insisted that Leslie Bricusse, an English composer-lyricist who had worked with him on *Dr. Doolittle*, be engaged to write the score.[2]

Champion felt considerable loyalty to the Previns, and he withdrew from the project. The film was eventually directed by Herbert Ross, himself a former choreographer, with the Bricusse score—but without Harrison. Ironically, Peter O'Toole, who had been an ardent Marge and Gower Champion fan in his youth, and Petula Clark finally played the unlikely lovers. Champion, meanwhile, continued to seek a project to film with the Previns. For a while, the three worked on a version of *Thieves' Carnival*, but the score was eventually shelved.[3]

Meanwhile, David Merrick, as usual, was searching for material to produce. He had hit on the idea of transforming Samuel Taylor's intimate French Canadian play *The Happy Time* (1950) into a musical. The original, based on short stories by Robert L. Fontaine, had starred Patrick Magee and Maureen O'Sullivan. At first Merrick had wanted Cy Coleman and Dorothy Fields to write the score. By January of 1967, however, they had withdrawn, taking with them Yves Montand, the French movie star slated to play the lead.[4] By early 1968, John Kander and Fred Ebb were at work on the score and N. Richard Nash was writing the book. The next step in Merrick's production schedule was, of course, securing a director.

When Merrick suggested the show to Champion, he was, as usual, not interested. Champion was never fond of living or working in the east, and his recent time in California with the Previns had proved to him that he did not want to work outside California, no matter what the material. Merrick, accordingly, flew Kander and Ebb to Los Angeles to play their score for Champion. The director was hooked. The agreement was that *The Happy Time* would be produced in Los Angeles, and only after previews would the production move to New York.[5]

Finding a suitable lead was a major hurdle, and Champion auditioned literally hundreds of possible candidates.[6] He flew to Paris for a round of auditions, then in New York heard hopefuls on the way back to California. He finally settled on Robert Goulet, who had not done anything significant on Broadway since his success as Lancelot in *Camelot* (1960).

Again as usual, Champion developed an overall conceit, a frame in which to place the story. The leading character was to be Jacques Bonnard, a successful commercial photographer who was visiting his home, a small town in Canada called St. Pierre. During his visit, he confronts various pieces of unfinished business—both with his family and with a previous romantic relationship. All of this is put into the perspective of photography and the fast-paced world in which Jacques had made himself a place. Champion, therefore, put the intimate story of a prodigal son's return home to an eccentric but loving family within a larger context of blank screens, upon which could be projected both moving pictures and still photographs supposedly taken by Jacques. The opening sequence perfectly illustrates the possibilities of this device.

Jacques appears on a stage empty except for a table on which is a vase with a rose in it. As he begins to photograph the rose, the pictures he takes, magnified hundreds of times, appear on the screens. Suddenly, a picture of the rose in a woman's hand appears, and the projected photographs begin to jump, seemingly taking on a life of their own. The rose is next seen in his grandfather's lapel. Other faces appear:

> JACQUES: You know, it's a very strange thing. The memory plays tricks. . . . You see, every time I take a picture of this rose, it reminds me of something else, something—another place—somebody—long ago![7]

The speech leads into the opening song, "The Happy Time," which explores the effect of happy memories on our lives. The effect was striking, a powerful tool with which to investigate a number of levels of meaning. Unfortunately it completely overpowered the family and the interrelationships being examined. The core of the show seemed lost, adrift in a sea of slick images and vast, dark spaces.

Perhaps because of this initial error, Champion was also unable to focus the narrative so that it would seem something other than simply episodic. As Laurie Mannon, Jacques' love interest, Champion originally cast Willi Burke, an actress roughly Goulet's age but who could play an older woman. It was the director's idea that Jacques should have had an affair with a woman slightly his senior, and then be confronted with it on his return. When this situation seemed to overshadow the rest of the story, rather than helping to develop it, Champion recast the role with a younger actress (first Linda Bennett and then Julie Gregg), thereby eliminating the narrative conflict. This sort of failure to focus the narrative line resulted in the episodic structure of *The Happy Time*, which did not stand up to the overpowering frame in which it was placed. The changes also wreaked havoc with the filmed aspects of the show, since each time the role was recast, all of the slides and motion picture film had to be re-shot.[8]

The idea of trying out a show in Los Angeles did not work to anyone's advantage. Champion felt that he had to prove himself to the California audiences, even with a track record of four hits behind him. For the first time there is evidence that he tried his hand at rewriting rather than simply demanding changes until he was satisfied.[9] Merrick discovered that the costs of constructing and shipping scenery outside New York crippled the budget. Moreover, he felt even more alienated from the production than he had previously because he needed to be on the east coast most of the time. His supervision of the entire production was minimal and, perhaps because of this, there were problems whenever he appeared.[10]

The Happy Time opened at the Ahmanson Theatre in Los Angeles on November 19, 1967, and at the Broadway Theatre in New York on January 18, 1968, in both cases to unenthusiastic reviews.[11] The show had cost over a quarter of a million dollars to produce (high for 1968), and the Merrick office was determined to get at least a year's run.[12] In fact, it closed on September 28, after 286 performances—the shortest run of any Champion musical up to that date. While it was playing, however, Champion had the distinction of having three shows on Broadway at the same time: *Hello, Dolly!*, *I Do! I Do!*, and *The Happy Time*. Clive Barnes, however, then the theatre critic of the *New York Times*, felt that Champion was a master at staging but that he should "leave the choreography to someone else."[13] From *The Happy Time* onward, that is precisely what he began to do.

Although the critics complained that *The Happy Time* was uninspired, it showed that Champion was searching for ways to expand the musical theatre stage to include other media. Because the frame in which the story was set completely dominated the show, however, it became, in effect, about media rather than about a family. Up to this point, all of Champion's musicals had employed a clearly defined chronological structure. *The Happy Time*, on the other hand, had clearly different time frames: Jacques, in his studio, remembering both his childhood (represented through still photographs) and his recent visit home (portrayed through live stage action). This use of flashback was only one of a number of cinematic effects and narrative devices with which Champion experimented.

During the rehearsals of *The Happy Time* in Los Angeles, Champion's mother had died. Her death was not an unwelcome end to a difficult relationship. Champion left rehearsals to attend the funeral, and went directly back. Any difficulty he experienced in the rehearsal hall at the time was really only a symptom of what was on his mind.[14] He was nearing fifty, and he no longer perceived himself as the "boy" that Ernest Belcher had called him. Gower Champion was entering a sort of crisis of limits—a time when he recognized that he was no longer the young ballroom dancer who had set Broadway on its ear. This age crisis seems to have been the root of any number of new behavior patterns.

Champion began a love affair with rock music, for instance, something that he had eschewed with vigor before. He and Marge would never have performed to rock and roll, or even the Latin rhythms that were popular when they were dancing together.[15] Champion gradually became interested in harder and harder sounds—and he loved to play his favorites at top volume while dancing to the music in a caftan. This interest would culminate in *Rockabye Hamlet*, a rock version of Shakespeare's *Hamlet*, in 1976.

But the most painful manifestation was the beginning of the dissolution of his marriage. When the Champions had stopped performing, Marge determined to be the model wife, and she had stayed resolutely in the background. Now that their sons no longer needed the constant attention that toddlers require, Marge began to spread her wings again. She took on a number of projects, among them many celebrity appearances supporting dance organizations, and teaching dance at the Mafundi Institute in Watts, the black ghetto of Los Angeles. Marge, the daughter of the foremost teacher of dance in the Los Angeles area, Ernest Belcher, was of course a classically trained dancer, and, moreover, a trained dance teacher.

Champion, on the other hand, had never developed a dance technique that was adequate enough for advanced ballet moves, in particular, lifts. He was always painfully aware that Marge was the one who had a solid dance technique. Further, he had often used her as a dramaturg, a person off of whom to bounce production ideas and concepts. Gower was the creative force, Marge, the editorial talent. Although he used her less and less after *Hello, Dolly!*, he still depended on her sharp observations and honest opinions. This relationship, Champion perceived, made him dependent on her. Increasingly he seemed to resent whatever Marge did.[16]

In addition, with *The Happy Time*, Champion had experienced his first Broadway failure, mild as it was. From the early months of 1968, Champion entered a period, more than a full year, of frustrating work, none of which materialized. He had turned down offers to direct movie versions of both *Bye Bye Birdie* and *Hello, Dolly!*. *I Do! I Do!*, however, could have a far different treatment on film than had been possible on a stage. He accepted the offer and for the first time in his life while preparing the film, Champion became a person with an office and a schedule. Dick Van Dyke, who had starred in *Bye Bye Birdie*, had been signed, along with Julie Andrews of *My Fair Lady* fame. In the end, the project was cancelled.

Then in March of 1967, Champion directed the Academy Awards presentation. For the first time in the history of the awards, some attempt was being made to give the show an overall feeling, and Champion's work marked the beginning of what was to be a more television-conscious awards program. In 1969 he directed Georges Feydeau's classic farce *A Flea in Her Ear* for William Ball's American Conservatory Theatre in San Francisco. Champion had conceived the play wholly in physical terms and the set was a gargantuan squirrel cage in which the actors could scamper and dart, caught in their own machinations.[17] The production was a success, and played in New York when the company made its yearly tour. But it did not generate a flood of new offers.

Champion's next Broadway show was *Prettybelle*, perhaps his most miserable failure. With book and lyrics by Bob Merrill, who had composed *Carnival!*, and a score by Jule Styne, a legendary Broadway composer, *Prettybelle* was an adaptation of a novel of the same name by Jean Arnold. Set in the contemporary South, it told the story of a schizophrenic and alcoholic southern belle (played by Angela Lansbury). Despite all of Champion's and Lansbury's efforts, it closed in Boston in February of 1971 after just two weeks of previews. The show was making its New York opening. But Champion and the rest of the creative staff felt that it needed one more week out of town. Unfortunately, his agent, mentor, and father figure, Lester Shurr, had died during rehearsal.

Champion was out of his element with the surreal, almost Tennessee Williams-like atmosphere of *Prettybelle*. He would slight the book scenes, hurrying through them in order to get to the business at hand— staging the numbers.[18] When he did get involved with directing the book, he acted as more of a moderator than a director, and he made only cursory attempts at exploring the psychological underpinnings of characters' actions. His rehearsals were closely moderated acting exercises based on the scenes rather than psychological explorations. Champion never did become a director of penetrating psychological nuance. Although none of the experiments he performed during the rehearsal period of *Prettybelle* seemed to result in a resounding success, however, the same methods would later yield richer rewards. The subtle interplay of myth, reality, and performance in *42nd Street* is, for instance, a direct result of the directorial exploration Champion was attempting in *Prettybelle*—and later in *Sugar* and *Mack and Mabel*.

Meanwhile David Merrick had conceived of a musical version of Billy

Wilder's comedy classic *Some Like It Hot* (1959), or as close to it as he could get. Although he was unable to obtain the rights to the movie, he *had* obtained the rights to the German film *Fanfares of Love* (1932), on which the film had been based. With a screenplay by Heinz Pauck, based on a story by Robert Thoeren (who later migrated to Hollywood) and Manfred Logan, director Kurt Hoffmann's film told the story of two unemployed musicians who don various disguises to get jobs with orchestras. Among the disguises are, of course, female drag to work with an all-girl orchestra (the conceit which Wilder expanded into *Some Like It Hot*). But the two also black their faces to work with a jazz band and wear bandannas and earrings in order to join a gypsy troupe. The humor in the original was broad, containing gags in which the two men shaved or smoked cigars while dressed as women. But there were, in addition, bits of darker humor such as hints of lesbianism and sadomasochism.

Working under the proviso that no hint of the Wilder movie or the Marilyn Monroe character could surface, Michael Stewart and Jerry Herman went to work. The writers set the story on the day after the war and went to work, producing a script and a skeleton score called *One of the Girls*.[19] The script portrayed two American GI musicians who, while escaping from a POW camp hours before liberation (with a string bass in tow), inadvertently capture a master German spy. He ends up presumed dead but in fact is living in the United States. Merrick disliked the script, and in his typically indirect way, blamed Herman when speaking with Stewart, and vice versa.[20] In the meantime, while in California, he had engaged Champion to direct. Recalling the pain of *Hello, Dolly!*, Herman dropped out of the project. *One of the Girls* folded.[21]

But—perhaps on that very trip to California—Merrick was able to obtain the stage rights to the Wilder film. Soured on both Herman and Stewart, he engaged Peter Stone and Jule Styne to write the new version of the show now called *Nobody's Perfect*, a reference to the last line of the Wilder screenplay.[22]

Champion had stuck by his contract to direct the show. At this point in his life all he could see was failure, and he was probably thankful for the diversion, to say nothing of the work. Then, too, after *The Happy Time* and the dismal failure of *Prettybelle*, Champion was desperate for a hit. He and Marge had separated, but no divorce proceedings had begun. Marge stayed in their house in the Hollywood Hills and he took a beach house in Malibu. Both were seeing therapists, but Champion, typically, chafed at anyone, even a professional, knowing the details of his private life.[23]

Rehearsals for *Nobody's Perfect* began in New York on December 13, 1971. The authors, particularly Styne, rankled under Champion's customary rehearsal protocol—that is, that no one could watch, not even the authors.[24] The resulting unhappiness of the authors was only a minor part of the problem. Champion was unable to focus on the show, and his direction was oddly fuzzy.[25] He had no visual hook into the material, and he depended on his performers not only for fine acting points, as he had always done, but to give the show style. Moreover, he had somehow lost his usual thoroughness about revisions. In addition, Jo Meilziner, the famed designer who had created the sets for such shows as *Death of a Salesman* and *Guys and Dolls*, had been engaged to do the scenery and lighting. Meilziner was old, and at this point, feeble. During the course of rehearsals, he became too ill to make the changes mandated by Champion.

The show, now titled *Sugar*, was scheduled to open in Washington, DC, at the Kennedy Center (the first musical to have its world premiere there) on January 17, 1972. At the opening, three, and possibly four, of the numbers printed in the program never appeared—so hazy was the structure that one reviewer was not sure about the exact number.[26] Moreover, the dingy Meilzeiner sets clearly needed to be replaced. Even Richard Coe, the critic for the *Washington Post*, who was one of Champion's most loyal supporters, called the staging "scrappy."[27] But it had become evident that Champion's lack of a clear visual concept was crippling the production.

A costly solution was needed for the problem of the setting. The production needed brightening, and yet it had been blocked and choreographed on a set that was now unusable. But the prospect of redirecting and re-choreographing on a totally new set was too daunting, and Robin Wagner, who had been Oliver Smith's assistant on *Hello, Dolly!*, flew to Washington and agreed to redesign the show using the Meilziner floor plans.

The opening in New York was pushed back week by week, and by the beginning of February the premiere had been postponed indefinitely.[28] Merrick, with so much already invested, decided to extend the tryout tour and booked the show successively in Toronto, Philadelphia, and Boston.[29] A line of show doctors began to appear, and Champion became frozen with indecision. At one point he could not even decide when to hand the actors the rewrites for the performance that night—before of after they were in makeup.[30]

The stars, Tony Roberts and Robert Morse, were battling each change in direction as well as each other, and Merrick was under considerable pressure to replace Champion.[31] Happily, a reconciliation with Marge was in the air, and she flew to Washington and was able to coax him into some of the decisions that could not be avoided.[32] Merrick asked the writer and director of his *Promises, Promises* (1968), another musical adaptation of a movie comedy, to help. Neil Simon took a look at the show and made some suggestions, but was not credited with any writing. It was reported that his suggestions were rejected by Champion.[33] Robert Moore reportedly took over the book scenes, but was given no billing.[34] Champion was having particular trouble with a ballet for Cyril Richard and Robert Morse in the second act, and he himself asked Donald Saddler to help with the choreography for that number.[35] Of the nineteen numbers in the score in Washington, only seven remained at the premiere in New York, on September 4, 1972.

Merrick was so concerned about the premiere that he had asked that no "legitimate producers" attend the opening.[36] With rumors flying that the show had been doctored by everyone from Simon "to Marcus Welby," Merrick had good cause to arrange as enthusiastic an opening as possible.[37] The reviews were mixed, and T. E. Kalem, writing in *Time*, confirmed one of Champion's worst fears—that he was no longer considered relevant to the musical theatre. "In the past three years," Kalem wrote, "*Company* and *Follies* [which had triumphed where *Prettybelle* had failed] have altered the critical perspective by providing a musical form that is spare, intelligent, ironic, mature, and capable of sustaining three-dimensional characters."[38] In fact, he said, *Sugar* was a musical of the old sort: integrated rather than daring, simple and buoyant rather than searing or searching.

Champion returned to California with Marge, his prospects as dim as he had ever seen them. Marge, on the other hand, had not let the devastation of their separation and seemingly inevitable divorce paralyze her. She had continued the activities that had begun accelerating in 1968 during the rehearsals of *The Happy Time*.

By 1969 she had become a regular participant in the services at the Bel Air Presbyterian Church. The pastor, Don Moomaw (a former all-American football player), and Merilee Zdenek (a fellow church member and author), approached Marge with the idea of an additional Sunday service that would explore alternate methods of worship, such as multimedia, folk music, and dance. As a result of the services they created, they wrote and published *Catch the New Wind*, a book that became a sort of *vade mecum* for the liturgical dance movement that flourished in the late 1960s and early 1970s.[39]

Moreover, because she performed in many of the services, Marge regained the fine tuning that a working dancer needs—despite the fact that at this point she was forty-nine and had not performed for almost ten years. This experience became a sort of bridge, bringing Marge from the relative seclusion of staying at home and having children into the limelight again.

The Champions divorced in January of 1973.[40] Marge remained in the house in the Hollywood Hills, and Champion eventually moved into a mammoth mansion in Beverly Hills complete with an indoor pool and retractable roof. He survived mostly on junk food—hamburgers and hot dogs bought from local vendors—and spent his days walking up and down his beloved beach.[41]

NOTES

1. Champion had made annotations in his script of *Birdie*. Champion, manuscript notes in *Bye Bye Birdie* (Los Angeles: Research Library of the University of California at Los Angeles, Special Collections).

2. Dory Previn, *Bog-Trotter* (Garden City, NY: Doubleday, 1980), p. 46.

3. Previn, *Bog-Trotter*.

4. *New York Post*, January 23, 1967.

5. *New York Post*, January 31, 1967; Interviews with Marge Champion Sagal, New York, January 6, 1984; Great Barrington, MA, May 25, July 5, and October 10, 1985; February 13, and March 28, 1986.

6. Gower Champion, audition notes for *The Happy Time* (Los Angeles: Research Library of the University of California at Los Angeles, n.d. [1967]).

7. N. Richard Nash, *The Happy Time* (Los Angeles: Research Library of the University of California at Los Angeles, n.d. [1967]).

8. *New York Daily News*, January 1, 1968.

9. Gower Champion, manuscript notes for *The Happy Time* (Los Angeles: University of California at Los Angeles Research Library, n.d. [1967]).

10. Dorian Kalem, " 'Happy Time' to Open at the Ahmanson," *New York Times*, October 10, 1967.

11. See, for instance, Walter Kerr, " 'Happy Time,' " *New York Times*, January 21, 1968.

12. *New York Daily News*, March 3, 1968.

13. Clive Barnes, " 'The Happy Time,' " *New York Times*, January 19, 1968.

14. The statements are universally supported by those who were closest to Champion during this period: Marge Champion Sagal, Karla Robertson Champion, Jess Gregg, Max Showalter and Gary Falco.

15. Sagal, Interviews.

16. Sagal, Interviews.

17. Daniel Sullivan, " 'Flea In Her Ear' at ACT," *San Francisco Chronicle*, November 2, 1969.

18. Interview with Jon Cypher, Los Angeles, August 31, 1984.

19. Michael Stewart, *One of the Girls*, Manuscript, Private Collection of Michael Stewart, New York.

20. Stewart, Interviews.

21. Stewart, Interviews.

22. When Jack Lemmon, disguised as Daphne, reveals to Joe E. Brown, his rich suitor, that he is really a man, Brown replies "Well, nobody's perfect!"

23. Sagal, Interviews.

24. Theodore Taylor, *Jule: The Story of Composer Jule Styne* (New York: Random House, 1979).

25. Interview with Tony Roberts, New York, May 14, 1985; Interview with Sheila Smith, New York, January 15, 1985.

26. Frank Getlein, " 'Sugar' Needs Sweetening," *Washington Evening Star*, January 18, 1972.

27. Richard L. Coe, " 'Sugar' Well on Its Way," *Washington Post*, January 18, 1972, p. B1.

28. "Deny That Simon, Moore Doctoring 'Sugar' Tryout," *Variety*, February 23, 1972. "Delay 'Sugar' Preem," *Variety*, February 2, 1972.

29. "May Extend Road Tour For 'Sugar,' " *Variety*, February 16, 1972, p. 67.

30. Smith, Interview.

31. Al Kasha and Joel Hirschhorn, *Notes on Broadway* (Chicago: Contemporary Books, 1985), p. 298.

32. Sagal, Interviews, and Smith, Interview.

33. "May Extend Road Tour For 'Sugar,' " *Variety*, February 16, 1972, p. 67.

34. "Deny That Simon, Moore Doctoring 'Sugar' Tryout," *Variety*, February 23, 1972.

35. Sagal, Interviews.

36. "Producer Merrick Asks Other Producers Shun 'Sugar' Preem; 'Spoilers'?" *Variety*, April 12, 1972, pp. 1, 93.

37. Liz Calhoun, "Merrick in a Flurry," *New York Times*, September 3, 1972.

38. T. E. Kalem, "The Girls In the Band," *Time*, September 1972.

39. Marge Champion and Merillee Zdenik, *Catch the New Wind* (New York: Random House, 1972).

40. Sagal, Interviews.

41. Interview with Ron Schwinn, New York, March 6, 1985.

Chapter 10

Fall and Rise
(1973–1979)

In February 1973 Champion answered a call for help that stemmed from a classic piece of Broadway miscasting. Harry Rigby, who had successfully mounted a revival of the classic 1925 musical *No, No, Nannette!* had again commissioned a revival.

Although *No, No, Nannette!*, Rigby's revival, used substantially the same score as its predecessor, by the time it opened at the new Minskoff Theatre in New York on March 13, 1973, its book bore only a slight resemblance to the original. The Cinderella theme, which the earlier play had made a musical staple of the 1920s, was still in evidence, but hardly anything else was. The new book was by Hugh Wheeler, whose collaboration with Stephen Sondheim, *A Little Night Music*, had opened a little over a month earlier. But the miscasting was obvious. The producers had hired John Gielgud to direct. When the production opened in Toronto for a tryout it was clear that it was not what it had been conceived to be—a star vehicle for Debbie Reynolds. Gielgud continued to work with the production when it went on to Philadelphia, but Reynolds and the director were not cooperating. The star called Champion, remembering how they had worked together before on, among other things, *Give a Girl a Break* (1953) and *My Six Loves* (1963).[1] Champion's problem in *Irene* was similar to Wagner's problem with *Sugar*: the show had already been completely choreographed, and Champion had been hired not to re-choreograph, but to make the show a hit. Champion and Peter Gennaro, the choreographer, worked together cooperatively, rearranging and revising numbers.[2]

Champion was ruthless about taking charge. He scrapped or drastically altered a number of big scenes, among them the grand finale, with Reynolds in her "Alice Blue Gown." The fountain that had been designed and built for the scene had developed insurmountable technical problems and was eliminated. In its place, Champion had Reynolds come out for her bow in a startling blue cape, only to remove it to reveal the tattered, Ninth Avenue shopgirl dress that she had worn earlier in the show,[3] a typically simple but effective touch. Joseph Stein (who had written the book for *Fiddler on the Roof* in 1964) and Bert Shevelove (who had worked with Sondheim on *A Funny Thing Happened on the Way to the Forum* in 1962) had also been hired to rewrite the book.[4] As a result of all their efforts, the show steadily improved through the run in Washington, DC, a city hastily added to the tryout tour.

Champion had felt uneasy about taking over at the last minute for the legendary Gielgud, who was making his Broadway debut as the director of a musical. At first, he accepted billing only as "production supervisor," although Gielgud was totally out of the picture. Merrick saw the production in Washington, and, in an atypical move, called Champion to tell him how good he thought it was. The producer then urged the director to take full credit. When Champion and Gielgud met to arrange the switch, neither showed much emotion. They rode down the elevator together. In the elevator, Champion recalled, "I said, 'The theater can be a terrible place sometimes, though it can be a beautiful place, too.' That was all. Neither of us showed any great feeling about what was happening. After all, we're theater people. These things happen all the time."[5] The production became a modest hit, but, although it ran two years to sellout houses in the cavernous Minskoff, it failed to show a profit.[6]

After his customary post-production vacation at his house in Topanga Canyon, Champion was offered a film to direct, *The Bank Shot*, starring George C. Scott. He accepted, surrounding himself with old friends like Max Showalter and Bibi Osterwald.[7] Champion prepared for production through the summer of 1973 and filmed in the fall. *The Bank Shot* was released in 1974 and was a disappointment. It had proved more enjoyable to work on than to watch, and it quickly went out of circulation.

In the midst of filming, Champion decided that while he loved the beach, it was too far from his theatrical contacts in Los Angeles, so he now bought a Beverly Hills estate. The house—complete with a retractable ceiling in the dining room and guest house in the back—was enormous, and he contacted Karla Russell, a long-time friend who was an expert at interior plantings, to help fill up some of the vast spaces. Karla and Gower had met during the making of *3 for Tonight*, although Champion had not remembered the young technical assistant when they met again, years later in the middle 1960s.[8] Now that the pain of the divorce had begun to settle, Gower and Karla had begun to see one another and a romance developed. Although she had not had as extensive a show business career as Marge, Karla offered Champion a kind of support he missed. She was willing to put up with silent suppers and his seeming total withdrawal during production, when all else—food, conversation, health, family—took a back seat to the project at hand.

Meanwhile, Jerry Herman had been working with Leonard Spiegelgass on a musical about the romance between Mack Sennett, of Keystone Kops fame, and Mabel Normand, who had starred in many of Sennett's early silent films. The project, at first tentatively called *Mabel and Mack* but then retitled *Hundreds of Girls*, had been initiated in 1971 by Edwin H. Lester of the Los Angeles Civic Light Opera, with the idea of opening his season with a world premiere of the show.[9] After working with Herman for a year with less than satisfactory results, Spiegelgass accepted a more attractive offer for a biography of Edward G. Robinson.[10] With a number of songs already written and what he considered an extremely viable property, Herman immediately called Michael Stewart, his collaborator on *Hello, Dolly!* and asked him to take over.[11] Stewart agreed, and they, of course, wanted Champion to direct.

Joe Kipness had produced such Broadway successes as *High Button Shoes* in 1947 and *Applause* in 1970. Between the two shows, he had produced *La Plume de Ma Tante* in 1958 with David Merrick. He and his partner, Lawrence Kasha, announced plans to produce *Hundreds of Girls*, but the team had not secured a release from Gene Fowler, whose biography of Sennett, *Father Goose*, the show closely resembled.[12] Herman and Stewart knew that Merrick was an expert at wheedling the rights out of recalcitrant authors and estates, and they approached him with the idea. At the time, another Kipness project, *Seesaw*, a musical version of *Two for the Seesaw*, was running into trouble. Kipness needed money and sold his interest in the Sennett musical to Merrick for ten percent of the profits.[13] Merrick attempted to remove Kipness' name from the credits and then claimed that his office had been burgled by Kipness' henchmen. The bizarre affair was investigated by the Rackets Bureau and was subsequently settled out of court.

Merrick, Herman and Stewart now approached Champion with the project. At that point, in the midst of a divorce and not wanting to leave his two sons in California, he demurred. Moreover, he was in negotiation with Paramount to direct a film version of Schmidt and Jones' perennial off-Broadway hit *The Fantasticks*. The project had progressed far enough for the three to make a trip to Sicily during the summer of 1973 to scout locations. Champion, an avid amateur photographer, took dozens of reels of 8mm research footage of the Sicilian countryside.[14] Paramount began to waffle, however, and Merrick once again offered the Mack Sennett musical, agreeing at least to try out the production on the West Coast. Champion assented.[15]

But the troubles were only beginning. As with *The Happy Time*, the rehearsals were to take place in New York.[16] Stewart and Herman went to Los Angeles for script conferences. It was decided that they would alternate, and that Champion would fly to New York to discuss details that could not be handled in California.[17]

The script had gone through an unprecedented number of full revisions. From January of 1972 through February of 1973, Stewart and Herman had produced seven different versions of the show, either in outline or in full script.[18] With Champion as director, they had again revised the script fully four times in as many months.[19] All during this period, of course, Champion was occupied with casting the roles that they were revising. The role of Mack, for instance, was offered to Jerry Orbach, who had played Paul in *Carnival!*. When Robert Preston, who had worked for Champion in *I Do! I Do!*, became available, he seemed to Champion a better choice, and Orbach was let go. Champion salved Orbach by telling him that he had another property in mind, and he was able to keep the promise with *42nd Street*.[20]

Casting the role of Mabel was an even longer series of trials and errors. When Champion first began, it was rumored among the theatre community that there would be no auditions for Mabel, and that Penny Fuller would play the role.[21] For whatever reason, auditions *were* held; Marcia Rodd, rather than Fuller, was cast, and she began rehearsals on May 6, 1974.[22] Two days later she was fired. The press was offered the reason that she lacked a certain "broken-wing quality" that Champion needed for Mabel.[23] Meanwhile, Champion had seen *Words and Music*. Among the performers was Kelly Garrett, whom he thought would make the perfect Mabel—and she was hired. A week later, however, she too was let go. Merrick had apparently guaranteed Garrett, an accomplished singer but a novice actress, that she would get help from a directorial assistant—a promise that Merrick had failed to communicate to Champion. The director, already feeling cornered, refused to have an assistant and Garrett was released.[24]

Meanwhile, Bernadette Peters, who had appeared in Stewart's *George*

M! in 1968, was visiting New York from Los Angeles to make an appearance on a television game show. Champion called her and asked her to read for the part, which she did, cold. She was thanked, but told that they were still looking. That night, her flight was delayed and she called her agent in Los Angeles to tell him that she would be late. At that very moment another call came in and he put her on hold. The call was from Champion, offering her the role.[25] She accepted and stayed in New York to begin rehearsals immediately.

After the disasters of *Prettybelle* and *Sugar*, Champion was at sea. Although he had always thought of himself as a winner, his recent failures had somewhat damaged his self-image. At fifty-four he was neither the *wunderkind* of *Bye Bye Birdie* and *Carnival!* nor the seasoned director who could take two characters and fill up a stage with *I Do! I Do!* He felt middle age acutely. Champion needed to "make his mark," and he sensed that a mark could not be made with the kind of material he had directed successfully for so long. He was searching for serious shows. Stewart and Herman saw a bright and happy show with a darker underside, a bite, and for that very reason the darker aspects of *Mack and Mabel* attracted him. Champion saw an opportunity to explore unhappiness, frustration, and drug addiction.

As a result of his exploration, during the rehearsal period of *Mack and Mabel*, he did something that he had never done before—he allowed the actors to improvise.[26] Champion had always kept a very tight rein on rehearsals. While he respected his actors' integrity and their contributions to the rehearsal process, he was always in complete control. As these methods began to fail him, however, he sought other, less familiar ways of dealing with scripts, ways that he would have rejected out of hand during *Hello, Dolly!* Earlier he had become fascinated with what he termed "Actors' Studio techniques," for example, and from *The Happy Time* (1968) onward, he began to let this approach creep into his work.[27]

Mack and Mabel opened in San Diego on June 17, 1974, and ran almost four months on the road. The rewriting was awesome—most days during that four months at least two, and often up to four pages of new script were tried out.[28] Perhaps the most fundamental change was a shift in the ending. From the very start of production Champion was uncomfortable with the resolution. His problem was that there really was no resolution—Mack and Mabel do not ever get together.

The show opened in New York at the Majestic Theatre on October 6, 1974.[29] *Mack and Mabel* closed sixty-six performances later with a loss of approximately $750,000.[30] Merrick had had four offers to film the musical before the opening, each of which evaporated in the face of the reviews.[31] To the press, Champion had been optimistic; he told them that he could "smell a hit."[32] Privately he had confided to friends that despite all his work, he thought the show was a turkey.[33]

After *Mack and Mabel*, Champion and Karla bought a house on Bentley Circle in Los Angeles and, as a tonic, Champion determined that he would take an active role in the planning of the interior, and also in its construction. He would rise every morning at 7:00 and be out on the construction site in a T-shirt and cut-off blue jeans by 8:00, hammer in hand.

In December of 1973, the Canadian Broadcasting Company aired a radio rock opera based on *Hamlet* called *Kronborg: 1582*.[34] Colleen Dewhurst, the American actress, who summered on Prince Edward Island, saw a stage production there and recommended that Lester Osterman consider producing it for Broadway.[35] She also recommended that Gower Champion be hired to direct it.[36] Champion first saw the show at Charlottetown in July of 1975. Along with Karla, he stayed in Canada for a number of weeks, taking notes and formulating an enlarged concept of the show.[37] Champion threw himself into the preparation of what he imagined could turn the tide of his career. *Kronborg: 1582* was playing right into his obsessions of the moment—rock music, unconventional theatrical forms, and, most important, serious material. What could be more serious than *Hamlet*?

Champion retained the interracial character of the Canadian production and cast Hamlet, Gertrude and Claudius with black actors, and Polonius, Ophelia, and Laertes as whites. The only major actor whom Champion retained from Canada was Beverly D'Angelo, who played Ophelia.

Rehearsals began in the newly renovated studios of Radio City Music Hall on December 15, 1975.[38] Champion had hired Tony Stephens, who had been the assistant choreographer for *Irene*. The tendency to delegate that started with *The Happy Time* had come to fruition—by now Champion had abdicated the details of dancing and was interested only in overall patterns, broad concepts of movement—the staging rather than the steps. This was, in fact, similar to the way that he had always dealt with musical arrangers and orchestrators. Champion would often suggest basic instrumentation or a musical style in which to set a piece, and would then demand revisions if he was in the least displeased.[39] In addition, the arrangements and orchestrations for *Rockabye Hamlet*, as the newly revised show came to be called, changed as rehearsals progressed.

The Canadian production's sound had been soft, utilizing a predominance of strings. But during rehearsals the sound gradually came to mirror Champion's interest in harder and harder rock.[40]

Thus, while Champion oversaw the development, step by step, of the choreography and the musical staging, he was not concerned with the creation of details. He had retreated, moreover, from toying with psychological motivations. During *Prettybelle* and *Mack and Mabel*, especially, Champion had experimented with what he perceived to be more serious directions. He had explored psychological nuances, and tried various theatre games, improvisations, and the like. During *Rockabye Hamlet*, on the other hand, he did not give even the slightest indication of providing actors with motivation—his concentration was totally on the assembling of the show's basic elements.

Champion's concept of the show was a staged rock concert with a plot. His concept for that staging, however, was parody—mostly of musical comedy clichés, but also of everything from Sonny and Cher to grand opera to Twyla Tharp.[41] When Rosencrantz and Guildenstern entered, for example, they were dressed in vaudeville costumes, complete with bowlers and wing collars, but with no shirts. They high-kicked down an incline that came to be known as the "Hello! Hamlet" ramp.[42] When Gertrude sang her final lament, "The Last Blues I'll Ever Sing," she stripped down to a slinky, sequined gown and, atop a piano, parodied the current *Sonny and Cher Show*, on which Cher would sing a torch song wearing an outrageously glamorous gown. Similarly, Ophelia committed suicide not by drowning, but by strangling herself with a microphone cord when she got caught up in a self-indulgent lyric.[43] Beyond this, Champion had asked Jules Fisher to portray the ghost of Hamlet's father using light.[44] Fisher had devised a series of lasers that would reflect off a cloud of stage smoke, giving an effect whose origin was almost indiscernible.[45]

Champion felt that he was once again in control and on the cutting edge of show business. Excitement about *Rockabye Hamlet* built throughout the previews (NBC wanted to buy into the production on the night of the last preview), but the show, which opened on February 17, 1976, closed eight performances later. With a single exception, the critics savagely panned it.[46] Champion was generally absolved of guilt.

He had staked more in *Rockabye Hamlet* than even he was accustomed to. His experimentation had been extreme; he was valiantly trying to create something young and innovative. Champion had failed at straight farce (*Three Bags Full*), social drama (*Prettybelle*), straightforward adaptation (*Sugar*), and a blend of all three (*Mack and Mabel*). With *Rock-abye Hamlet* Champion struck out in a completely different direction. In his mind he was attempting to salvage a career careening out of control.

The Champions left New York and drove to Florida where they spent two weeks incommunicado. Champion would take long walks along the beach, just as he would have done had they been in California. There was silence and solitude as he tried to sort out the experience. Late in February the pair traveled cross country, again by car, pausing in New Orleans and San Antonio—simply taking their time. Back in California, Champion bought a house in Mandeville Canyon, west of Los Angeles. He and Karla were married in the house on July 23, 1976, with Champion, of course, staging the entire production.[47] But he did not recover from *Rockabye Hamlet* as he had from other flops—his spirit seemed broken.[48]

Champion did accept the direction of a revival of *Annie Get Your Gun* for the Los Angeles Civic Light Opera. The production was to star Debbie Reynolds as Annie Oakley; and, because of this, Irving Berlin had given his permission not only for a revival, but for a complete revision of the show. It was on these terms that Champion agreed to the project.[49]

From the beginning of rehearsals, Champion seemed a changed person—intense, yet able to keep business in perspective. Dancers who had worked for him previously had generally been frightened of asking him about any problem, but in this show he seemed somehow more approachable, even good humored, almost mellow. Perhaps he had finally resigned himself to the kind of musical theatre he could produce. For whatever reason, Champion felt that *Annie Get Your Gun* was going to be his final show.[50] During rehearsals for "There's No Business Like Show Business," he confided to his assistant, Will Mead, that his staging of the number was his "farewell to show business."[51]

Annie Get Your Gun opened at the Orpheum Theatre in San Francisco in late May of 1977. It went on to tour Los Angeles, Dallas, and Miami—and rumor had it that it was going to play a theatre on Broadway before touring Russia.[52] At length, however, Reynolds decided that she was not quite ready for another Broadway run and the show did not play New York.

In the early fall, John Kander and Fred Ebb, who had written *The Happy Time*, asked Champion to help with their current musical, *The Act*, which was in trouble out of town. Liza Minelli was playing the lead, a faded movie star hoping for a comeback with a Las Vegas nightclub act. After working with Minelli for one afternoon, Champion enthusiastically accepted, and told his friends that he had worked with one of the most talented people he had ever encountered.[53]

Champion helped reconstruct the book of the show. Kander and Ebb had conceived the musical numbers to be done by the star in her act, rather than to be expressions of her personal life. Champion convinced the collaborators that whether or not they intended it, the audience was reading the numbers as relating not only to the act but to the star's personal history. They needed to build and to have some relation to the larger story being told. The show was rewritten and opened in New York on October 29, 1977, to generally favorable reviews, running a very respectable 233 performances.[54] When co-star Barry Nelson went on vacation, Champion stepped into the part, the first time he had been on a Broadway stage since *3 for Tonight* in 1955. He loved the experience and began sketching plans for a new acting career.[55]

Meanwhile, the Los Angeles Civic Light Opera, enthusiastic about the reception (and the receipts) that *Annie Get Your Gun* was getting, asked Champion to take over the artistic direction of the company. Once again he had an office on the West Coast and swore that he wanted nothing to do with New York theatre.[56] His first project was a revival of Rodgers and Hart's *Pal Joey*, with an interracial cast. But after massive casting and conceptual controversies, Champion withdrew from the project—a unique event in his career.[57] Once again, lasting work in California had eluded his grasp.

Meanwhile, Mary Tyler Moore Enterprises, the television producing company, offered him a very attractive special. Champion had not worked in television for years, aside from an occasional commercial for one of his shows. By May of 1977, however, negotiations were far enough advanced that he was offered a contract.[58] Champion had conceived a fantasy about Moore on the beach interacting with various animals and other denizens of the California coastline. Eventually Champion pulled out because Moore's representatives insisted that the broadcast be a classic variety show, with high-kicking chorus lines.

Champion now accepted an offer to direct Thornton Wilder's *Our Town* in Long Beach, California. During the rehearsals for the show, a natural disaster demonstrated to Champion just how much he had changed from his early, maniacally serious days. In October of 1978 a brush fire threatened to destroy Mandeville Canyon, where he and Karla lived. Champion was in Long Beach in rehearsal and was unaware of the gravity of the situation. Karla, along with their menagerie of pets, was evacuated. A neighbor told Karla that their house had been totally destroyed by the flames. Debating whether or not to call Gower out of rehearsal, she finally decided that he should be informed. He had cancelled rehearsal—a move that would have been out of the question ten years earlier—and had talked his way through the barricades to discover that their house was in fact safe.[59] Champion told Karla that he was calling her from their dining room.

Late in 1978, Champion's friends Charles Strouse and Lee Adams asked the director to attempt to salvage their show, *A Broadway Musical*. Champion went to New York and worked on it for about a month, from mid-November to mid-December. The show was interracial, and had two refugees from *Rockabye Hamlet*, Larry Marshall and Alan Weeks, in the cast. The story was unclear, and Champion's efforts to get William F. Brown, who had written the book, to clarify the plot line were largely in vain. When he called in his assistant from *Rockabye Hamlet* to be another eye at a rehearsal, he could not discern a plot at all.[60] The show opened on December 21, 1978, after two torturous weeks of previews. It lasted one performance.

When Champion returned to California after his stint in *The Act*, he felt as if he had the flu—a feeling that persisted and worsened. He made an appointment at the Scripps Institute for tests and was diagnosed as having Waldenstrom's macroglobulemia, a variant of leukemia. The syndrome is a cancer of the lymphocytes, the white blood cells. The malignancy causes the cells to secrete massive amounts of globulin, or antibody, which renders the blood thick. At the same time, platelets are unable to clot; the globulin has coated them so they cannot stick together.[61] No cure is currently known. The only treatment is a process called plasmapheresis, a cleansing of the blood via a machine that drains the blood, filters out ninety percent of the excess globulin, and then pumps the liquid back into the veins.[62] It is a painful and time-consuming operation, not unlike dialysis. The treatment is deceptive because, immediately after weeks of feeling tired, a patient's energy is immediately renewed. The sensation, however, is only temporary, for the cancer is still active and the blood cells continue to produce excess globulin.

Champion's doctors had told him that his prognosis was poor (Waldenstrom's patients very rarely live ten years beyond diagnosis, the median being three). They warned him against taking on any projects, because overexertion and stress would exacerbate his condition.[63] Meanwhile, he began treatments at Cedars of Lebanon Hospital in Los Angeles, and with the combination of plasmapheresis and chemotherapy, the symptoms seemed gradually to subside.[64]

Completely ignoring his doctors' advice, Champion considered a number of projects, both stage and film scripts, and by August of 1979 he began working on a screenplay by E. Olinger and D. A. Segal called *The Impresario*. The film was to be shot in Czechoslovakia, which excited the director. But ultimately the location could have played a large part in his deciding against the project. Champion always kept a tight rein on his emotions, and he was loath to reveal himself even to those closest to him. To a person who had considered himself the perpetual boy, this period of declining health, juggling possibilities of treatment with the prospect of directing a major film (something he had always wanted to do) was maddening. Champion did not want to divulge the gravity of his health problem for fear that he would lose the chance to direct. On the other hand, insurance would have depended on his always being in close proximity to treatment—something that would have been quite tricky on location. He was finally spared having to face the dilemma, since financing for the film did not come through. Some of the projects he had previously refused, however, were still active. In fact, a phone call from Michael Stewart, asking him to reconsider directing an adaptation of the classic 1936 film *42nd Street*, would end Champion's period of enforced leisure.

NOTES

1. Leo Seligsohn, "Gower: A Champion at Performing Miracles," *Newsday*, April 22, 1973, Part II, p. 3.

2. Interview with Jack Lee, New York, November 14, 1984.

3. Seligsohn, "Champion."

4. Seligsohn, "Champion."

5. Seligsohn, "Champion."

6. Gerald Bordman, *American Musical Theatre: A Chronicle* (New York: Oxford University Press, 1978), p. 674.

7. Interview with Bibi Osterwald, Boston, August 18, 1984. Interview with Max Showalter, Los Angeles, March 20, 1985.

8. Interviews with Karla Champion, Los Angeles, March 19 and June 4, 1985.

9. Ellen Stock, "Mack and Mabel: Getting the Show Off the Road," *New York*, October 7, 1974; Richard F. Shepard, "To 'Mack' Writers, Custard Man Is the Icing on Cake," *New York Times*, October 8, 1974.

10. Shepherd, " 'Mack.' "

11. Stewart, Interviews.

12. " 'Good Evening' and 'Mack' to End Run on Broadway," *New York Times*, November 28, 1974, p. 47.

13. "A Plot on 'Mabel' Suspected Here," *New York Times*, January 15, 1975, p. 48.

14. Champion, Interviews. The films remain in the possession of Karla Champion.

15. Stock, "Mack & Mabel."

16. Ibid.

17. Interviews with Robin Wagner, New York, September 19 and November 1, 1984.

18. The versions are: 1st outline, January–February 1972; 2nd outline, May 29, 1972; 1st draft, November 5, 1972; revised 1st draft, December 3, 1972; 2nd revised 1st draft, December 3, 1972; 2nd draft, December 14, 1972; and the revision handed to Gower Champion on February 24, 1972. Collection of Michael Stewart, New York.

19. Those are: 1st Champion revision, January 7, 1974; 2nd Champion revision, January 23, 1974; 3rd Champion revision, February 14, 1974; and 4th Champion revision (rehearsal version), April 7, 1974. Collection of Michael Stewart, New York.

20. Various interviews.

21. Stock, "Mack and Mabel."

22. Earl Wilson, "Who's 'Mabel' Now? . . . ," *New York Post*, May 14, 1974.

23. Wilson, "Who's"; Stock, "Mack and Mabel."

24. Wilson, "Who's." Garrett was immediately hired to star on a television revival of *Hit Parade*.

25. Interview with Bernadette Peters, New York, April 29, 1985.

26. Stewart, Interviews; Peters, Interview; Interview with Igors Gavon, Washington, DC, April 14, 1984.

27. Interview with Jess Gregg, New York, January 14, 1985.

28. Stewart, Interviews. His memory is corroborated by sheaves of rewrites. Collection of Michael Stewart, New York.

29. Interview with Anthony Manzi, New York, June 3, 1986.

30. *Variety*, December 4, 1974, p. 64.

31. Amy Archerd, "Merrick Film Delay; Wants Maximized Legit Run on 'Mack and Mabel,' " *Variety*, July 3, 1974, p. 23.

32. Karin Winner, "Gower Champion 'smells' a hit in 'Mack and Mabel,' " *Women's Wear Daily*, August 28, 1974, p. 17.

33. Champion, Interviews.

34. Sidney Fields, "Only Human: 'Hamlet' Without Dialogue," *New York Daily News*, February 17, 1976, p. 30.

35. Interview with Risa Schwartz, November 11, 1983.

36. Marjorie Osterman, "It'll Win a Tony," unpublished manuscript, n.d., p. 162.

37. Champion, Interviews.

38. Betty Lee Hunt Associates, press release, n.d. [week before December 15, 1975], Billy Rose Theatre Collection, New York Public Library at Lincoln Center.

39. Interviews with Gordon Lowry Harrell, New York, November 21 and 24, 1983.

40. Interview with Cliff Jones, Toronto, March 31, 1984.

41. Interview with Larry Carpenter, New York, October 4, 1984; Robb Baker, "Daze in Black Leather," *Soho Weekly News*, February 26, 1976.

42. Howard Kissel, " 'Rockabye Hamlet' . . . or Something's Rotten in New York," *Women's Wear Daily*, February 18, 1976.

43. Carpenter, Interview. Ophelia was wearing a simple white dress with strips of cloth criss-crossing her body—a parody of a straight jacket.

44. Interviews with Jules Fisher, New York, November 14 and 17, 1983.

45. Interview with John Butz, New York, November 27, 1983; Harrell, Interviews; Interview with Alan Weeks, New York, November 27, 1985.

46. The single exception was Audrey Kopito in a radio review. Typescript of radio review of *Rockabye Hamlet*, Greater New York Radio, n.d., The Billy Rose Theatre Collection, New York Public Library at Lincoln Center.

47. Champion, Interviews.

48. Champion, Interviews.

49. Interviews with Will Mead, New York, September 4 and 11, 1984.

50. Mead, Interviews.

51. Similarly, he had told Karla that it was his "love letter to show business."

52. Interviews with Bibi Osterwald, Marc Pluff, and Don Potter, Boston, August 18, 1984.

53. Osterwald, Interview.

54. Al Kasha and Joel Hirschhorn, *Notes on Broadway* (Chicago: Contemporary Books, 1985), p. 198.

55. Champion, Interviews.

56. Champion, Interviews.

57. Interview with George Boyd, New York, October 14, 1985.

58. Letter from Michael S. Ovitz (Champion's agent) to Arthur Price (of Mary Tyler Moore Enterprises), Los Angeles, May 23, 1977. Collection of Karla Champion.

59. Champion, Interviews.

60. Carpenter, Interview.

61. D. J. Weatherall, J. G. G. Ledingham, and D. A. Warrell, eds., *Oxford Textbook of Medicine* (New York: Oxford University Press, 1983), nc. 19,183.

62. Kurt J. Luelbacher, Raymond D. Adams, Eugene Braunwald, Robert G. Petersdorf, and Jean D. Wilson, eds., *Harrison's Principles of Internal Medicine*, ninth edition (New York: McGraw-Hill, 1980), p. 336.

63. Champion, Interviews.

64. Champion, Interviews. In addition to plasmapheresis, Champion was administered leukeran, which reduces the white blood cell count, and dibenzalene to contain infection.

Chapter 11

42nd Street
(1976–1980)

On September 7, 1980, an advertisement appeared in the theatre section of the *New York Times*:

A Comment from David Merrick, Producer of the Musical Extravaganza "42ND STREET" (only New York is Bigger).

There is a story appearing today in this section of the *New York Times* that purports to be an account of the rehearsal period leading up to the opening night of "42nd Street." I disagree with its content.

The only authentic and true document of the bizarre and lurid happenings during the production and rehearsal period of this fabulous show, with all of the suspense, pathos, hilarious incidents, romance, poetry and ultimate drama of "42nd Street's" memorable opening night are being chronicled by me. When I have finished, I will place the story in my vault at the Chase Manhattan Bank, only to be released twenty-five years after my death. Will it be news-worthy then? Of course! The show will still be running.

David Merrick[1]

Whether Merrick was actually concerned about telling the "true" story, or whether this was just another of his publicity stunts will probably never be known. It was, however, a barometer of the level of tension that existed even two weeks after *42nd Street* had opened. It was Gower Champion's final show and, by all accounts, responsible for his death.

The story of *42nd Street*, at least the Broadway version, begins in a revival movie house on New York's West Side, sometime in the spring of 1976. Michael Stewart was viewing the Warner Brothers classic backstage musical *42nd Street*. It occurred to him that it had the makings of a first-class Broadway musical. He asked his good friend Mark Bramble, with whom he had worked on *Barnum* and *The Grand Tour*, to take a look at the movie and report back what he thought. When Bramble saw it, he was even more enthusiastic than Stewart.[2]

The Warner Brothers film of Bradford Ropes' sensational novel had successfully rescued that studio from bankruptcy. Released in 1933, it had also revived the genre of the movie musical, which had recently fallen on hard times. The screenplay of *42nd Street* was by Rian James and James Seymour, with a score by Al Dubin and Harry Warren. The director was Lloyd Bacon, and the inspired dance director was Busby Berkeley. Ruby Keeler, playing Peggy Sawyer, was the first-time chorus girl who fills in for the ailing star (Bebe Daniels). Dick Powell, as Billy Lawlor, the juvenile lead, provided love interest for Keeler. There were five songs in the film, "Young and Healthy," "Shuffle Off to Buffalo," "It Must Be June," "You're Getting to Be a Habit With Me," and, of course, "42nd Street."[3]

By late summer of 1976 Bramble and Stewart were confident enough of the property to begin securing the stage rights. They quickly discovered, however, that the rights to the motion picture did not include them. When Warner Brothers bought the book from Simon and Schuster, the publisher had retained stage rights.[4] Their search led them to Mexico and a Mrs. Emil Bigue, Bradford Ropes' sole heir. They obtained the rights from her by early 1978.[5]

At the same time the authors were looking for a producer. Stewart had had difficulties with David Merrick. But he approached him and by late 1978 Merrick was in negotiations with United Artists to secure rights so that he could begin raising money for the project.[6] *42nd Street* would also mark something of a return to Broadway for Merrick. Since *Sugar* in 1972, he had not produced a musical from the start; and not since 1976 had he produced theatre in New York.[7]

Stewart thought that the only director worthy of the project was Gower Champion. He submitted the idea to Champion in the form of an outline, and by September of 1978, lawyers were drawing up papers detailing an agreement between Stewart and "Champion VII," as Champion's companies were called.[8] It would be his full-scale return to Broadway after the disastrous *Rockabye Hamlet* in 1976.

On Monday, July 31, 1978, Stewart and Bramble met to create a first outline.[9] By early spring of 1979, however, Champion had withdrawn from the project.[10] In a heartfelt letter to Michael Stewart, Champion explained that he left *42nd Street* for personal, not professional, reasons.[11] In fact the main reason was undoubtedly his worsening medical condition. Waldenstrom's Syndrome meant greatly reduced energy, and his doctors warned him that three things would shorten his life considerably and possibly prove immediately fatal: exposure to sunlight, any substance abuse, or extreme tension.[12] For Champion that meant that he could absolutely not direct a show.

Champion remained in California and began preliminary work on a screenplay called *The Impresario*.[13] Although he had always wanted to direct a major motion picture and make a name for himself in films, even this project was half-hearted.[14] He simply did not possess the enthusiasm that he had had earlier. He and Karla had bought a house in secluded and scenic Mandeville Canyon, a twenty-minute drive from Hollywood. He spent his days either working on the script, tending his beloved azaleas, or—in spite of the doctors' warnings—taking long walks on the beach.[15]

Stewart, Bramble and Merrick moved quickly, and by May they had offered *42nd Street* to Michael Bennett.[16] Bennett declined, telling Stewart that after the phenomenal success of *A Chorus Line* and *Dreamgirls* he did not want to do another backstage musical.[17] They also approached Bob Fosse, who also declined.[18] But Merrick still felt that despite his problems with him, Champion was simply the best man for the job.[19] With no director to guide them, Stewart and Bramble continued to work under the producer's guidance.

At the same time, Stewart and Bramble were staging backers' auditions—tabloid versions of a revised show for prospective investors. Champion flew from California to attend one of these on October 25 and decided that he could not resist the property.[20] Before February of the following year he was sent the first draft of the script, which was still being revised.[21] With the draft in hand, Champion began assembling the people with whom he wanted to work on what he knew could very well be his last production. Although his doctors had warned him against going into production again, he felt that life without meaningful work was merely existing.[22]

Without exception, publicity for the show stated that Champion never knew how to tap dance.[23] It was not precisely true. At this point in his career, Champion choreographed in a very individual manner. He had not tapped in years, but he had spent a not inconsiderable time in 1946 studying the form intensely.[24] In subsequent years, however, his style had grown more airborne. Tap dance requires a subtle combination of surrender and control, *ballon* and weight. Champion's style had become lyric, but extremely controlled—precise, yet sweeping. It was not a style even vaguely related to tap. For this reason he hired Karin Baker and Randy Skinner, two dancers for whom tap was a specialty.

His assistants were responsible for most of the actual steps, and Champion took this raw material and shaped and edited it into choreography.[25] It was as if he were a writer with an assistant constantly at a thesaurus, suggesting interesting words. Thus, even if Champion had been a crack tap dancer, he probably would have hired assistants to work out the steps.

Champion moved to New York in February of 1980 for the intense pre-production work he knew was coming. He took rooms in a newly renovated condominium at the corner of Sixth Avenue and West 56th Street, and began to feel more energetic as he took the time to furnish the apartment to his taste, including a piano.[26] That feeling of "conquering the city" came back—he again enjoyed the bustle of New York.[27] Almost immediately he began auditions and conferences with his designers. He held the usual round of Equity principal calls and open chorus auditions, and seemed to be assembling a strong cast. He offered the role of Julian Marsh, the director trying to make a comeback, to Jerry Orbach, and Orbach accepted. Tammy Grimes was signed to play Dorothy Brock, despite the seeming modesty of the role and an initial refusal.[28]

The pre-production period of *42nd Street* was significantly different from any other Champion production on Broadway—he was now living in New York. He had developed a rather close personal friendship with Robin Wagner, his set designer, and they often had dinner together. They both had teenage sons, about the same age, and could compare crises and resolutions.[29] During these evenings, Champion would talk over the show endlessly, "noodling," as he called it, with Wagner much the way he had done with Priborsky thirty years earlier and with Marge during his first four New York shows. And, of course, there were long working sessions with his old friend Michael Stewart, with whom he had collaborated on four earlier shows, and with his new partner, Mark Bramble.

During this time, two themes pervaded Champion's thoughts. The first was that *42nd Street* would be a summation of what he knew about musical theatre. Traces of this theme are evident everywhere, even in his choice of a theatre.[30] Where a show would play was always very important to Champion, and he would tour empty houses, trying to imagine what the show would look like in each environment. For *42nd Street* he chose the Winter Garden, mainly because of the long, low proscenium arch. Into this "documentary" frame, he asked Wagner to put scenery that was strictly symmetrical, giving the story a sort of monumental atmosphere.[31]

The second theme revolved around the fact that Champion wanted only three locations: backstage, the show, and limbo. He was apparently conceiving *42nd Street* in terms of a production about show business as an institution—a fable celebrating the best of what Broadway can be—rather than as a representation of particular events. This kind of idea is one he discovered when planning *I Do! I Do!*[32] Since that production in 1966, musical theatre had undergone a revolution: Stephen Sondheim and Hal Prince had presented *Company* in 1970, and the "concept musical" had become firmly established as a genre. Although Champion never carried the idea as far as Sondheim—to whom the origin of the "concept musical" has been imputed—he had nonetheless begun conceiving musical theatre in terms of a unity not based on an integrated narrative involving conventional scenes and songs.

Rehearsal for *42nd Street* began in mid-April 1980, with only Champion, the two juvenile leads, the dance assistants, and the dance arranger in attendance. During these approximately four weeks of rehearsal, Champion worked out the dance vocabulary he would use for the rest of the show. (He also worked out the delicate process of functioning with two dance assistants. His energy seemed at full force, so it is likely that he was using the dance assistants not so much as dancers when his limited energy supply dimmed, but as resources for tap steps.) He would choreograph a general movement and dictate, either by clapping or speaking, a rhythm which he wanted the tap steps to establish. The climactic tap duet started up-tempo, but soon relaxed into what a tap dance rarely is—a slow, seductive dance about two people falling in love. It was Champion's concept that the two should have a conversation in tap, and that is exactly what emerged. Although the duet is all tap dancing, something that he and Marge never did, the choreography is very reminiscent of their duets and is pure Champion, with arching, lyric lines and interweaving steps.

In May 1980, the full chorus was first called to rehearse at the Minskoff Studios, a complex of large modern rehearsal halls in a relatively new building on Broadway. During the first week they learned a basic tap vocabulary and Champion experimented with patterns—circles, interweaving, and the like. He wanted the chorus to begin to get a feeling of what the style of the show would be. And so it all began; Champion arranged and revised as he had done ever since *Bye Bye Birdie*. To cast

members who had never worked with him before, he seemed unbeliev-
ably concentrated.[33] He would stand in the middle of the floor with the
entire cast around him, staring off into space, visualizing what he wanted.
He would instruct one group to enter in such-and-such a way on the first
eight bars, another group on the second, and still another to begin upstage
on the third beat of the second group of eight. Then the cast would run
what he had described. He would stop and, like a painter, arrange and
change and modify until the number began to take the shape he had
imagined.

The Minskoff Studios, large as they were, were not quite large enough
to choreograph the mammoth chorus numbers to be performed on the
stage of the Winter Garden, and rehearsals moved downtown to Michael
Bennett's Quadrille Studios, near Union Square.[34] As the time for the
opening in Washington, DC, grew closer, Champion seemed merely to
sketch some numbers in. About the "Lullaby of Broadway," for example, he frankly told the cast that he was merely giving them some
movement with which to open the show, and that he would greatly refine
it in Washington. The dancers did not like what he gave them, because
it was achingly simple—merely a series of step-touches in various patterns with outstretched arms.[35] Little did they realize that Champion
would not change a step of the number out of town; it was exactly what
he wanted. Moreover, it was as simple and effective on its own terms
as the "Hello, Dolly!" number had been in the show of the same name.
Champion had choreographed a moment in a way which only he could
do so effectively.

During the last weeks of rehearsal in New York Champion held his
first run-through. It was a rag-tag affair, with missed entrances, barely
continuous scenes, and floundering continuity. After the rehearsal, however, Champion was clearly pleased—his face shone with pride. He knew
that he had the bones of a successful musical, a musical in his own style.
Wanda Richert, who was playing Peggy Sawyer, wrote him a note, expressing her admiration, thanking him for all he had done for her.[36]
Champion, always the gentleman, wrote her back, thanking her in turn
for her hard work.[37] From these pleasantries developed a relationship
that was to figure prominently in the publicity after the opening, for the
parallels between Julian Marsh and Gower Champion, and Peggy Sawyer
and Wanda Richert, had become too obvious to be ignored.

A week before the opening at the Kennedy Center Opera House on
June 24, 1980, the cast left for Washington. They spent the last week in
technical rehearsals. The reviews of that opening performance indicated

that much work remained before the New York opening.[38] The story, still skeletal at this point, was simply not hanging together. By the time the show closed in Washington on July 27th, the running order had been considerably revised. It was decided that it would remain the same when the show opened in New York—now, as far as Champion was concerned, only a final polishing of some spots seemed to stand between Washington and success on Broadway. But, although Merrick had announced the New York opening for August 11, by the Washington closing he had postponed that date indefinitely.[39] He was still dissatisfied with various moments and, although it was now evident that Champion was not in good health, he demanded revisions. Moreover, Champion and Merrick were no longer on speaking terms, and both used Robin Wagner, the set designer, as a go-between.[40]

The company arrived in New York on July 28, and at first rehearsals were held at various hired studios. But *42nd Street* was to open at the Winter Garden, a house owned by the Shubert Organization, and Merrick had struck a deal with Bernard Jacobs, its president, so that he did not have to pay rent on the theatre for technical rehearsals. The company moved to the Winter Garden. Even with free rent on a theatre, Merrick was paying over $100,000 each week for salaries and the building of new scenery.[41] But as the rehearsal period lengthened and it was clear that the production was under revision rather than simply in technical rehearsals, Jacobs made it clear to Merrick that the theatre would not be available indefinitely.[42]

Each afternoon Champion would rehearse numbers that he thought needed work. Each evening he would hold a run-through, complete with costumes, make-up, lights, and full orchestra. All this to an empty house. Champion became increasingly ill and depressed. The cast became increasingly disheartened. And Merrick became increasingly paranoid, both about Champion's ability to complete the show and about the potential reviews.[43] To deter intruders, the producer initiated a security system, complete with armed guards at the theatre and clip-on photograph identification badges for every member of the cast, crew, and support staff.[44] On August 9, Merrick ran an advertisement in the *New York Times*, explaining the delay in opening: "The Great Man way up there has said that this show is ready, that it can be a memorable musical. He will give the word when He feels the show is ready. I am waiting for the courier to arrive."[45]

On August 10, 1980, Merrick released a number of tickets to the Democratic National Committee, then having a meeting in New York.

The cast was ecstatic to have an audience after almost four weeks of playing to empty houses. The next night Merrick released four hundred tickets to TKTS, the half-price ticket booth in Times Square.[46] Merrick, however, suspected that John Corry, a reporter for the *New York Times*, had disguised himself to sneak past the guards who had been alerted to keep any press out of the preview. Indeed, Corry had been in the audience. Merrick's fanaticism about this supposed intrusion was most unusual. He would normally have welcomed any press coverage. It is possible, in fact, that he hired guards and established the elaborate security procedures purely for the coverage that it would undoubtedly engender. Yet Merrick *had* imposed a blackout before the show had left Washington, telling the press that he wanted to avoid the publicity overkill that he blamed for the failure of *The Great Gatsby*. Merrick, or so he informed the press, wanted "*42nd Street* to sneak into town on tiny feet."[47]

In any event, for whatever reason, Merrick appeared onstage and announced that the performance was cancelled because there were "technical problems."[48] The theatre was cleared, but a complete run-through was held. The next day he told the press that "a snake was loose in the house."[49] The cast, triggered by having finally had an audience after nearly a month of playing to empty houses, at last rebelled. The night of August 13, they filled the front rows with stuffed animals and their resume pictures, just so it would seem that there was somebody watching them.[50] On August 15 Merrick announced that *42nd Street* would finally open on Monday, August 25, with previews on Friday and Saturday.[51]

Although they had been divorced for almost seven years, Champion had never lost contact with Marge, whose career had taken its own path. Now Marge Champion Sagal, wife of a television director, she was in New York doing pre-production work on *The Day the Circus Came to Town*, a television special. Champion invited her to one of the previews so that he could pick her brain about some spots that were still troubling him.

Meanwhile, his health was rapidly declining. After the run-through on August 22nd, Richert entered his apartment to find it dark and seemingly empty. On searching she found Champion in bed in the dark. He told her he was fine, and that he was simply tired. Alarmed, she called Marge.[52] Richert then called Larry Carpenter, who, in turn, called paramedics. When the lights were finally turned on, they discovered Champion in a pool of blood.[53] He was immediately taken to Sloan-Kettering Memorial Cancer Institute.

With Champion in the hospital and near death, the calls went out to gather the family. Karla, Gregg and Blake began a vigil (along with Merrick, Wagner and Musser) in the waiting room outside the intensive care unit.[54] Although Merrick insisted that Champion's condition be withheld from the cast as well as the press, Richert was summoned to the hospital for a brief visit. Only then did she discover how very near death Champion actually was.[55] The doctors were furiously attempting to cleanse Champion's blood, but the syndrome had overtaken the blood's ability to regenerate. As a last resort, one of Gregg's veins was tapped and a transfusion performed directly.

By noon on August 25, 1980, it was clear that Champion's chances of survival were infinitesimal. Merrick became even more adamant that no one from the outside be told about the events, whatever they might be. He hovered around the pay telephone in the waiting room, either expecting a call himself or making sure that no one else from Champion's room made a call.[56] At 1:00 P.M. the doctors pronounced Champion dead. Without a word of sympathy to anyone, Merrick ordered everyone to keep strict silence about the event. Then he left.

The opening performance was scheduled for 6:15 P.M. By 6:00 the limousines were arriving at the entrance to the Winter Garden, bringing a glittering array of stars to witness what they all hoped would be Champion's triumphant return to Broadway. In the audience were Ethel Merman, Joshua Logan, Joseph Papp, Bob Fosse, Ruth Gordon, Joan Fontaine, Neil Simon—a glamorous assembly even for a Broadway opening.[57] Merrick's ploy had apparently worked, for nobody in the audience had an idea that Champion had died.[58] The cast certainly did not.[59] As Richert made up, however, a note from Champion that she had taped to a shelf in her dressing room fluttered down to the floor. She knew that he had died.[60]

The performance was a smashing success, and the applause spontaneously turned into a standing ovation. After ten curtain calls, Merrick appeared on stage and the applause increased. He hushed the audience. He told them that a great tragedy had happened. Unaware, the audience thought he was making a joke, and laughed. He then announced that Gower Champion had died.

There was a general gasp of disbelief from the house. In an instant the cast was brought from the peak of excitement to the reality of death. They turned to face each other, numb with shock. Jerry Orbach shouted to Steve Zweigbaum, the production stage manager, to bring down the curtain. The orchestra began the music that plays the audience out of the house, but the razzmatazz ending music was a jarring incongruity as most people left in stunned silence.

Backstage, pandemonium had broken out. Some chorus members had fled to the wings, crying in corners, others hugged each other, still others had returned to their dressing rooms, unable to comprehend the fact.[61] Champion's wife Karla had come to the theatre and went backstage to offer her sympathy to the distraught cast. She embraced Richert, sharing a mutual grief. Slowly and mournfully, the company of *42nd Street* dispersed.[62]

The next day, at the suggestion of the League of New York Theatres and Producers, all the lights on Broadway theatres were dimmed for five minutes, reportedly the first time such a unified display of mourning had ever occurred.[63] A memorial service was held in the Winter Garden, with Merrick himself as master of ceremonies. Marge spoke of his search for identification. His son Gregg related stories about how his father, so often absent when he was growing up, took care to remain close in unusual ways. At one point, while on the telephone, he said, his father had asked him to look out the window. He reminded his son that they were looking at the same moon. David Hartman, who played the head waiter, Rudolf, in the original production of *Hello, Dolly!* also spoke. A recording of "Lullaby of Broadway" was played as Merrick stood at the side of the stage, crossing his arms like Julian Marsh. When the service was finished, Merrick waved grandly at the audience, said "Gower says thanks for coming," and walked upstage into the darkness.[64]

Champion's body was cremated. At a service held at his favorite place on the Malibu beach in California, his ashes were spread on the Pacific Ocean. Karla, Marge and Jeanne Tyler Estridge, his first partner, were in attendance.[65] One of Champion's many friends who spoke at the service was Max Showalter, actor and composer.[66] Showalter was one of the few friends that Champion had allowed to stay close. Among the personal things that Champion shared with Showalter was a love of azaleas. They would telephone each other as the blooming season approached, and afterward compare notes about how to care for their bushes in order to get them to flower again. Showalter's porch on Hollywood Boulevard was full of plants given to him by the director. Unusually, the day before the service, the plants on his porch had burst into glorious bloom. Showalter had filled the pockets of his jacket with the blossoms and at the end of the service went down to the shoreline and sprinkled the blooms on Champion's ashes as they washed out to sea.

NOTES

1. David Merrick, Advertisement in *New York Times*, September 7, 1980.

2. Interviews with Michael Stewart, New York, May 5 and 17, 1984; June 25, July 20, August 27, and September 3, 1985.

3. Clive Hirschorn, *The Hollywood Musical* (New York: Crown, 1981), p. 75.

4. Stewart, Interviews; and letter from Helen Harvey [Stewart's attorney] to Bea Hurwitz [of Simon and Schuster] (November 16, 1976), Collection of Michael Stewart.

5. Contract between Michael Stewart and Mark Bramble and Bess Bigue, John S. Pottinger, Peggy Koll and Dorothea Anderson (February 27, 1978), Collection of Michael Stewart.

6. Letter from Dean Charles Stolber [Vice President in Charge of Business Affairs for United Artists] to Michael Stewart (December 15, 1978), Collection of Michael Stewart.

7. Richard Hummles, "Trade Ponders '42nd St.' Puzzle From Man-of-Mystery Merrick; Is 'No Publicity' the Best Kind?" *Variety*, August 13, 1980, p. 85.

8. Each successive corporation Champion formed to produce the shows he directed was named "Champion" with Roman numerals to denote the number. Letter from Alvin Deutsch to Michael Stewart (September 5, 1978), Collection of Michael Stewart.

9. Michael Stewart and Mark Bramble, first outline of *42nd Street* (July 31, 1978), Collection of Michael Stewart.

10. The exact date of Champion's decision is unclear, but by May 9, 1979, Stewart wrote to Michael Bennett, inviting him to direct the show.

11. Letter from Gower Champion to Michael Stewart, June 7, [1979], Collection of Michael Stewart. The idiosyncratic capitalization is Champion's.

12. Interviews with Marge Champion Sagal, New York, January 6, 1984; Great Barrington, MA, May 25, July 5, and October 10, 1985; February 13 and March 28, 1986.

13. E. Olinger and D. A. Segal, *The Impresario*, typescript, Collection of Karla Champion, Los Angeles.

14. Gower Champion, Notes on "The Impresario," manuscript, Collection of Karla Champion, Los Angeles, California. Champion's notes on the film are slim indeed.

15. Karla Champion, Interviews; and John Corry, " '42nd Street,' " *New York Times*, August 14, 1980, sec. III, p. 20.

16. Letter from Michael Stewart to Michael Bennett, May 9, 1979, Collection of Michael Stewart.

17. Stewart, Interviews.

18. Corry, " '42nd Street.' "

19. Interview with Helen Nickerson [David Merrick's business manager] New York, April 8, 1986.

20. Stewart Interviews. Also see Corry, " '42nd Street.' "

21. Again, the date of Champion's decision is unclear, as are the precise reasons. Stewart invariably listed the director on the title page of his working scripts, and Champion is named ("Directed and Choreographed by") in Michael Stewart and Mark Bramble, *Forty-Second Street*, First Draft, February 5, 1980, typescript, Collection of Michael Stewart, New York. Moreover, Champion's own schedule for pre-production activities begins on February 1, 1980, and so his decision must have preceded this date. Gower Champion, pre-production notes for *42nd Street*, manuscript and typescript, Collection of Karla Champion, Los Angeles.

22. Champion, Interviews.

23. See, for instance, Corry, " '42nd Street.' "

24. Letter from Gower Champion to Marjorie Bell, Los Angeles, July 7, 1946. Collection of Marge Champion Sagal, Stockbridge, MA.

25. Carpenter, Interview.

26. Interviews with Anthony Manzi [Stage Manager for *Rockabye Hamlet* and *Mack and Mabel*], New York, July 25 and September 3, 1985.

27. Champion in letter to Stewart.

28. Letter from Tammy Grimes to Michael Stewart, Toronto, n.d., Collection of Michael Stewart.

29. Interviews with Robin Wagner, New York, September 19 and November 1, 1984.

30. Interviews with Lucia Victor, New York, April 11 and 18, 1984, and April 4 and 11, 1985; and Interview with Larry Carpenter, New York, October 4, 1984. Toward the end of his career, Champion would often turn to his assistant and comment that he wished he could figure out *why* something worked the way it did.

31. Wagner, Interviews.

32. Victor, Interviews.

33. Interviews with Wanda Richert, New York, December 13 and 20, 1984. Interviews with Carole Banninger, New York, January 10 and 17, 1984.

34. Banninger, Interviews.

35. Banninger, Interviews.

36. Richert, Interviews.

37. Letter from Gower Champion to Wanda Richert, n.d., Collection of Wanda Richert.

38. Richard Coe, "42nd Street," *Washington Post*, June 25, 1980.

39. " '42nd Street' Postpones Opening," *New York Times*, July 29, 1980, p. C7.

40. Wagner, Interviews.

41. *New York Times*, August 9, 1980.

42. Wagner, Interviews.

43. During this difficult period, Champion did not discuss his health with anyone connected with the show. Wagner, however, feels that Champion knew his death was imminent, despite tentative plans to do *Sayonara*. One evening Wagner returned to the theatre after a supper break to find Champion sitting in the darkened house alone. Merrick had just announced yet another delay of the opening. Wagner feels that Champion simply hung around the theatre, knowing that his days in the theatre, indeed his days on earth, were numbered.

44. Stewart, Interviews.

45. David Merrick, Advertisement in *New York Times*, August 9, 1980.

46. Corry, "42nd Street."

47. Ibid., p. 37. Merrick's publicist had sent actual warnings to the press: "If you come to see the show, we will refuse to cooperate in any way" and "If you take a jaundiced view of the show, you'll be made out to be a fool."

48. Corry, "42nd Street," p. 37.

49. Ibid.

50. Banninger, Interviews; Stewart, Interviews; Wagner, Interviews.

51. *New York Times*, August 15, 1980, p. C3.

52. Sagal, Interviews.

53. Richert, Interviews; Sagal, Interviews; Carpenter, Interview.

54. Karla Champion, Interviews; Wagner, Interviews.

55. Richert, Interviews.

56. Wagner, Interviews.

57. John Corry, "Gower Champion Dies Hours Before Show Opens," *New York Times*, August 26, 1980, p. 1.

58. Wagner, Interviews.

59. Banninger Interviews; Interview with Don Percassi, New York, December 15, 1983; Interview with Roy Reams, New York, December 3, 1983.

60. Richert, Interviews.

61. Banninger, Interviews; Percassi, Interview.

62. Champion, Interviews; Interview with Carole Cook, Los Angeles, July 22, 1985.

63. Corry, "42nd Street."

64. Sagal, Interviews; and Corry, "Champion."

65. Champion, Interviews; Sagal, Interviews. Interview with Jeanne Tyler Estridge, San Bernadino, CA, June 5, 1985.

66. Interview with Max Showalter, Los Angeles, July 11, 1985.

Chronology of Champion's Life

Champion was director/choreographer for all his shows after 1960. Film listings continue until 1960, when the peak years of Hollywood movie musical production ended and Champion began to work exclusively in theatre. Broadway listings give composer/lyricist credit. Film musical listings give principal performer(s). Except where noted, stage and film musicals appeared in the year listed.

Date	Events in Champion's Life	Theatre and Film Musicals
1919	Born June 22 in Geneva, IL, to John and Beatrice Champion	*Broadway*: George M. Cohan: *The Royal Vagabond* Irving Berlin: *Ziegfeld Follies of 1919* George Gershwin: *La La Lucille* (Gershwin's first complete Broadway score) Fred and Adele Astaire: *Apple Blossoms* Busby Berkeley (performer): *Irene* (New York stage debut)
1922	Recently divorced, Beatrice Champion moves to Los Angeles with Gower and older brother John Jr.	*Broadway*: George Gershwin: *George White's Scandals* George M. Cohan: *Little Nellie Kelly* Irving Berlin: *The Music Box Revue*

Fred and Adele Astaire: *The
Bunch and Judy*
Busby Berkeley: Directing stock
productions in New England and
Canada

1931   Champion begins dance and piano instruction at Norma Gould
School of Dance in Los Angeles.

Broadway:
George Gershwin: *Of Thee I Sing*
Fred and Adele Astaire: *The
Bandwagon* (final stage appear-
ance as team)
Film:
Busby Berkeley: *Whoopee!* (film
version of Eddie Cantor stage hit)

1933   Gower Champion and Jeanne Tyler perform a tango at their first
recital in Los Angeles.

Broadway:
George Gershwin: *Let 'Em Eat
Cake*
Cole Porter: *Gay Divorce*
Jerome Kern: *Roberta*
Irving Berlin: *As Thousands
Cheer*
Film:
Fred Astaire and Ginger Rogers:
Gay Divorcee (their film debut
and first duet, to Cole Porter's
"Night and Day")
Busby Berkeley: *42nd Street*
(first film for Warner Brothers)

1936   Tyler and Champion win the
"Veloz and Yolanda Waltz to
Fame" contest and perform professionally for the first time at
the Coconut Grove nightclub. Engagements follow in San Francisco and Chicago as "America's
Youngest Dance Team."

Broadway:
Cole Porter: *Red, Hot and Blue*
George Gershwin: *Porgy and
Bess*
Rodgers and Hart: *On Your Toes*
(choreography by George Balan-
chine)
Film:
Busby Berkeley: *Gold Diggers of
1937* (last film for Warner Broth-
ers)
Fred Astaire: *Swing Time*

1937   Tyler and Champion tour with
Guy Lombardo, Eddie Duchin
and other dance bands in nightclubs and vaudeville.

Broadway:
Rodgers and Hart: *Babes in Arms*
(choreography by George Balanchine)

I'd Rather Be Right (George M. Cohan's last Broadway appearance)
Film:
Fred Astaire: *Shall We Dance*
Busby Berkeley: *Gold Diggers of 1937*

1939   Tyler and Champion make first Broadway appearance in Olsen and Johnson's revue *Streets of Paris*.

Broadway:
Cole Porter: *Du Barry Was a Lady*
Jerome Kern: *Very Warm for May*, (Kern's last Broadway show)
Film:
Fred Astaire: *The Story of Vernon and Irene Castle*
Judy Garland: *The Wizard of Oz*

1940   The team performs at Radio City Music Hall and the Rainbow Room.

Broadway:
Irving Berlin: *Louisiana Purchase*
Cole Porter: *Panama Hattie*
Rodgers and Hart: *Pal Joey*
Film:
Judy Garland: *Strike Up the Band*
Fred Astaire: *Broadway Melody of 1940*

1942   Tyler and Champion's last Broadway show, *Count Me In*. Gower joins the Coast Guard.

Broadway:
Irving Berlin: *This Is the Army*
Rodgers and Hart: *By Jupiter*
Film:
James Cagney: *Yankee Doodle Dandy*
Bing Crosby: *Holiday Inn*
Fred Astaire: *You Were Never Lovelier*

1943   Champion tours in Coast Guard revue, *Tars and Spars*, by Vernon Duke and Howard Dietz. Jeanne Tyler marries and retires from show business.

Broadway:
Rodgers and Hammerstein: *Oklahoma!* (choreography by Agnes de Mille)
Cole Porter: *Something for the Boys*
Film:
Judy Garland: *Girl Crazy*
Gene Kelly: *As Thousands Cheer*
Ethel Waters: *Cabin in the Sky*

1945 Released from military duty, Champion signs contract with MGM. Makes first film appearance, a fifteen-second dance sequence in *Till the Clouds Roll By*. Begins seeing Marjorie Belcher, daughter of his former dance teacher, Ernest Belcher.

Broadway:
Rodgers and Hammerstein: *Carousel*
Leonard Bernstein: *On the Town* (choreography by Jerome Robbins)
Film:
Fred Astaire: *Blue Skies*
Robert Alda: *Rhapsody in Blue*
Gene Kelly: *Anchors Aweigh*

1947 Champion and Belcher first perform as a team under names "Christopher Gower and Marjorie Bell" in Montreal and Chicago. They are married in October and rechristen their act "Marge and Gower Champion."

Broadway:
Lane and Harburg: *Finian's Rainbow*
Styne and Cahn: *High Button Shoes*
Lerner and Loewe: *Brigadoon*
Rodgers and Hammerstein: *Allegro*
Film:
Betty Grable: *Mother Wore Tights*
Comden and Green: *Good News*

1948 Champion debuts as a Broadway choreographer with two revues, *Lend An Ear* and *Small Wonder*.

Broadway:
Cole Porter: *Kiss Me Kate*
Frank Loesser: *Where's Charley?*
Film:
Fred Astaire, Judy Garland: *Easter Parade*

1949 The Champions make first television appearance, *The Admiral Broadway Revue*, and are on the cover of *Life* magazine after a performance for President Truman at the White House Correspondents' Dinner. In Hollywood, they film two dance sequences for a Paramount Bing Crosby film, *Mr. Music*, and sign a two-year contract with MGM.

Broadway:
Styne and Robin: *Gentlemen Prefer Blonds*
Rodgers and Hammerstein: *South Pacific*
Film:
Fred Astaire: *The Barkleys of Broadway*
Gene Kelly: *On the Town*

1951 MGM releases first film with the Champions, a remake of *Show Boat*. Gower choreographs *Make A Wish* on Broadway with Nanette Fabray.

Broadway:
Frank Loesser: *Guys and Dolls*
Irving Berlin: *Call Me Madam*
Rodgers and Hammerstein: *The King and I*

Film:
Gene Kelly: *An American in Paris*
Fred Astaire: *Royal Wedding*

1952   The Champions' first two starring roles in film released by MGM: *Everything I Have Is Yours* and *Lovely to Look At.*

Broadway:
Lerner and Loewe: *Paint Your Wagon*
Harold Rome: *Wish You Were Here*
Film:
Gene Kelly: *Singin' in the Rain*
Ray Bolger: *Where's Charley?*

1953   MGM releases its third film featuring the Champions, *Give a Girl a Break*, score by Ira Gershwin and Burton Lane.

Broadway:
Cole Porter: *Can-Can*
Leonard Bernstein: *Wonderful Town*
Film:
Fred Astaire: *The Band Wagon*
Kathryn Grayson: *Kiss Me Kate*

1954

Film:
Judy Garland: *A Star Is Born*

1955   The Champions appear in Esther Williams' last film, *Jupiter's Darling*, and their only joint Broadway show, *3 for Tonight*, which Gower directed.

Broadway:
Cole Porter: *Silk Stockings*
Adler and Ross: *Damn Yankees* (choreography by Bob Fosse)
Film:
Frank Sinatra: *Guys and Dolls*

1957   Champions' last film, *The Girl Most Likely*, released by RKO. Their first child Gregg is born. Gower injured in car accident prior to filming their first television series, "The Marge and Gower Champion Show." Show cancelled in July. Nightclub appearances and guest spots on television continue.

Broadway:
Leonard Bernstein: *West Side Story*
Meredith Wilson: *The Music Man*
Lerner and Loewe: *My Fair Lady*
Frank Loesser: *The Most Happy Fella*
Film:
Fred Astaire: *Silk Stockings*
Elvis Presley: *Jailhouse Rock*

1959   Champion directs television revue, *Accent on Love*, for CBS. Marge and Gower tour Russia with Ed Sullivan. Champion hired for first director/choreogra-

Broadway:
Rodgers and Hammerstein: *The Sound of Music*
Styne and Sondheim: *Gypsy*
Bock and Harnick: *Fiorello*

pher assignment on Broadway, *Let's Go Steady*, which would become *Bye Bye Birdie*.

Film:
Gwen Verdon: *Damn Yankees* (1958)
Shirley MacLaine: *Can-Can* (1960)

1960   *Bye Bye Birdie* opens; Champion's first show with Michael Stewart; 607 performances.

Broadway:
Lerner and Loewe: *Camelot*
Frank Loesser: *Greenwillow*
Meredith Wilson: *The Unsinkable Molly Brown*

1961   *Carnival!* opens; Champion's first show for David Merrick; 719 performances.

Broadway:
Frank Loesser: *How to Succeed in Business Without Really Trying* (choreography: Bob Fosse)
Jerry Herman: *Milk and Honey*

1963   Champion hired by David Merrick to direct and choreograph a musical version of Thornton Wilder's *The Matchmaker*.

Broadway:
Lionel Bart: *Oliver!*
Bock and Harnick: *She Loves Me*
Schmidt and Jones: *110 in the Shade*

1964   *Hello, Dolly!* opens; 2,844 performances.

Broadway:
Styne and Merrill: *Funny Girl*
Bock and Harnick: *Fiddler on the Roof*
Strouse and Adams: *Golden Boy*

1966   Champion directs *I Do! I Do!*, a musical version of *The Four-poster*, with Mary Martin and Robert Preston; 560 performances.

Broadway:
Kander and Ebb: *Cabaret*
Jerry Herman: *Mama*
Coleman and Fields: *Sweet Charity*

1968   *The Happy Time* opens to mixed reviews; 286 performances.

Broadway:
MacDermot, Ragni, Rado: *Hair*
Kander and Ebb: *Zorba*
Bacharach and David: *Promises, Promises*

1971   *Prettybelle*, score by Jule Styne and Bob Merrill, closes in Boston after two preview weeks.

Broadway:
Stephen Sondheim: *Follies* (choreography by Michael Bennett)

Lloyd Webber and Rice: *Jesus Christ Superstar*
Stephen Schwartz: *Godspell*

1972   *Sugar*, stage version of Billy Wilder's film *Some Like It Hot*, opens in New York to mixed reviews.

Broadway:
Stephen Schwartz: *Pippin* (choreography by Bob Fosse)
Jacobs and Casey: *Grease*

1973   Champion takes over direction of revival of *No, No, Nanette!* (with Debbie Reynolds) from John Gielgud. Gower and Marge Champion divorce.

Broadway:
Stephen Sondheim: *A Little Night Music*
Woldin and Brittan: *Raisin*

1974   *Mack and Mabel* opens in New York after four months on the road to negative reviews, and closes after 66 performances.

Broadway:
Bernstein and Wilbur: *Candide* (revival)
Stephen Schwartz: *The Magic Show*

1976   *Rockabye Hamlet* closes after eight performances. Champion marries Karla Russell in Los Angeles.

Broadway:
Kander and Ebb: *Chicago* (director: Bob Fosse)
Stephen Sondheim: *Pacific Overtures*
Hamlisch and Kelban: *A Chorus Line* (director: Michael Bennett)

1977   Champion directs *Annie Get Your Gun* for Los Angeles Civic Light Opera. Takes over direction of Kander and Ebb musical, *The Act*. Gower plays male lead opposite Liza Minelli for three weeks, his first Broadway role since 1955.

Broadway:
Strouse and Charnin: *Annie*
Rodgers and Hammerstein: *The King and I* (revival)
Coleman and Stewart: *I Love My Wife*

1978   Champion is diagnosed with a rare, incurable blood disorder and undergoes dialysis and chemotherapy. Against his doctors' advice, he begins work with Michael Stewart on a stage version of Busby Berkeley's 1933 film *42nd Street*.

Broadway: Various Composers: *Dancin'* (direction/choreography: Bob Fosse)
Fats Waller: *Ain't Misbehavin'* (revue)
Coleman, Comden and Green: *On the Twentieth Century*
Carol Hall: *The Best Little Whorehouse in Texas*

1979   Champion withdraws from *42nd Street* project in early spring. Michael Stewart approaches Bob Fosse and Michael Bennett to direct and choreograph. Both decline.

Broadway:
Stephen Sondheim: *Sweeny Todd*
Lloyd Webber and Rice: *Evita*
Hamlisch and Sager: *They're Playing Our Song*
McHugh, Fields and others: *Sugar Babies* (idealized version of classic burlesque show by Ralph Allen and Harry Rigby)

1980   Champion rejoins *42nd Street* in February and begins rehearsals in April. Show opens in Washington and runs June 24–July 27. Scheduled New York opening on August 11 is postponed to August 25. On August 22 Champion is rushed to the hospital. He is pronounced dead at 1 P.M. on August 25, five hours before the opening night performance. David Merrick announces Champion's death from the stage of the Winter Garden theatre after the show. *42nd Street* ran 3,486 performances in New York.

Broadway:
Coleman and Stewart: *Barnum*
Gilbert and Sullivan: *Pirates of Penzance* (1981)
Kander and Ebb: *Woman of the Year* (1981)
Lloyd Webber and Rice: *Joseph and the Amazing Technicolor Dreamcoat* (1981)
Krieger and Eyen: *Dreamgirls* (1981) (director/choreographer: Michael Bennett)

Selected Bibliography

INTERVIEWS AND LETTERS

Ballard, Kaye. Interview. New York. October 10, 1985.

Banninger, Carole. Interviews. New York. January 10 and 17, 1984.

Boyd, George. Interview. New York. October 14, 1985.

Butz, John. Interview. New York. November 27, 1983.

Carpenter, Larry. Interview. New York. October 4, 1984.

Champion, Karla. Interviews. Los Angeles. March 19 and June 4, 1985.

Cook, Carole. Interview. Los Angeles. July 22, 1985.

Cypher, Jon. Interview. Los Angeles. August 31, 1984.

Drylie, Pat. Interview. New York. April 29, 1985.

Estridge, Jeanne Tyler. Interviews. San Bernadino, CA. March 20 and June 5, 1985.

Fisher, Jules. Interviews. New York. November 14 and 17, 1983.

Gavon, Igors. Interview. Washington, DC. April 14, 1984.

Gregg, Jess. Interview. New York. January 14, 1985.

Hallow, John. Interview. New York. November 4, 1985.

Harrell, Gordon Lowry. Interviews. New York. November 21 and 24, 1983.

Herman, Jerry. Interview. New York. April 2, 1985.

Jones, Cliff. Interview. Toronto. March 31, 1984.

Jones, Tom. Interview. Sharon, CT. October 15, 1985.

Kerr, Walter. Interview. New York. April 23, 1984.

Kresley, Ed. Interview. New York. October 27, 1984.

Lee, Jack. Interview. New York. November 14, 1984.

McEnnis, Pat. Interviews. Dallas, TX. October 18, 1984; Princeton, NJ. October 25, 1985.

Manzi, Anthony. Interviews. New York. July 25 and September 3, 1985; June 3, 1986.

Maricle, Marijane. Interview. New York. November 14, 1983.

Mead, Will. Interviews. New York. September 4 and 11, 1984.

Mitchell, James. Interviews. New York. September 26 and October 3, 1985.

Morris, John. Interview. New York. February 13, 1985.

Nickerson, Helen. Interview. New York. April 8, 1986.

Osterwald, Bibi. Interview. Boston. August 18, 1984.

Pan, Hermes. Letter to the author. June 12, 1985.

Percassi, Don. Interview. New York. December 15, 1983.

Peters, Bernadette. Interview. New York. April 29, 1985.

Pluff, Marc. Interview. Boston. August 18, 1984.

Potter, Don. Interview. Boston. August 18, 1984.

Preston, Robert. Interview. Santa Barbara, CA. July 22, 1985.

Priborsky, Richard. Interview. Los Angeles. March 23, 1985.

Reams, Roy. Interview. New York. December 3, 1983.

Richert, Wanda. Interviews. New York. December 13 and 20, 1984.

Roberts, Tony. Interview. New York. May 14, 1985.

Sagal, Marge Champion. Interviews. New York. January 6, 1984. Great Barrington, MA. May 25, July 5 and October 10, 1985; February 13 and March 28, 1986; July 11, 1987.

Schwartz, Risa. Interview. November 11, 1983.

Schwinn, Ron. Interview. New York. March 6, 1985.

Showalter, Max. Interviews. Los Angeles. March 13 and 20, and July 11, 1985.

Smith, Sheila. Interview. New York. January 15, 1985.

Stewart, Michael. Interviews. New York. May 5 and 17, 1984; June 25, July 20, August 27 and September 3, 1985.

Torrey, Tracy. Interview. Washington DC. May 6, 1985.

Trott, Pat. Interviews. Boston. August 18, 1984; June 1, 1985.

Victor, Lucia. Interviews. New York. April 11 and 18, 1984; April 4 and 11, 1985.

Wagner, Robin. Interviews. New York. September 14 and 19, October 25, and November 1, 1984.

Weeks, Alan. Interview. New York. November 27, 1985.

SCRIPTS AND RELATED EPHEMERA

Champion, Gower. Letters. Collection of Marge Champion Sagal, Stockbridge, MA.

———. Manuscript gloss on mimeographed script of *Goodbye, Birdie, Goodbye* [*Bye Bye Birdie*]. Special Collections, University of California at Los Angeles Research Library.

———. Manuscript notes for *Bye Bye Birdie*. Special Collections, University of California at Los Angeles Research Library.

———. Manuscript notes for *Carnival!*. Special Collections, University of California at Los Angeles Research Library.

———. Manuscript notes for *Dolly, A Damned Exasperating Woman* [*Hello, Dolly!*]. Special Collections, University of California at Los Angeles Research Library.

———. Manuscript notes on typewritten audition schedules for *The Happy Time*. Special Collections, University of California at Los Angeles Research Library.

———. Manuscript notes for *The Happy Time*. Special Collections, University of California at Los Angeles Research Library.

———. Manuscript notes for *I Do! I Do!*. Research Library of the University of California at Los Angeles.

Lend An Ear. Souvenir Program. New York: 1948.

Miller, Warren, and Millian, Raphael. *Let's Go Steady*. Wisconsin Center for Theatre Research, Madison.

Nash, N. Richard. *The Happy Time*. Los Angeles: Research Library of the University of California at Los Angeles, n.d. [1967].

Olinger, E., and Segal, D. A. "The Impresario." Collection of Karla Champion, Los Angeles. (Typewritten.)

Rabinovitch, Reuben. *News Release*. June 5, 1958. Billy Rose Theatre Collection, New York Public Library at Lincoln Center.

Radio City Music Hall. *Program*. June 13, 1940.

Record Corporation of America. *Press and Information*. n.d. [1966].

Ryan, Elisa. Program for a recital. Elisa Ryan Studio of Dance, May 29, 1933. Collection of Jeanne Tyler Estridge, San Bernadino, CA.

———. Program for *Good News*. Cathay Circle Theatre, March 30, 1935. Collection of Jeanne Tyler Estridge, San Bernadino, CA.

Sabinson, Harvey. News Release, August 11, 1960. Billy Rose Theatre Collection, New York Public Library at Lincoln Center.

———. News Release, March 9, 1961.

Stewart, Michael. *Dolly*. Manuscript in Collection of Michael Stewart, New York.

———. *42nd Street*. Manuscript in Collection of Michael Stewart, New York.

———. *Let's Go Steady*. Manuscript in Collection of Michael Stewart, New York.

———. *Mack and Mabel*. Manuscript in Collection of Michael Stewart, New York.

———. *Mack and Mabel*. 1st Outline, January–February 1972. Typescript, Collection of Michael Stewart, New York.

———. *Mack and Mabel*. 2nd Outline, May 29, 1972. Typescript, Collection of Michael Stewart, New York.

———. *Mack and Mabel*. 1st Draft, November 5, 1972. Typescript, Collection of Michael Stewart, New York.

————. *Mack and Mabel*. Revised 1st draft, December 3, 1972. Typescript, Collection of Michael Stewart, New York.

————. *Mack and Mabel*. 2nd Revised 1st Draft, December 3, 1972. Typescript, Collection of Michael Stewart, New York.

————. *Mack and Mabel*. 2nd Draft, December 14, 1972. Typescript, Collection of Michael Stewart, New York.

————. *Mack and Mabel*. Champion Version, February 24, 1973. Typescript, Collection of Michael Stewart, New York.

————. *Mack and Mabel*. 1st Champion revision, January 7, 1974. Typescript, Collection of Michael Stewart, New York.

————. *Mack and Mabel*. 2nd Champion revision. Typescript, Collection of Michael Stewart, New York.

————. *Mack and Mabel*. 3rd Champion revision. Typescript, Collection of Michael Stewart, New York.

————. *Mack and Mabel*. 4th Champion revision, April 7, 1974. Typescript, Collection of Michael Stewart, New York.

————. *One of the Girls*. Manuscript in Collection of Michael Stewart, New York.

Waldorf-Astoria Hotel (New York). *Waldorf-Astoria Daily Bulletin*, December 31, 1937, vol. 7, no. 92, p. 1.

Zolotow, Sam. "Stage News" (Press Release), December 12, 1958. Billy Rose Theatre Collection, New York Public Library at Lincoln Center.

PUBLISHED WORKS ABOUT GOWER CHAMPION

Alameda Times-Star. February 1950.

Baral, Robert. *Revue: The Great Broadway Period*. New York: Fleet Press, 1962.

Billboard. 1937–1955.

Bordman, Gerald. *The American Musical Theatre: A Chronicle*. New York: Oxford University Press, 1978.

Boston Globe. September 1966.

Boston Herald. 1941–1966.

Boston Record. January 1948.

Boston Sunday Post. September 1942.

Brooklyn Daily Eagle. March 1951.

Caesar, Sid, and Davidson, Bill. *Where Have I Been? An Autobiography*. New York: Crown, 1982.

Caughey, John, and Caughey, Laree. *Los Angeles: Biography of a City*. Berkeley: University of California Press, 1976.

Champion, Marge, and Zdenik, Merillee. *Catch the New Wind*. New York: Random House, 1972.

Chicago Daily Tribune. February 1953.

Chicago Times. April 1949.

Christian Science Monitor. October 1942.

Cleveland Press. January 1948.

Collier's Magazine. July 1952.

Daily Variety. 1955–1958.

Dance Magazine [The American Dancer]. 1927–1980.

Detroit Free Press. February 1948.

Dietz, Howard. *Dancing in the Dark.* New York: Random House, 1975.

Engel, Lehman. *The American Musical Theatre.* rev. ed. New York: Collier Books, 1975.

———. *American Musical Theatre: A Consideration.* New York: CBS Books, 1968.

Farnsworth, Marjorie. *The Ziegfeld Follies: A History in Text and Pictures.* New York: Bonanza Books, 1956.

Flinn, Denny Martin. *Musical! A Grand Tour.* New York: Schirmer Books, 1997.

Gaynor, Charles. *Lend an Ear.* New York: Samuel French, 1971.

"Gower Champion, Marge Champion." *Current Biography* (September 1953): 39.

Green, Stanley. *Encyclopedia of the Musical Film.* New York: Oxford University Press, 1981.

Hawley, Renee Dunia. *Los Angeles and the Dance, 1850–1930.* Ph.D. dissertation, University of California at Los Angeles, 1971.

Hellman, Lillian. *My Mother, My Father and Me.* New York: Random House, 1963.

Hirschhorn, Clive. *The Hollywood Musical.* New York: Crown, 1981.

———. *The RKO Story.* New York: Crown, 1982.

Hollywood Citizen-News. February 1953.

Hollywood Reporter. 1949–1968.

Indianapolis News. July 1958.

Indianapolis Star Magazine. July 1958.

Kasha, Al, and Hirschhorn, Joel. *Notes on Broadway.* Chicago: Contemporary Books, 1985.

Kissel, Howard. *David Merrick: The Abominable Showman.* New York: Applause Books, 1993.

Krueger, Miles. *Show Boat: The Story of a Classic American Musical.* New York: Oxford University Press, 1977.

Leiter, Samuel. *The Great Stage Directors.* New York: Facts on File, 1994.

Life. May 1951.

Loney, Glenn. *Unsung Genius: The Passion of Dancer-Choreographer Jack Cole.* New York: Franklin Watts, 1984.

Los Angeles Daily Mirror News. June 1955.

Los Angeles Examiner. 1936–1958.

Los Angeles Herald and Express. August 1957.

Los Angeles Times. 1936–1980.

Luelbacher, Kurt J., Adams, Raymond D., Braunwald, Eugene, Petersdorf, Robert G., Wilson, Jean D., eds. *Harrison's Principles of Internal Medicine,* ninth edition. New York: McGraw-Hill, 1980.

Malnig, Julie. *Exhibition Ballroom Dancing and Popular Entertainment.* PhD dissertation, New York University, 1987.

Merman, Ethel, with George Eells. *Merman.* New York: Simon and Schuster, 1978.

Miller, Merle. *Plain Speaking.* New York: Scribner's, 1973.

Montreal Daily Herald. July 1937.

Montreal Gazette. June 1937.

Motion Picture Herald. September 1955.

Mueller, John. *Astaire Dancing.* New York: Knopf, 1985.

New York. October 1974.

New York Daily Mirror. 1942–1960.

New York Daily News. 1942–1976.

New York Herald Tribune. 1940–1965.

New York Journal American. 1949–1965.

New York Morning Telegraph. 1948–1966.

New York Post. 1939–1974.

New York Star. October 1947.

New York Sun. January 1938.

New York Times. 1939–1980.

New York World Journal Tribune. November 1966.

Newark Daily News. September 1948.

Newark Evening News. September 1942.

Newark Star-Ledger. May 1953.

Newsday. April 1973.

Oakland Tribune. August 1959.

Osterman, Marjorie. "It'll Win a Tony." Unpublished manuscript, n.d.

Philadelphia Inquirer. February 1960.

Playgoer (Los Angeles). June 1948.

Previn, Dory. *Bog-Trotter.* Garden City, NY: Doubleday, 1980.

St. Louis Daily News. July 1947.

St. Louis Globe Democrat. June 1947.

St. Louis Post Dispatch. June 1947.

San Diego Union. July 1957.

San Francisco Chronicle. November 1969.

Sennett, Ted. *Your Show of Shows.* New York: Collier Books, 1977.

Showmen's Trade Review. October 1955.

Soho Weekly News. February 1976.

Strouse, Charles, and Adams, Lee. *Bye Bye Birdie*, Vocal Score. New York: Edwin H. Morris, 1960.

Suskin, Steven. *Showtunes: 1905–1985*. New York: Dodd, Mead, 1986.

Syracuse Herald Journal. January 1955.

Taylor, Theodore. *Jule: The Story of Composer Jule Styne*. New York: Random House, 1979.

Terry, Walter. *I Was There*. New York: Audience Arts, 1978.

Thomas, Lawrence B. *The MGM Years*. New York: Columbia House, 1972.

Time. 1951–1972.

Variety. 1936–1980.

Washington Evening Star. 1947–1972.

Washington Post. June 1980.

Washington Times-Herald. November 1947.

Weatherall, D. J., Ledingham, J. G. G., and Warrell, D. A., eds. *Oxford Textbook of Medicine*. New York: Oxford University Press, 1983.

Women's Wear Daily. 1974–1976.

Index

About the Author and Editors

DAVID PAYNE-CARTER was an Assistant Professor of Drama at New York University at the time of his death in 1991. He previously taught at Oberlin College and at the University of Delaware. He traveled extensively as a performer, writer, musician, and director for a USO tour in Central and South America; studied at the Catholic University of America, Southwest Texas State University, St. Vincent Benedictine Monastery, and the Royal Conservatory of Music in Madrid; and continued to write and direct during his career as an educator.

BROOKS MCNAMARA is Professor of Performance Studies at New York University and Director of the Shubert Archive. He is the author or editor of 12 books, numerous articles on the theater and related subjects, and a contributing editor of *Film History*. He has lectured at many universities and museums, and has appeared on radio and television. Professor McNamara has been a Fulbright Scholar and a Guggenheim Fellow.

STEVE NELSON teaches musical theatre and popular performance in the Department of Drama at New York University and produces an historical recordings series of noted songwriters performing their own songs, including Cole Porter, Frank Loesser, and Yip Harburg. He is also co-editing (with Robert Kimball) *The Complete Lyrics of Frank Loesser*, scheduled for publication in 2000.

ISBN 0-313-30451-3

HARDCOVER BAR CODE